INFORMATION TECHNOLOGY AND DEVELOPMENT

INFORMATION TECHNOLOGY
AND
DEVELOPMENT

Editor

ARUN BAVEJA

KALPAZ PUBLICATIONS

Delhi-110052

INFORMATION TECHNOLOGY AND DEVELOPMENT
(Information technology)

ISBN: 81-7835-001-7

Published in 2000 in India by
Kalpaz Publications
C-30, Satyawati Nagar
Ashok Vihar Phase-III
Delhi-110052
E-Mail: kalpaz@hotmail.com

Laser Typeset at A.S. Printers
Printed at Mehra Offset Printers, New Delhi

Preface

The great leap forward in information technology and the media has been witnessed in the past decade has already begun to shape the thought processes that give a society in strengths and weaknesses. Information technology has come to occupy the centre-stage of development, with the approach of 21st century.

Information technology concerns the storage, communication and processing of information. In the past we have witnessed independent development of the three, for example, microfiche, photo libraries, book libraries, video-tapes, etc. For information storage AM and FM broadcast, cable and satellite communication for information movement and successive generation of general-purpose and special-purpose computers.

In the last decade the three aspects have come together through developments in technology. Some important contributing factors are conversion of more and more information into digital form, development of data compression techniques, and reduced cost of digital storage, and transmission and processing of information.

The main aim of the book is to encourage a critical debate on the role of information technology in the developmental process and to contribute to more informed decision making concerning information technology development, adaptation, transfer and utilisation.

The book will be used as a vehicle for information exchange and sensitisation on the growing gap between the developed and developing world, the role of information technology in this process, and its impact on the excluded and included sectors of society, especially with reference to the current globalisation trends.

Editor

Contents

1

Personal Computers

A major segment of the market involves entertainment: personal computers offer a growing array of games, music, and art far more sophisticated, in terms of speed and capability, than video material based only on television. This advantage results from the ability of computers to store and quickly retrieve large amounts of information. The future will bring many more uses for computers in both business and home. Indeed, the possibilities are virtually endless. A great variety of computers, large and small, are now available. A personal computer is a machine or system meeting all the major qualifications.

The system is designed to accept secondary memory devices to supplement the primary, built-in memory, the user is expected to interact with the system continuously, not only at the beginning and end of a problem, at least one general language (BASIC, FORTRAN, COBOL, PASCAL, ADA, or C) is available for this interaction, the system is usable for a wide variety of problems and is not designed for any single application and the computer is distributed through mass-marketing channels, with the marketing emphasis on the first-time computer user.

A typical modern personal computer consists of a circuit board with a silicon chip microprocessor and one or more memory chips attached. The microprocessor can perform hundreds of thousands of calculations every second, and the memory chips provide the primary storage for instructions and data.

External storage devices, such as cassette tape units or small recording disks (floppy disks), augment the memory capacity and provide a storage medium that can be physically transferred from one personal computer to another. (Typical users begin with cassette units but soon change to disks to gain the advantages of greater speed and capacity.) Input is through a typewriter-like keyboard unit. Output typically takes the form of words and numbers displayed either on a television screen or a similar specialized screen called a monitor. Most monitors are designed to display 24 lines of letters and figures, with each line containing a maximum of 80 characters. Adding a printer unit permits output in the form of a printed paper. A special device, called a "modem" (for modulator/demodulator), permits the computer to receive and transmit data over a conventional telephone line. But the significant factor in defining a personal computer is not its physical features but the characteristics of the operating system.

Designers of personal computers and software attempt to provide a friendly human-machine interface, even at the expense of brute computing power. Optional programs are also available so that the computer can be used for many different purposes. Although word processors and hobby computers have many characteristics of personal computers, they lack this flexibility.

Recent trends in microelectronics, memories, input--output mechanisms, and software suggest that the trend in microprocessors is toward larger "words" and higher circuit speeds. A computer capable of handling larger "words" is able to perform a complete operation in fewer machine cycles and to operate directly with larger memory. Both these assets enhance performance by increasing the speed of operations and the number that can be performed in a sequence without the operator's intervention. In addition to greater speed and memory access, these larger microprocessors have the advantage of greater accuracy.

The first wave of personal computers used 8-bit microprocessors-that is, microprocessors in which 8 binary digits (0 or 1) can be processed in parallel, giving the capacity to process in a single operation any number up to 256, or to address any of up to 256 points in the memory. Processing larger numbers with an 8-bit microprocessor requires multiple operations, which take more time. Newer systems use 16-bit microprocessors, and 32-bit microprocessors are now available.

The primary memory in personal computers is of two different types: read-only memory (ROM) and random-access memory (RAM). In the forme information is fixed in the memory at the time of manufacture and is not lost when computer power is switched off. The role of such a ROM is to guide the computer through a fixed procedure, such as calculating square roots translating a user's program into machine language. In a RAM, information such as special programs and data files can be "written in" or "read out" a frequently as desired, with any storage location directly accessible. RAMS are of two types: dynamic RAMS, which are cheaper but lose their store information unless they are "refreshed" often, and static RAMS, which are costlier but do not need to be "refreshed." If power is lost, both types of RAM lose their stored information.

Over the past decade, the number of memory circuits per unit of area on chip has increased by a factor of 64, and cost on a unit basis has been reduced by a factor of 50. Both these trends will continue. So-called

64K dynamic RAMs (each contains 65,536 bits of information [K = 2 10 = 1024; 64K = 64 x 10241) are expected to remain popular until about 1984, when the much larger memory capacity of 256K dynamic RAMs is expected to become standard.

Most manufacturers supply system programs on ROMs, and this practice will continue because programs are secure against power failures and users are less able to duplicate programs in this form. Computers' main memories will be supplemented by secondary storage devices that offer larger and relatively inexpensive, though slower, capacity for long-term storage of program and data files. The most popular of these is a so-called "floppy disk"—a disk of mylar coated with magnetic material on one or both sides. Data are stored in a series of spots—either magnetized or demagnetized—along the concentric tracks. Heads for reading or writing data can be moved radially across the disk to reach a specified segment of circular track.

Storage capacity depends on the format used for the stored data, the quality of magnetic surface, and the design of the reading-writing head. Floppy disks in current use typically have capacities of 1 to 4 million bits, sufficient to store 20,000 to 80,000 words of English text. During the next four years, higher-density floppy disks will be common. Indeed, disks offering capacities of 50 to 100 million bits are already becoming popular, but they are much costlier than floppy disks.

The primary display device used in all personal computer systems is a cathode-ray tube (CRT), either standing alone or as part of a television receiver. This system will continue through the foreseeable future. Output is typically presented in alphanumeric form-letters and numbers. Charts and game boards can be presented, but the memory and software required to display such graphical images is often complex and expensive. The letters and numbers in alphanumeric displays are patterns of dots programmed in special ROMs known as "character generators." The quality of the image depends on the number of points (or pixels) on the screen that can be addressed by the computer-that is, the number of points at which dots can be located. A typical low-resolution screen has a field of 6144 (128 times 48) pixels (picture elements-dots on the screen). High-resolution systems (100,000 pixels or more) allow sophisticated graphics for animation or detailed figures and may provide colour as well.

The market and the players

The personal computer industry has grown as a direct result of the evolution of the microprocessor. This evolution began when Intel in 1971 packaged a complete, if somewhat limited, processor with a 4-bit word size in a single integrated circuit. The company followed with the first 8-bit processor in 1972 and an improved version in 1974. One year later Micro Instrumentation and Telemetry Systems, Inc. (MITS), an Albuquerque firm, developed the first personal computer around Intel's 8-bit processor. The basic system sold for $395 in kit form and $621 in assembled form, not including accessories (peripherals).

Though the MITS system is no longer manufactured, its method for connecting peripherals and the main computer has become an industry standard. Within three years after it was introduced, Radio Shack, Apple, and Commodore had entered the market. Now makers of large computers such as IBM and Honeywell, as well as minicomputer leaders such as Digital Equipment Corp. and Data General Corp., are also making personal computers, having observed their traditional markets being eroded by the new low-priced products. The results are rapid development of the market and growing popular interest and faith in personal computers.

The pioneering manufacturers did not survive beyond the initial phase of personal computer development results from the preoccupation with the needs of hobbyists. New entrants such as Radio Shack, Commodore, and Apple captured a major share of the market in 1978 by promoting fully assembled, ready-to-operate systems that were easier to use. Though the success of the companies now in the competition will depend at least partly on their financial and technical resources, their products' ease of use (or "user-friendliness," in trade jargon) is a significant competitive feature.

The personal computer market can be divided into four segments in terms of the computer's intended use: business, home, research-technical, and educational. The business segment, by far the largest at present, accounted for 750,000 sales (retail value of $2 billion) in 1982, or 54 percent of the units sold and 65 percent of the dollar sales. This segment will continue to be a major factor, with more sales than all other segments put together. No wonder, then, that the leading makers of personal computers are concentrating their sales efforts on the business sector.

The most visible segment of the personal computer "revolution" is in homes, where computers are used for entertainment and education, sending messages, and home finances. The development of appropriate software will soon enable sophisticated users to pay bills, manage bank accounts, compute taxes, and even buy household items without written transactions.

The potential market for personal computers in education has barely been tapped. Computer manufacturers recognize that schools are the logical environment in which to develop computer skills, and they have reason to expect that students will purchase the machine on which they first learn computing. So manufacturers are offering many price incentives to the educational sector. Yet the educational sector will continue to account for only about 15 percent of total sales of personal computers for the rest of this decade, as school funding will be limited.

Although they want to serve all four segments, the industry leaders (Apple, Radio Shack, Commodore, IBM, and Xerox) are focusing on the business market. Vector Graphics is also emphasizing this market by tailoring personal computer systems to the needs of particular industries. Atari (Warner), Intellivision (Mattel), and Texas Instruments are focusing on the home market. Hewlett-Packard is offering a highly specialized compact product with built-in printer, tape memory, and video monitor especially for the scientific community.

In general, both prices and manufacturers' profit margins are failing, and mass marketing is becoming the rule. The major competitors win each spend over $10 million in 1983 on advertising aimed at expanding the market and establishing their place in it. The dynamics of the entire personal computer market may be changed substantially by new entrants by 1990. Traditional barriers to entry into this field have crumbled. For example, manufacturing capability is not essential: the IBM personal computer is assembled almost entirely from premanufactured components not of IBM origin.

By contrast, strength in marketing and distribution is a significant advantage, and many organizations with this capability may seek to replicate IBM's strategy for rapid entry into the field. Organizations such as General Electric, Procter and Gamble, Phillip Morris, and Du Pont all have the ability to enter the personal computer market in this way.

Selling personal computers

Strategies for marketing mainframe computers are not appropriate for marketing personal computers-profit margins are not large enough to justify hiring internal sales forces to sell directly to end users. As a result, producers are now experimenting with a wide variety of distribution strategies.

Franchised retail chains constitute a major distribution channel. For example, the Computerland chain sold $200 million worth of computers and related accessories in 1981. These stores distribute the products of many vendors, and their volume is large enough to support a technical and maintenance staff.

Manufacturer-owned retailed stores have been used successfully by Radio Shack. IBM, Digital, and Xerox have also opened such stores but only to supplement existing distribution channels. Except for Xerox, each manufacturer's stores sell only that manufacturer's products, and a prospective buyer is thus obliged to visit several stores to compare equipment of different makes.

Department store outlets have generally been unsuccessful. Mass merchandisers depend for profits on fast-selling commodities. According to computer industry data, personal computer buyers make four shopping trip totalling as much as seven hours when selecting their machines. These buyer also expect sustained support and maintenance services that department stores are unaccustomed to providing.

Office equipment stores specializing in copiers, typewriters, word processors and other office equipment are well positioned to reach the most Promising future market for personal computers and auxiliary equipment. If these stores can provide adequate servicing, they will become very popular.

Consumer electronics stores such as Tech Hi-Fi have been marketing personal computers with some success, but the lack of expertise at the store level has been a constraint. Japanese manufacturers have also established ties with such stores as distributors of other Japanese products. These channels will become a major factor as the Japanese increase their share of the personal computer market.

Independent retailers often lack the capital required to compete vigorously and are therefore not gaining in numbers and importance as quickly as other retail channels.

Catalog showrooms have been used by Texas Instruments, but personal computers require follow-up support that such showrooms have been unable to provide.

Mail order firms offering discounts ranging up to 30 percent appeal to price-sensitive customers, but their total lack of continuing support disenchants users. Price-cutting penalizes the full-service dealers on which manufacturers want to rely as major sales outlets. Accordingly, major companies are trying to discourage sales through mail order firms.

Direct sales staffs are used for large-volume sales to government, educational institutions, and major corporations who prefer dealing directly with the manufacturer. But such direct sales tend to antagonize dealers by dipriving them of some of their most profitable opportunities, and profit margins are inadequate to support direct sales to small-volume and individual buyers.

Value-added houses serve specialized users with coordinated hardware and software, such as printing companies that need word-processing and typesetting capabilities but have little or no internal computing expertise.

Though franchised retail outlets are the largest sellers of personal computers in the us, the one compelling characteristic of personal computer distribution today is diversity. No one form of vendor or market approach is dominant.

Selecting a personal computer

No one should select a personal computer system without taking into account the tasks for which it will be used and the environment in which it will function. Even within a single business, personal computer users come from different areas-personnel, accounting, management, manufacturing, research, sales-and have different computing needs.

Even within departments there are many possible uses. The personnel department will run personnel files on a regular basis but also may want to study policy questions-the likely benefits in terms of increased revenue from a larger sales force, for example. Furthermore, different users have different strategies for using a computer for ad hoc applications. Thus, the person who will use a personal computer should-almost by definition-choose it, partly on the basis of the services it will provide and partly on the basis of its apparent user-friendliness.

Indeed, the machine's responsiveness to its user's needs and style is the critical technological breakthrough. But it is not necessarily so simple. In many organizations, personal computers create and fill completely new needs that were not originally anticipated. Consider the example of a personal computer acquired to improve one lay worker's access to a main computer facility. While retrieving data from the main computer to run programs locally, this user finds that the personal computer can help evaluate alternative business strategies, answering, "what-if... ?" questions instantaneously. The original application for which the personal computer was purchased becomes secondary. Given that the uses and benefits of personal computers are hard to predict, and that a wide range of systems and software are available, how should a potential buyer decide what and when to buy? And should such a buyer postpone action, expecting costs to decline in the future as they have in the past?

There are two arguments against postponing purchase in anticipation of a lower future price. One is the high cost of waiting, based on the computer's great (and often unexpected) uses. The other is that prices are expected to decline less dramatically in the future than in the past: future systems will offer technological improvements that increase performance at unchanged cost. Prices seem likely to stabilize at around $1500 for a full personal computer system.

Future personal computers are likely to offer increased memory size, increased processor power (16-bit and even 32-bit instead of 8-bit microprocessors), improved printers, more powerful programming languages that give the user more compact and natural communication with the computer, improved user access (better keyboards supplemented or replaced by touch screen and voice systems), and greater flexibility (the computer will be able to intermix and manipulate text, numbers, and graphics more easily). Yet today's personal computers may rapidly become obsolete, reflecting the rapid pace of change in semiconductor technology.

Changes in the microprocessor, the heart of any personal computer system, are most likely—and most serious. A computer with a 16-bit microprocessor cannot operate on hardware and software designed for an 8-bit microprocessor. Though many vendors provide add-ons that enable a new microprocessor to support old software, there is never total compatibility.

Software for a personal computer is expensive, and for most users new software development is impractical. So the amount and utility of the software available with a particular system is the key question in the buyer's choice of a personal computer. The variation can be large: 11,000 programs are available for the Apple ii and Apple ii Plus computers, whereas fewer than 100 widely distributed programs exist for the IBM personal computer, a more recent introduction. Of course, the IBM programs may be just the ones the buyer needs, and more software will be developed for the IBM.

Price is also an important variable, including not only the manufacturer's suggested price but the range of discounts offered by different retail computer sources. But discount alone does not tell the story. The critical factor is the ability of the distributor to provide both routine hardware maintenance, usually at the retail outlet, and software support and maintenance. A company store is likely to offer very good service on that company's product line but not necessarily on any other line, while a retail computer store is likely to offer moderately qualified service and support for many different manufacturers' systems. Mail order sales offer very little service but usually have the highest discounts.

The ultimate question for the purchaser is that of system configuration: what combination of hardware and software is appropriate for a buyer's current and projected needs? Perhaps the most important options are off-the-shelf software. To be sure they buy what they need, buyers should gain some experience with available programs before making the purchase; otherwise they risk having to modify their needs to fit the software they've purchased or embarking on the costly and time-consuming route of software development.

The programming tools on most personal computers are primitive compared with the equivalents available for mainframes, and the widespread dearth of good programmers is a complicating factor. Indeed, trying to develop special programming for a personal computer is inadvisable except under extraordinary circumstances. Memory capacity is another important variable. Most computers based on 8-bit microprocessors have no more than 48 or 64 kilobytes of built-in accessible memory (RAM), while the newer 16-bit processors can have 1, 4, or even 16 megabytes. (One byte is a string of 8 binary digits that represents one alphabetic character.)

Additional memory can be inserted into most personal computers by plugging cards into slots or inserting extra chips directly onto the microprocessor board. Storage capacity of the main memory for programs and instructions can also be supplemented by secondary devices, of which floppy disks are the most popular form. Disks with capacities ranging from 100,000 bytes to several megabytes now come in two standard sizes: 8 inches and 5¼ inches in diameter. But personal computer buyers should be aware that disks designed for one system will not generally operate in another maker's system because of different data-formatting conventions.

The critical performance characteristic of a floppy disk is the response time to a read-write request, which may range from 200 to 500 milliseconds. Though the response time for such a single file request is very short, a single compilation or word-processing command may involve 20 or more accesses to a floppy disk, and access time may account for 80 percent of the total command execution time. Where better performance and/or capacity are required, "hard" disks in the same format as the 5¼-inch and 8-inch floppy disks are useful. They offer storage capacities ranging from 5 to 50 megabytes and response time averaging 20 to 40 milliseconds, but their high cost (around $2000, including interfaces) can double a buyer's total investment in hardware.

All personal computer systems use cathode-ray tubes as output devices. If "hard copy" is required, buyers have a choice of several printing devices. Thermal printers, costing under $500, create images by applying points of heat to special paper. A dot-matrix printer, costing from $500 to $1500, has a vertical array of 7 to 10 dot-printing elements. These are activated by the computer as the printing head passes across the paper, forming alphanumeric characters and also graphs and drawings.

The limited number of elements results in a somewhat stylized character, but the process is as fast as thermal printing—50 characters per second. If letter-quality printing is required, a printing mechanism with precisely machined character matrices that strike the paper through a ribbon is required. Such printers cost $750 or more and print between 30 and 90 characters per second. Various accessories such as floppy disks and printers—or "peripherals"—are attached to personal computers through special "slot" receptacles. The IBM personal computer offers five such slots for peripherals such as printer, colour display, dual floppy-disk controller, communications channel, and memory module.

All business-oriented personal computers offer text editing for word processing. Some permit use of a light pen to directly indicate on the screen the word to be edited, and a few check spelling against a mini-dictionary stored in the computer memory. Business data manipulation is facilitated by "spreadsheet" packages such as VISICALC—a very popular package that enables users to see on the CRT the impact of altering one figure (say, retail price) on all other figures (profit margin, corporate profit, return of investment).

Software is now becoming available for generating displays such as those accompanying this article with only a few minutes' effort. For example, ExecuVision permits displays combining information in numbers, text, and pictures. It also provides animation that can add emphasis to presentations. Though personal computers are today viewed primarily as stand-alone work stations for individual users, the ability to transmit and receive data and programs is an important attribute of most contemporary systems. Personal computers are already serving as intelligent terminals for retrieving and manipulating files from large computers. These networking and communication capabilities are important considerations in selecting a personal computer. Unfortunately, no industry standard for communication protocols and interfaces exists. Different vendors use different protocols, so it is difficult to link various personal computers in a single network.

Technological advances in communications are expanding the power of personal computers. For example, owners of personal computers can now receive current stock market quotations by telephone. Personal computers can be connected with nationwide electronic funds transfer systems, so users have access to full banking facilities. They may transfer funds from one account to another and buy and sell financial instruments.

In homes, personal computers are now primarily used for recreational activities such as computer games. But these applications should not be underrated.

Computer games test and develop mental capabilities while generating familiarity with computer operations. Home computers are also used for office work at home, and many other applications are--or soon will be-possible. For example, a tax return can be prepared with the aid Of VISICALC. The user can analyse which forms and deductions to use for paying the minimum taxes. A personal computer can be used to balance checkbooks and plan investment strategies. And, of course, word-processing capabilities are useful in writing letters and professional papers.

As commercial databases such as Dow Jones News/ Retrieval and the Source are expanded and their subscription costs reduced, personal computers will be useful for locating stores and services, comparing prices, and placing orders. This would be especially appropriate for products or services whose prices fluctuate rapidly, such as those of the airline industry. Computers are being used increasingly for security applications. Traditional home security systems are limited, often failing to distinguish between a natural event and an intrusion by an unwanted visitor. Computer-controlled home security systems can include a variety of routines to analyse the signals from sensors before generating an alarm. Such an analysis can distinguish, for example, between the entry of a cat and the entry of a human being, or between the noise of a telephone ringing and a door opening.

Another home-oriented application is a medical information system that performs some of the diagnostics of a medical doctor. Perhaps the most useful application of this is a database for poison or first-aid: the user reports what substance the patient has ingested or the nature of an accident, and the computer responds with a step-by-step first aid plan. Children turn out to be heavy users of home computers. They enjoy computer games and seem able to learn computer languages faster than their elders. They find personal computers intriguing for recreation, school assignments, and self-paced courses that are now becoming available. Even though today's personal computers are equivalent in basic computing power to the mainframes of the 1960s and the minicomputers of the 1970s, they should not be used as substitutes for the earlier machines. Rather, users should capitalize on the new technical developments, including the diminishing cost of computing, and the Englishlike languages that replace the cumbersome digital languages of early machines, to make personal computers supplement, not displace, mainframe computers.

Personal computers should be used to analyse more issues in greater detail than ever before-not to do the more routine work typically assigned to mainframes. In the 1960s and 1970s, computers were used principally for well-structured, periodic jobs such as payroll accounting. Today's personal computers are especially useful for more casual, ad hoc analyses and problem solving, such as studies of the impact of cost of living increases, new tax regulations, or alternative hiring and layoff policies.

Consider the stock analyst who uses data from company balance sheets to evaluate investment risks. The balance sheets contain detailed, current information on assets and liabilities. But interest rates fluctuate, markets rise and fall, taxes change, competition falters or gains. Each such change affects a company's current performance and future prospects.

Using a central computing facility is an expensive way to analyse such problems, resulting in time delays and partial answers. But using a personal computer in the interactive mode linked to the central computer and a financial database makes it possible to understand the impact of changes quickly and accurately.

Psychology of personal computers

Manufacturers, media, and computer scientists have presented the public to computers the way one might have presented Aladdin to his lamp. Here was the genie, the workhorse that we could mount today and ride onto the new millennium. By the end of the 1970s, with the mass manufacture of personal computers, the promises extended into the home. Home computers would teach us French, help us with financial planning, even do our taxes. For many Americans, the first thing that computers brought into their homes was not a more efficient medium for work but new worlds to conquer in play.

"Space Invaders" became a household word for people with home computers or the machines' junior siblings, computerized video games. The experience of the decade has resulted in a widely shared public rhetoric. When people talk about the computer and their futures, they tend to fall back on the two images they know best: the computer as tool and the computer as toy; objective instrumentality and engrossing play. But there is another dimension. What people do with computers weaves itself into the way they see the world. People use a discourse about computers for thinking and talking about other things, about politics, religion, education, and about themselves and other people.

The subjective dimension of the computer presence is not merely a matter of discourse, of using the computer intellectually as a metaphor or model. There is another, and more emotionally charged, aspect which does not engage *ideas* about computers as much as the immediate quality of an individual's *experience* when working with them. Working with computers can be a way of "working through" powerful feelings. In this essay we develop this idea by using as a case study a group of computer users for whom issues related to control are particularly salient. For a first generation of computer hobbyists, controlling the computer is a way to deal with frustrations and desires, both personal and political, that have nothing to do with the computer *per se.*

The subjects of my study are men and women who bought personal computer systems in the four years that followed the 1975 announcement of the "Altair"—the first computer small enough to sit on a desktop, powerful enough to support high-level language programming, and that you could build for only $420. My study began in 1978 with a questionnaire survey answered by 95 New England computer hobbyists (their names had been drawn from the roster of a home computer club and from the subscription list of a personal computer magazine), and continued during 1978 and 1979 with nearly 300 hours of conversation with 50 individuals who owned home computers. What we found can be read historically: a study of the pioneer users of an increasingly ubiquitous technology. But most central to the intent of this essay is to use the story of the early hobbyists as a window into the highly personal ways in which individuals appropriate technologies. It is a case study of the "subjective computer," the computer as a material for thinking, for feeling, for "working through."

We are emphasis on the subjective is at odds with a widespread ideology that quickly grew up around the emergent computer hobbyist culture. The Altair, aimed at a strictly hobby market, was followed by other small systems—the Pet, the Sol, and, most successfully, the Radio Shack TRS-80 and the Apple, marketed to less specialized audiences of small businessmen and curious householders. With this explosion of hardware came a lot of rhetoric about a personal computer revolution. Most of the talk, both from the companies that marketed the machines and from those who claimed to be the most visionary spokesmen for the people who bought them, was about all of the things that a home computer could do for you.

The utilitarian, "genie in the bottle," ideology is expressed in the content of hobbyist conventions and magazines, filled with articles on how to make your home computer dim your lights, control your thermostat, run an inventory system for your kitchen or toolroom. And it is also found in writing on the personal computer from outside the hobbyist world. The view from the "outside" was well illustrated when, on May 14, 1979, the *Wall Street Journal* reported on its own little "evaluation experiment." The paper had drafted one of its staff reporters, Mitchell Lynch, into the ranks of the "home computer revolution." It presented him with a TRS-80 and asked him to take it home. His assignment was to report back six months later on what it had been like.

The terms of Lynch's evaluation are instrumental: what can the computer do? On these terms it fails, and when he goes to the experts for an explanation of what went wrong, he encounters an official "instrument" ideology from within: "Experts say that people like me have neither the technical training nor technical inclination to make a home computer strut its stuff." The point of having the computer, says the expert, is to make things happen. And, reassures the expert, they will happen with a better operator or a simpler computer. This instrumental view is an important ingredient of the hobbyist ideology but it is not the whole story. In the course of my work I found a very different answer from within.

Most hobbyists do make their computers "strut their stuff," but their sense of engagement and energy are found primarily in the non-instrumental uses of the technology. When asked in a questionnaire "What first attracted you to computers?" more than half the respondents gave reasons that were highly subjective. In response to an open-ended question, 26 percent said that they were first attracted to computers by an appeal that was intellectual, aesthetic, involved with the fun of what I would call "cognitive play." They wrote of "puzzle solving," of "the elegance of using computer techniques to handle problems," of the "beauty of understanding a system at many levels of complexity." They described what they did with their home computers with metaphors like "mind stretching" and "using the computer's software to understand my wetware."

Another 26 percent wrote of reasons for getting involved that seemed more emotional than intellectual. They wrote of the "ego boost" or "sense of power" that comes from knowing how to run a computer, of the "prestige of being a pioneer in a developing field," of the "feeling of control when I work in a safe environment of my own creation." The hobbyists who responded to my survey seemed familiar with Lynch's brand of scepticism, with people who ask them what they do with their computers and who won't take "cognitive play" for an answer. David, a 19 year-old undergraduate at a small engineering school, put it this way: "People come over and see my computer and they look at it, then they look at me, then they ask me what useful thing we do with it, like does it wash floors, clean laundry or do my income tax—when we respond no, they lose interest." David said that when he started out, he was attracted to the computer because "we liked the idea of making a pile of hardware do something useful, like doing real time data processing ... like picking up morse code with an amateur radio and transcribing it automatically into text," but in his list of things that he currently does with his computer.

Thirteen percent of those who responded to my questionnaire told a similar story. Like David, they began their relationship with personal computation for instrumental reasons (they had an image of a job to do, a specific task), but they became absorbed by the "holding power" of something else. A full two-thirds of my survey sample either began with or ended up with a primary interest in what I have called the "subjective computer," the computer seen in its relationship to *personal meaning.* Clearly, to understand what people are doing with their home computers we must go beyond the "performance criteria" shared by the hobbyist magazines and the *Wall Street Journal.* The simplest way of thinking about the subjective computer is through the metaphor of "the computer as Rorschach"—that is, seeing the computer as a projective screen for other concerns. In the Rorschach test, one is presented with a set of ink blots and asked to make some sense of them. Some people see the blots as threatening; others see them as benign. Some focus on small, complex details; others on global form. So too, the computer presents us with an ambiguous stimulus. For example, although most people think of the computer as an object without real intentionality, they accord computers enough autonomy in action to make "blaming the computer" a commonplace of daily life.

The very fact that the computer is a machine that touches on a sphere—intelligence—that man has always considered uniquely his is enough to make many people experience the computer as an object "betwixt and between," hard to classify, hard to pin down. Sometimes people deny the irreducibility of computation by asserting that, no matter how complex the computation "product," a move in a chess game for example, "all the computer really does is add." Of course in a certain sense this is correct. But saying that a computer "decided to move the Queen by adding" is a little bit like saying that Picasso "created Guernica by making brushstrokes."

Reducing things to this level of localness gives no satisfying way to grasp the whole. Just as in theoretical psychology there is a tension between the gestalt and the atomic, so too in computation there is a pervasive tension between the local simplicity of the individual acts that comprise a program or a computation, and what one might call the "global complexity" that can emerge when it is run. The elusiveness of computational processes and of simple descriptions of the computer's essential nature, the tension between local simplicity and global complexity, all contribute to making the computer an object of projective processes, and exemplary "constructed object." Different people apprehend it with very different descriptions and invest it with very different attributes. In views of the computer's internal process, individuals project their models of mind.

In descriptions of the computer's powers, people express feelings about their own intellectual, social, and political power—or their lack of it. Looking at the computer as Rorschach, as projective, puts the emphasis on aspects of the individual—from cognitive style to personal fears—that are revealed through behaviour with the machine. But of course the computer is more than a Rorschach. The Rorschach ink blots are evocative, revealing, but they stay on the page. They do not enter the life of the individual. The computer does. It is a constructive as well as a projective medium. For readers who have not had the experience of programming a computer, this idea may be sharpened by an analogy with another technology. In my own studies of people's emotional relationships with technologies, airplanes emerge as startlingly like computers in respect to the issues they raise for their hobbyists. Specifically, both are powerful media for working through the issue of control.

Local versus global and the question of control

There is always a compelling tension between local

simplicity and global complexity in the working of a computer and in the appreciation of a computer program. Locally, each step in a program is easy to understand; its effects are well defined. But the evolution of the global pattern is often not graspable. You are dealing with a system that surprises. This play between simplicity and complexity allows programmers, as pilots do with flying, to make of computation very different experiences that provide a context for working through different needs in relation to issues of personal control. Depending on how the programmer brings the computer's local simplicity and global complexity into focus, he or she will have a particular experience of the machine as completely understandable, under control, or as baffling, even as controlling. By focusing on the local, the line by line, you can feel in control. By focusing on the global, you can feel control slip away. In their style of programming a computer, people betray different levels of tolerance for temporary losses of control.

Some will avoid it at all costs; but others will seek it out, and enjoy "playing" with sensations of risk and danger. And so different people end up with very different relationships to controls and power in their programming work. To illustrate this point, it is useful to begin with an example at one extreme. We see a first style in Howard, an ex-programmer, now a university professor, who describes himself as "having been a computer hacker." Howard was not in my sample of hobbyists. He has a terminal at home which links to a large timesharing system, but when asked about home computers, he winced in distaste and said that he "wouldn't touch the stuff. It's too simple." His case, in which we see a love of programming for the feeling of "walking near the edge of a cliff," is meant as a contrast for what we found to be a prevalent and more conservative "hobbyist style." Howard described his longtime fantasy that he would walk up to any program, however complex, and "fix it, bend it to my will." As he described his intervention, he imitated the kind of hand gestures that a stage musician makes toward the hat before he pulls out the rabbit.

Wizards use spells, a powerful kind of local magic. Howard's magic was local too. He described his "hacker's approach" to any problem as a search for the "quick and dirty fix." For Howard, what was most thrilling about the experience of programming was "walking down a narrow line," using the program's flexibility (for him defined as the possibility of making a local fix) in a struggle to keep the whole under control. Weekends at the terminal with little to eat and little or no rest were frequent, as was the experience of not being able to leave the terminal while debugging a program, even when the obvious need was for sleep and looking at the whole in the morning, instead of trying to "fix it" by looking at it line by line all night. For Howard, the urgency of these encounters was tied to his sense that through them he was grappling with a computational essence—the struggle to exert control over global complexity by mastery of local simplicity.

A second programmer, Bob, is a computer professional, a microprocessor engineer who works all day on the development of hardware for a large industrial data system. He has recently built a small computer system for his home and devotes much of his leisure time to programming it. Whereas, for Howard, the excitement of programming is that of a high-risk venture, Bob likes it as a chance to be in complete control. Although Bob works all day with computers, his building and programming them at home is not more of the same.

At work he sees himself as part of a process that he

cannot see and over which he feels no mastery or ownership: "Like they say, we are just a cog." At home Bob works on well defined projects of his own choosing, projects whose beginning, middle, and end are all under his control. He describes the home projects as a compensation for the alienation of his job. He works most intensively on his home system when he feels furthest away from any understanding of "how the whole thing fits together at work."

Howard and Bob have very different opinions about what is most satisfying about programming. These translate into different choices of projects, into different choices of programming language and level to program at, and ultimately into what we might call different computational aesthetics. Howard likes to work on large, "almost out of control" projects; Bob likes to work on very precisely defined ones. Howard finds documentation a burdensome and unwelcome constraint; Bob enjoys documentation, he likes to have a clear, unambiguous record of what he has mastered. Indeed, much of his sense of power over the program derives from its precise specifications and from his continual attempts to enlarge the sphere of the program's local simplicity.

Hobbyist programmers mean different things when they say that machine language programming "puts them in control." For some, the reference seems objective. Given the primitive higher-level languages available on the first and second generation of hobby computers, machine-level programming seems to them the best instrumental solution. For others, the issue is more subjective. Many hobbyists who said they felt uneasy using systems programs for which they didn't have the source code also admitted never looking at the source code listing which they felt they had to have. Having access to the code was symbolic.

In other cases it was apparent that machine language programming was valued because the experience of doing it was pleasing in itself. It meant that the programmer was writing instructions that acted directly on the machine, no "building on top of" somebody else's interpreter. Most hobbyists have relationships with computation at work which involve sharing the machine with countless and nameless others. In personal computation they see a chance to be independent and alone.

The machine comes to them virgin. They have full possession. Finally, there is the issue of asserting control over an inferior. Bob, like many of the other hobbyists I spoke with, is a middle-level worker in the computer industry. He does not feel very good about the importance of his job. Proving that he is "better than any dumb compiler" gives a sense of importance. Using the computer to assert control was a central theme in my interviews with hobbyists. It was expressed directly, and also wove itself into four other issues that characterize the hobbyists' "subjective computer." These are using the computer to strengthen a sense of identity; to construct a completely intelligible piece of reality that is experienced as "transparent" and safe; to articulate a political ideology; and to experience a sense of wholeness that is absent in one's work life. It is these four issues to which I now turn.

Building identity

In achieving a sense of mastery over the computer, in learning about the computer's "innards," people are learning to see themselves differently. Among other things, they are learning to see themselves as "the kind of people who can do science and math." This was most striking among hobbyists who had no technical background. But it also came up among hobbyists who did see themselves as "technical people" but who for one reason or another had gotten "scared out of real science." Barry is 28 years old, an electronics technician at a large research laboratory. He went to college for two years, hoping to be an engineer, then dropped out and went to technical school. He has always loved to tinker with machines and to build things. His current job is to calibrate and repair complex instruments, and he is very happy with it because he gets a chance "to work on a lot of different equipment." But he came to his job with a feeling of having failed, of not being "analytic," "theoretical," of not being capable of "what is really important in science."

Five years ago, Barry bought a programmable calculator and started "fooling around with it and with numbers the way I have never been able to fool around before," and says that "it seemed natural to start working with computers as soon as I could." To hear him tell it, numbers stopped being theoretical, they became concrete, practical and playful, something he could tinker with. I'll pick up the calculator, and if we don't know how to do a problem I'll play with the calculator a few minutes, or a few hours and figure it out. It's not so much that the calculator does a particular calculation, but you do so many, have so much contact with the numbers and the results and how it all comes out that you start to see things differently ... The numbers are in your fingers.

When the calculator and the computer made numbers seem concrete, the numbers became "like him," and Barry felt an access to a kind of thinking that he had always felt "constitutionally" shut out of: "When I write in assembler I feel that mathematics is in my hands . . . and I'm good with my hands." Barry claims to have "grown out of" his aspiration to be an engineer. He says he doesn't keep engineering as a pipedream or think of his computer skills as something that could make it real. In terms of his career he says that "nothing has changed." But a lot has changed. Barry has always thought of himself as a bundle of aptitudes and ineptitudes that define him as the kind of person who can do certain things and cannot do others.

Working with the computer has made him reconsider his categories. We really couldn't tell you what sort of thing I'm going to be doing with my computer in six months. It used to be that I could tell you exactly what we would be thinking about in six months. But the thing with this, with the computer, is that the deeper you get into it, there's no way an individual can say what he'll be thinking in six months, what we are going to be doing. But we honestly feel that it's going to be great. And that's one hell of a thing. For Barry, the world has always been divided between the people who think they know what they'll be thinking in six months and those who don't.

And in his mind, his home computer has gotten him across that line and "That's one hell of a thing." For Barry, part of what it means to have crossed the line is to start to call the line into question. When he was in school, his inability to do the kind of mathematics he had "respect" for made him lose respect for himself as a learner, The computer put mathematics in a form that he could participate in. Barry has three children, has bought them their own calculators, and encourages them to "mess around with the computer." He feels that they are going through the same problems with math and science that he had and he wants them to have "a better start." For Barry, the computer holds the promise of a better start, not because it might teach his children a particular subject, but because it "might change their image of themselves. They might think of themselves as learners." Personal computers are certainly not the only hobby that people use to enhance their sense of identity. For my informants, "hobbies" have always been a way of life. Almost 90 percent of them had been involved in a hobby other than computation, most usually in another "technical" hobby, such as photography, ham radio, or model railroading.

Fifteen percent of the hobbyists surveyed were using their computers to "augment" their participation in another hobby—for example, using the computer to keep an inventory of motorcycle parts, figure out ideal compression ratios for racing cars, interface with amateur radio equipment. For nearly a third of them, their home computer had completely replaced another hobby. People spoke of these abandoned hobbies as "fun" and as "good experiences," but their remarks about past hobbies underscored several ways in which in our day and time a computer hobby can be special. In particular, people spoke about their "switch to the computer" as making them part of something that was growing and that the society at large "really cared about."

Gregory is in his mid-forties, and has been in the electronics industry for all of his working life, as a technician, a programmer, and currently as a products designer. For two years, his computer shared space in his study with an elaborate model railroad system. A year and half before we met him he had bought a new hard copy printer and a graphics plotter. In the overcrowding that followed, the trains had finally found their way to storage in the basement.

We heard many echoes of Gregory's phrase, "it's part of the real world too." Hobbyists spoke about the computer offering them a connection with something beyond the hobby. For some, having a computer and "getting good at it" means crossing a frontier that separates "tinkering" from "real technology." They feel that the world sees their computer hobby as serious (several commented that friends and neighbours hardly even look at it as a hobby, as though the word were reserved for frivolities), and they start to see themselves that way too. Most first-generation hobbyists have technical educations, but many of them, like Barry, feel they have never been part of what is most exciting and important in the scientific and technical cultures. They see themselves as the low men on the totem pole.

Working with computers, even small computers, feels technologically "avant garde." A smaller group of hobbyists (but a group whose numbers are growing as new generations of personal computers become more accessible to the nonspecialist) have always felt completely left out of the scientific and technical worlds. For them, owning a computer can mean crossing a "two Cultures" divide. Alan, a 29-year-old high school French teacher who describes himself as "having a love affair with a TRS-80," has always felt he wasn't "smart enough to do science."

Alan majored in French ("It was easy for me ... my mother is from Montreal") and took up carpentry as a hobby. And although he was good at it, it only reinforced his sense of not being able to do intellectual things, which in his mind meant not being able to "*do anything technical.*" When Barry began to do mathematics with his calculator, he felt that he started to cross a line to become the kind of person who could expect change and excitement in his intellectual life. For Alan, his TRS-80 led him across a line to become a member of a different culture, a scientific culture, a culture of "powerful people." For Barry, Alan, Gregory, relationships with computation enhanced self-image.

There is another way in which working with a computer can influence an individual's sense of identity.

Ideas about computers, about how they work and what they can and cannot do, can be used to assert ideas about people. They can provide metaphors for thinking about oneself Many hobbyists, fascinated by the idea of someday being able to trace out the complex relationships of electronic events, machine and assembly language instructions, and higher-level language commands within the computer, used the image of these many levels of intelligence to think about how people might work, about how people might, or might not, be like machines.

Some of this epistemology was implicit, for example when people made comments about "using the computer's software to think about my wetware." And sometimes, although less frequently, the issue became quite explicit. Conversations that began with descriptions of household "robotics" projects, such as a plan to build an energy monitoring system, led to reflections on how these projects would require programs that could represent the system's knowledge to itself, and from there into formal epistemological reveries: were these the kind of *self-representing programs* that ran inside people's heads? Do people have different kinds of self-representation programs for representing different kinds of knowledge, such as the knowledge of a dream and the knowledge of being awake? What kind of self-representation program might be running within people that allows them to remember and then forget their dreams?

Constructing reality

Hobbyist's descriptions of what it is like to work with their own computers frequently referred to the idea that the computer provides a safe corner of reality. Other hobbles can give a similar sense of security but often exact a price. For example, people can feel safe but limited. Alan, the French major, now "in love with his TRS-80," felt secure in his carpentry hobby, but he experienced it as a safety that came from refusing challenge. "It was an 'artsy' hobby. We couldn't see myself any other way." The computer is more likely than most other media to allow the experience of playing worlds (let us call them "microworlds") that are secure and also adventurous enough to allow for mind-stretching explorations. Almost all of the hobbyists we interviewed described some version of a limited, safe, and transparent microworld that was embodied in their personal computer.

For Alan just the fact of working with a computer created such a world. For others, it was more specific: a morse code microworld; a text editor microworld; and, most generally, the assembly language microworld. This use of the computer as a place to build a microworld is particularly salient for children when they are put in computational environments in which they have access to programming. Elsewhere I shall report on my study of elementary schoolchildren and adolescents who have gone through an experience with a LOGO computer system—a system designed to allow children to work in visually represented microworlds that are sufficiently constrained for a child to be able to understand and control them, yet sufficiently open-ended to give a child a real experience of intellectual power. Here I will mention only briefly one child and what she made of the computer as a medium for world building. Deborah at 11 years old was the baby of her family, the youngest of three children. Her childhood, had been spotted with illnesses which further exaggerated her "baby" position.

The members of her family were always doing things for her, insisting that she was not old enough to do the things that she wanted to do most: take out the laundry, baby-sit, stay over at a friend's house, choose her own hair style and her own clothes. Dependent on others at home, very overweight, and with an image of herself as sick and weak, Deborah had little sense of her own boundaries, her ability to say no, to assert control. Even at 11, she had become involved with a crowd of older kids who were smoking, drinking, using drugs. Towards the end of her eleventh year a LOGO computer came into Deborah's classroom as part of an educational experiment. At first, she found the computer frightening and threatening: until one day she hit upon the idea of confining the designs she made with the computer to ones in which the lines always came together in multiples of 30 degrees. She called it her "30 degrees world."

This restriction defined for her a space in which she felt safe but in which she was able to produce designs of great ingenuity and complexity. When I interviewed her two years later I found that she had used her experience with the "30 degrees world" as a kind of model, an experience-to-think-with. In her mind it represented how you could take control and make things happen by the judicious use of constraint. In Deborah's words, it was the first time that she ever "laid down her own laws." It was a turning point in her ability to take control of other situations. She lost 20 pounds, has given up smoking and drugs, and says that she "only sometimes" has a drink. For Deborah and for many adult hobbyists the sense of safety with the computer derived from the feeling of working in a sphere of intelligibility and transparency, a sphere that is protected, much as the space of a psychotherapeutic or psychoanalytic relationship is set off, bracketed.

People talked about feeling safe and secure in the world they had built with their home computers, a world where there were few surprises and "things didn't change unless you wanted them to." Of course, there was much talk of problems, of false starts, of frustrations. There are "bugs" in hardware and in programs. Things don't work; things go wrong. But bugs, with time, are either fixed or become "known" bugs. Joe is an insurance salesman in a small North California suburb who owns a second-hand Commodore Pet "with a lot of hardware problems." To Joe the bugs in his system "have become almost like friends": "We turn on the machine and we systematically check for my 'old friends,' and we swear, finding them there has a certain reassuring element."

Political ideology

The use of the computer as a medium for building a transparent and intelligible world brings us to how it can be used to think through questions of political ideology. Fred sells components for a large electronics supply house. He narrowly escaped starvation in a prisoner of war camp during World War II, and from that experience he says that he took "a sense of optimism." "we mean, if there is something out there and you want to do it—do it, understand it, act." Fred has tried to live that way. He is active in local politics; he keeps up with the news; he writes letters to the editor of his town newspaper. He bought his TRS80 on an impulse because "it seemed that you wouldn't be able to understand American society any more if you didn't know about computers." When it comes to working with his computer, Fred wants to know "exactly how things work": "There is a big gap in my own mind between the fact that an electrical circuit can be on or off and the binary number system ... and again from there to the BASIC language. I've got to understand all of that."

When hobbyists like Fred spoke about "wanting to know exactly how things work" in their computers, they were usually talking about wanting to know how their systems were built up from level to level, from electrical circuit to high-level language command. Fred, for example, expressed sharp frustration at gaps in his ability to follow the system through: "we can't really follow the continuum. I'm going to a user's group meeting, I'm talking to people and reading books and some of it is helping, but I am really frustrated.

We want to be able to follow the whole thing through." Larry, 35, lives in a Boston suburb. His computer offered him the first way he ever found to challenge the school's judgments of his child's abilities. A year before we met him, Larry had bought an Apple computer for small business use and ended up bringing it home so that his children would be able to play with it. His 12-year-old son Todd had been judged "backward" by his teachers through six years of schooling. His math scores were low; he could barely read. But Todd picked up the Apple manual, taught himself how to use the game packages, and then taught himself how to program in BASIC. As far as anyone knows, the Apple manual was the first book that Todd had ever read. In three weeks Todd was writing his own games, games that demanded an understanding of variables and a knowledge of geometry that his teachers claimed he didn't have. Larry is starting to demand more from his son's teachers. His experience with Todd has made him optimistic about what computers will mean for politics because "people will get used to understanding things, of being in control of things, and they will demand more." This optimism is widely shared among hobbyists, part of a distinct style of talking about computers and politics.

Hobbyists, like Fred and Larry, take what is most characteristic about their relationships with the computer—using computers to build safe microworlds of transparent understanding—and turn it into a political metaphor. Hobbyists associate images of computational transparency and of "knowing how the machine works" with a kind of politics where relations of power will be transparent, where people will control their destinies, where work will facilitate a rich and balanced cognitive life, and where decentralized power will follow from decentralized information resources. For many hobbyists a relationship with their home computer carries longings for a better and simpler life in a more transparent society. *Co-Evolution Quarterly, Mother Earth News, Runner's World,* and *Byte Magazine* lie together on hobbyists' coffee tables.

Small computers become the focus of hopes of building cottage industries that will allow people to work out of their homes, have more personal autonomy, not have to punch time cards, and be able to spend more time with their family and out of doors. Some see personal computers as a next step in the ecology movement: decentralized technology will mean less waste. Some see personal computers as a way for individuals to assert greater control over their children's education, believing that computerized curricula will soon offer children better education at home than can be offered in today's schools. Some see personal computers as a path to a new populism: personal computer networks will allow citizens to band together to send mail, run decentralized schools, information resources, and local governments. In sum, many of the computer hobbyists I have interviewed talk about the computers in their livingrooms as windows onto a future where relationships with technology will be more direct, where people will understand how things work, and where dependence on big government, big corporations, and big machines will end. They imagine the politics of this computer-rich future by generalizing from their special relationship to the technology, a relationship characterized by simplicity and a sense of control.

Alienation from work

Over 40 percent of those who responded to my survey worked, or had once worked, as computer programmers. The programmer is typically in a situation where he or she is in touch with only a very small part of the problem that is being worked on. Increasingly, programmers work in large teams where each individual has very little sense of the whole, of how it all fits together.

Programmers have watched their opportunities to exercise their skill as a whole activity being taken away (for those who are too young, the story of the process remains alive in the collective mythology of the shop). They have watched their work being routinized, being parcelled out into the well defined modules that make up the tasks of the structured programming team. They mythologize a golden age. This lived experience at work made programmers particularly sensitive to the parcellization of knowledge and to the alienation from a sense of wholeness in work. And they bring this sensitivity to their home computer hobbies.

Hannah worked as a programming consultant for a large business system for ten years before starting her own consulting company through which she offers her services to other computer hobbyists. To her, nothing is more depressing than working on a tiny piece of a problem. In her old job, "most of the time we didn't even know what the whole problem was." She likes working with computers at home because she has more control of her time and can spend more time with her family. But she says that what is most important about working with a personal computer is that "we can finally think about a whole problem." Hannah's feelings were widely shared among the hobbyists interviewed, most notably among programmers, ex-programmers, and "team engineers." Images of lack of intellectual balance, of fragmentation, of not being connected, came up often, with the computer at home usually placed in the role of righting what had been wrong at work. As Hannah put it: "With my computer at home we do everything, we see my whole self, all my kinds of thinking."

For these people, having a computer at home meant "thinking experiences" where they could see what their real capacities were, where they had a chance to try things out. Karl, for example, who worked for a long time as a programmer and who is now an engineer in a microprocessor firm, had thought a lot about his mental "ecology."

> In the first half of an engineering project there is literally nothing coming together and that's when we find that we need to go home and put something together. We used to make lamps like those in the living room out of glass bottles. But then towards the middle of an engineering project, things did start to come together and wel would lose the need for cutting glass. But if you never or rarely get to finish things at work, if your job is basically to make little pieces and it's somebody else's job to make them fit into a whole, then working with the computer at home can give you an experience of getting it all together. You do the whole thing—building up from machine code to finished project. It makes you feel in balance.

When we spoke with Karl he was at a point where everything at work seemed "pretty disconnected." Or, as Karl put it, if he hadn't had his home computer, it would have been "glass cutting time." Karl saw his current work with the computer as a corrective to fragmentation on the job. During our interview, he spoke to me about his current plans for revamping his computer system. Computer systems like his which have several components (keyboard, display screen, printer) have to be connected by using devices, usually simple circuits, called "interfaces." Karl's plan called for using a separate microprocessor as an interface for each component. He had conflicts about the "rationality" of his project.

After all, he admitted, it was far from economical if one measures economy in terms of the cost of the hardware. Each interface circuit needed only a few specialized and inexpensive chips. There was no need for a general-purpose microprocessor at each node. Specialized chips could do the job more cheaply, but could not satisfy his desire to experience the system as maximally coherent. By replacing the special-purpose circuits by separate, but identical, general-purpose microprocessors, the whole system, at least in Karl's eyes, became uniform, intelligible, and systematic. Karl could not help concluding: "We guess you could say that my choice of projects is not always rational." But from the perspective of using a relationship with computation as a way of "working through" personal concerns, Karl's rationale was clear. For Karl the "inexpensive" solution, using a collection of opaque, *ad hoc* circuits, felt unintelligible. It felt to him like his work situation. His plans for his multiprocessor system were dictated by the logic of compensation rather than by the logic of material economy.

The mind and body of the machine

In studying the hobbyist experience we have found people, largely people with technical backgrounds, in intense involvement with machines. They describe their work (or rather their leisure) with the computer as different from what they have done before with other hobbies. They describe it as an involvement with greater personal consequence. Some of the sense of consequence comes from an historical moment: the computer hobby is seen as signifying a place in the "avant garde." Although in some circles "computer person" is a term of derision, the hobbyist experiences it with pride.

Some of the sense of consequence comes from experiencing an individualistic and independent relationship with computation that can be mythologized as belonging to a now-past "golden age" of the programmer. But most of the sense of consequence comes from the holding power and intensity of the time spent with the computer. What is there about these people and these machines that makes possible relationships of such power and such intensity? For me, the relationships that hobbyists form with their home computers can be partially captured with a metaphor of the "mind" and the "body" of the machine.

The "mind" of the computer is that side of computation that involves thinking in terms of high-level programs. In this metaphor, relating to the "body" of the computer means not only working on hardware, but also, and indeed especially, working with programs in a way that is as close as possible to the machine code—that is to say, as close as possible to the core of the computer, its central processing unit (CPU). In terms of this metaphor I have found that the prototypical hobbyist is trying to get into a relationship with the body (rather than the mind) of the machine, to assert power and control in the relationship with the computer, and to create safe worlds of transparent understanding. In trying to find concepts for thinking more clearly about what draws the hobbyist to this kind of relationship with the CPU and about what its meaning might be, we find three issues particularly salient. We think, moreover, that, although we formulate them here in terms of computers, they are relevant to understanding relationships with other technologies as well. The first issue goes back to control.

The hobbyist complains of a work situation where everyone suffers from the constant presence of intermediaries. Bureaucracies stand between the programmer and the computer, a bureaucracy that schedules the computer, that decides its up and down time, that apportions the work for its software design and decides on priorities and procedures for access to it. At work, when something goes wrong with the system it is usually the fault of an intermediary person, one of the many "somebody elses" who deal with the machine. Or it may be the fault of a technical intermediary, one of the many elements in the computer system that mediate between the user and the bare machine: a compiler, an interpreter, an operating system, someone else's program. At home, the hobbyists feel themselves as working directly with the CPU, in complete and direct control of the machine's power.

And when something does blow up, the situation has a special immediacy. It is between them and the bare machine. When a FORTRAN program is run on a large IBM machine the events in the machine are far from being in one-to-one correspondence with the steps of code written by the programmer. Two factors contribute. First, it is in the nature of higher-level languages to work in a conceptual space different from that of the machine. FORTRAN works in a "formula" space, COBOL works in a "business" space, both very different from the space of bits and bytes. Second, the sense of indirect relationship is exacerbated when the compiled code is run by an operating system which allocates memory, mediates control of peripheral devices, and even interleaves the program with other programs. At home hobbyists can follow machine-language programs step by step as their instructions pass through the CPU. They can envision the changes in state of the whole system as being produced by specific actions of the CPU.

And if they suspect that there is a bug in the hardware they can pull out an oscilloscope and see whether the CPU is doing what it should in response to a given instruction. They can figure out where the signals should be going, they can collect their own evidence for what is going wrong, trap and fix the bug themselves. Again and again in my interviewing I heard about the pleasures of debugging—of "going in with meters and scopes and tracking it down." The procedure exhilarates. With every successfully tracked bug comes an affirmation of direct control over the machine. The issue of control was often explicitly recognized by the hobbyists we interviewed. But they lacked a language for naming a second issue which has to do with a notion referred to as "syntonicity" within the psychoanalytic tradition.

Syntonicity implies that we should look for "body-to-body" identification in every powerful relationship with a technology—the body of the person and the body of the machine. It implies that we should understand the appeal of machine language in terms of people's ability to identify with what is happening inside the machine. The CPU of the hobbyist computer lends itself to personal identification with its primary action: moving something that is conceptually almost a physical object (a byte of information) in and out of some thing (a register) that is almost a physical place. The metaphor is concrete and spatial. One can imagine finding the bytes, feeling them, doing something very simple to them, and passing them on. For many of the people that we met in the hobbyist culture, getting into this kind of identification feels safe. It makes the machine feet real. There is a third issue raised by the hobbyists' relationship to the CPU. It is an aesthetic one.

The generation of hobby computers that was born in the 1970s are very primitive machines. The hobbyist thinks of much about them as "klugey," a computerist's way of saying that one is dealing with a compromise, a collection of patches whose structure has been dictated by arbitrary corporate decisions, by economic necessities. The corner of the hobbyist machine that seems to them to have the greatest "intellectual integrity," that distills what they feel to be a tradition of some of the best ideas in computer science, that comes closest to being "clean," is the CPU. And so it is natural for the hobbyist to seek the closest possible contact with it. For a culture in which there is a widely shared aesthetic of simplicity, intelligibility, control, and transparency, getting into the "un-klugey" part of the machine and working in machine code seems the most aesthetically satisfying way to use the personal computer as an artistic medium.

2

Using Computers

Recent years have seen both a decline in the price and a rise in the power of personal computers. You can get a fairly basic word-processing kit, including a monochrome monitor, dot matrix printer and word-processing software, for around £400; Whereas £1,500 would buy you a powerful and sophisticated IBM-compatible personal computer (PC) with a built-in integrated suite of software (word processing, database, spreadsheet, graphics, communications, etc.), DOS and Windows operating systems, colour monitor and a bubblejet printer.

There may be a temptation for a community information service to assume that a computer is now a necessity for its work, before asking the obvious question: 'What do we need one for?' Consideration also needs to be given to the question of who is expected to use the computer. If your service relies on volunteers, they may have an aversion to new technology or simply not work long enough to become familiar with and confident in using a computer. Before plunging into the murky waters of information technology (IT), you should first of all ask the kind of basic questions that needed to be addressed when setting up your service, such as 'Why do we need IT?', 'What functions do we want it to perform?, 'What system is going to meet our needs?,' 'Who is going to use the system?', 'Where can I get advice?', 'What training will be required?', and so on. There are many reasons why an information service might want a computer but they may not necessarily all be the right reasons. Some wrong reasons are:

— everybody else has got one;

— to improve the image of the service;

– to sort out our database/statistics/financial accounts, which are in a mess.

This latter brings to mind the computer cliche 'garbage in, garbage out', namely that if you put rubbish into a computer, you can expect to get rubbish out. Before inputting any information into a computer, you must first have a logical and organized manual system. The computer won't do it for you.

Some right reasons might be:

— to provide faster and more timely access to information;
— to facilitate access to a wider range of information;
— to provide more sophisticated access to information;
— to enable more people to have direct access to information.

Before making a decision on what equipment to purchase, consider what functions you want the computer to perform. These might be one or several of the following:

— database management;

– recording *statistics* and, possibly, producing these in graphic form, i.e. as bar or pie charts, graphs, etc.;

– running *welfare benefits* and other programs;

— running a local *viewdata* system;

— *online access* to other external databases;

- word processing;
- financial accounting;
- desktop publishing.

If you require most of these functions, a fairly powerful machine would be necessary but you might be better advised to consider more than one computer or even linking them in a *local area network* (LAN). A LAN enables personal computers to communicate with each other and share resources such as software and printers. Usually, a LAN is driven by a computer with a large hard disk which contains the software programs and the data input by the rest of the PCs or terminals on the system. It also provides access to shared printers on the network and to central back-up facilities.

Choosing the right equipment and software

There are several ways in which you might set about choosing a computer, depending on the level of knowledge of staff in your organisation. Let us assume elementary or no knowledge of computers, in which case the options might be the following:

Dealers—may be OK if you know one who can be trusted or is recommended, but computer salesmen, like car salesmen, frequently try to get you to buy a machine of a higher specification than you need and blind you with technical jargon. Also limits your ability to shop around.

Consultants—usually expensive unless you can beg or borrow their services. Have a tendency to recommend separate software packages for each function or even writing a program to match needs exactly, rather than considering integrated packages which may require some compromise. OK if all the separate parts can work or are not required to work together.

Other organisations in the same sector who use computers in their work may' be able to recommend equipment and software from their own experience. However, they may be reluctant to admit shortcomings and the equipment/software they use may be out of date, given the speed of developments in this area.

Networks who support advice services or community and voluntary organisations, such as Community Computing Network (65 Litchfield Road, Cambridge. CBI 3SP) or the Computer Development Unit of LASA (2nd Floor, Universal House, Wentworth Street, London El 7SA Tel. 071-377 2798). Apart from giving direct advice themselves, they may be able to put you in touch with others who can help.

Within the space of this book, it is not possible to consider -all the potential uses to which a community information service may wish to put a computer. I have therefore concentrated on those aspects which, though not peculiar to information services, are a major feature of their work, namely database management (including viewdata and access to external databases), welfare benefits programs and enquiry statistics.

Database management

There are a number of reasons why a community information service would want to keep its information file on computer:

— beyond a certain point, a manual information file becomes unwieldy to use and update, whereas a computer database offers speed of access and ease of updating;

— complex searches involving, for example, subject, place and clientele, are extremely difficult and well nigh impossible to carry out with a manual system. A good computer database management system allows searching of the database by a combination of terms;

— individual records or subsets of the database can be printed out on demand in a variety of formats, e.g. as mailing labels, lists, standard letters;

— through networking, online or exchange of disks a computer database can be shared with other workers or organisations;

— customers can be given direct access to the database through public access terminals in your centre(s) or through a viewdata system (see below);

— entries can be fed into a word-processing or desktop publishing package and printed out as leaflets, directories, handbooks, etc. either directly or, more usually, by preparing a master copy which is then printed by offset litho.

A computer database is made up of two parts—the software, sometimes referred to as DBMS (database management system) and the database file, which is very much like a manual card index system in that it contains individual records made up of a number of fields (e.g. name, address, telephone number, hours of opening, etc.), into which bits of information (data) are entered (input). Most database systems store data in a highly structured form but there are some exceptions, known as free-form' or text-retrieval databases, which automatically index all significant words in a document.

Some database systems allow information to be viewed or edited either in tabular form, with each record represented by a row and fields as columns, or a record at a time. The tabular approach is fine if the fields in each record are short but is less convenient where you have lengthy fields. This can usually be circumvented by limiting the number of characters in each field, but then you cannot see the record as a whole. There are basically two types of database management systems: a *simple* DBMS produces a single file (sometimes called *flat file) of* records that have a predetermined number of fields and field lengths. This does not mean that field lengths cannot be varied or fields added or deleted, but any changes affect all the records in the file. A flat file may be adequate, say, for a database of community organisations, provided you have reasonably anticipated all the fields and field lengths that you are likely to require.

However, it will not be suitable for a situation where YOU want to create several different files and have the ability to link them. For example, in addition to the database of community organisations, you may want databases of leaflets, booklets and pamphlets; 'hard' information; individuals who can provide help; and enquiries plus the ability to search on all of them simultaneously. In those circumstances, you are more likely to need a *relational* DBMS, which would enable you to form links between the different files through the use of common denominators, such as subject or classification fields, client reference number, etc.

Examples of flat file systems are Cardbox Plus (used by Help for Health for its database), Q&A, and FileMaker Pro. Most database functions that come as part of a suite of integrated software, such as LotusWorks, will be flat file systems and may not be sophisticated enough to cope with anything but a simple database. Some of the leading relational systems are DataEase, Paradox, and dBase systems (dBase IV, FoxPro, Clipper). I have used for a number of years a system called Superfile which, at the time, had the advantage of not requiring any programming knowledge from the user. However, most of the database systems have become more user-friendly over the years.

The price you can expect to pay for a DBMS can range from £250 to £750 but some suppliers offer substantial discounts to voluntary organisations and charities.

Choosing the software

Before choosing a database management system, you should first of all draw up a shopping list of requirements and questions that YOU need to ask, such as the following:

— Is there a maximum size of file that the system can handle? In most cases this will depend on the size of your computer's memory but some systems may operate more slowly as the database grows beyond a certain size.

— Is there any limit on the size of records, the number of fields in a record, or the size of a field? If so, is this likely to be a problem?

— Is it possible to add, expand or delete fields from a record without difficulty?

— Is it possible to print out all or a selection of records and fields within records in a structured format?

— Can the data be fed into other software packages to produce lists, standard letters, mailing labels, etc.?

— What features does the system provide for searching records? For example, wildcards (* ? =) are a means of truncating search terms to take account of varying forms or spelling, e.g. ORGAN will find any first word in a field beginning with the letters O R G A N, such as 'organize', 'organisation' etc.; 'sounds like' will find records with similar sounding words to the search term, e.g. FAIR and FARE; or Boolean logic will logically link or exclude terms to narrow the field of search, e.g. A and B, A or B, A-G but not C, etc.

— Is there a facility to check on the validity of entered data?
— Is there provision for constructing user-friendly menus?
— How much knowledge is required to set up a database? How long does it take to acquire that knowledge? Can it be self-taught?
— How good is the documentation that accompanies the system?
— Is there a multi-user version of the software?
— What support is offered by the supplier? Is there a us;; group?

Creating a database

Having bought your software and installed it on the computer, the next step is to create the database(s). Each database management system will have its own methods for setting up the database and this section can give only a few tips from experience that should apply to whatever system you have chosen. First determine a *structure* for your database. If you are moving from a manual database, that structure may already exist.

The method of determining a structure for a database is similar to that for a manual system, as set down in Chapter Four. However, in addition to identifying what fields you require, you will also need to determine field lengths. Be generous, if your system will allow, so that you are not continually changing field lengths. Separate fields will need to be given field *names or tags* to which the computer attributes information that is being input.

For example, you might decide to call the 'organisation' field ORG and the 'address' field AD. Where a field consists of several lines, such as an address, it is advisable to split these into separate fields, particularly if you want to search on individual elements of an address field or to print them out as separate lines. An address field might thus be divided into two or three separate fields for building/house name, street, community/neighbourhood/village and fields for town, county and postcode. So your tags might look like AD1, AD2, COM, TOWN, COUNTY, PCODE. In some cases, a record might contain several repetitions of the same field types, e.g. names and addresses. Every time these occur you could give them the same tags, but this may cause problems when conducting searches or printing out information.

For example, if you wanted to see or print out a list of organisations in, for example, the 'Parkside' neighbourhood, the computer would also throw up records for, say, the secretary or second contact who lives in the 'Parkside' neighbourhood, if they all have the tag COM. The simplest way to get round this is to add to the root name for tags a separate number for each occurrence within your record structure, e.g. COM1, COM2, COM3, etc.

There are occasions when it is advantageous to use the same tag for several fields:

1. You might, for instance, want to have several fields for subject headings. By giving them the same tag name, this will ensure that, in whatever subject field a particular term is entered, the computer will throw up the record when a search is made under that term. It will also ensure that when records are printed out, the record will appear under each subject heading.
2. When you want to link files in a relational database system, this can be achieved by having a field with the same tag name appearing in each file, e.g. subject, name of organisation, client, etc. A search on

that particular field will throw up records in all the files bearing the term entered.

It is advisable to have the database form in the same order as the form that you send out to organisations for their information, as this makes it easier for the person inputting the information. One of the advantages of having a computerized database is that it enables you to automate administrative processes.

For example, update letters can be customized and printed out as you determine. If you want to update continually throughout the year rather than in one session, then you will need to build into your record structure, field that enables you to do this, e.g. date record last updated, or added, AGM date. Dates must be entered in a consistent form. Alternatively, you could update a section of the file each month by the initial letter of each organisation, e.g. Month 1: A-B, Month 2: C-D, and so on. When sending out update letters or forms for information about new organisations, if people's names and addresses are going to be recorded, make sure that you conform to the requirements of the Data Protection legislation by including a statement to the effect that: 'This information is being stored on a computer. Please indicate any items of information that you do not wish to be recorded.' Details of the Data Protection legislation are available in a series of free booklets from the Office of the Data Protection Registrar, Springfield House, Water Lane, Wilmslow, Cheshire SK9 5AX.

When sending out an update letter, it is also helpful to send a printout of the organisation's current entry as a prompt for any changes that may have occurred and to save the secretary time in filling out information that has not changed.

All database systems will have some facility for sorting records according to predetermined parameters, e.g., alphabetical by subject, then alphabetical by name of organisation or by date, record number, place, etc. You can usually set up several sort codes for different purposes. The sorting facility is used mainly as a prerequisite when printing out records as a list. For this, you will use another element of a database management system, the report function. (name may vary according to DBMS used). This enables you to print out information in a predetermined format, using all or a selection of fields in a record. Again, more than one report can be set up to take account of different uses. In some integrated packages, the database records have to be fed into the word-processing package for printing out.

Uses of the database

You will need to consider potential uses of the database. Is it a tool for the staff alone to use in answering enquiries? Are you going to allow public access to records either as printouts or through an online terminal? Are you going to make the database available to other organisations through exchange of disks or even sell it to interested parties? The answers to some of these questions will have implications for the kind of hardware and software you choose, and therefore need to be decided at an early stage.

For example, if you decide to allow public access via an online terminal, apart from the additional terminal and keyboard you will also need a multi-user version of the software which must be capable of building in safeguards to prevent the public either accidentally or deliberately erasing or changing records. Some database systems offer *runtime* versions of the software at a substantially lower price. These allow the system to be run but cannot be used to Make changes to it or to develop something new. A good example of this is Help for Health's Cardbox database, where subscribers receive a runtime version of Cardbox and regular updated disks of the database. Obviously, a runtime database will not be as up to date as a true online system but could be a cheaper and safer alternative. You can also get *videotext* packages which run on PCs and enable you to marry attractive graphics with a database. A good example is the TAP (Training Access Point) terminals located in various public buildings to dispense information on training opportunities, both local and national. The national information was obtained through online links with remote databases. The local information database is maintained on a master PC and then transferred by disk at regular intervals to the PCs driving the TAP terminals. The advantages of this, kind of system are:

— eye-catching graphics can be used to overcome the public's reluctance to use computers;
— protects your main database;
— less staff-intensive.

The disadvantages are:

— the information is not as up to date as a true online system;
— a PC is occupied just in running that function;
— it can become monopolized by young people who think it's the latest arcade game;
— if a printout facility is offered, this can easily be abused, requiring frequent staff attention;
— there is a need to make the equipment inaccessible or tamper-proof

PC-based videotext terminals have been used to good effect by some commercial organisations to provide local information and advertising. You find these most often in the windows of tourist information centres, the computer display being operated by a touch-sensitive keypad attached to the window. Another variation is to get a graphics package, such as Animator, which has the facility of enabling the computer to rotate a series of frames of information at set intervals. Several years ago COIC (Careers & Occupational Information Centre) offered a videotext package called Rotaview which enabled users to create colourful graphics and link these with a database.

The system was used to prepare an offline database, to access or download frames of information from Prestel, or to operate as a mini-viewdata service with users dialling into the database for information. Another attraction of Rotaview was its carousel feature that enabled up to 80 frames of information to be scrolled at intervals. A particular use for this type of feature in an information centre would be to display essential information to the public out of hours. Rotaview was marketed at schools, colleges and public libraries but, alas, was developed only for the BBC micro and is no longer available. However, with infinitely more powerful PCs around today, there must be similar software on the market, if you are interested in this way of displaying information.

Other database systems

Using a PC is not the only way of setting tip a community information database. There are other options which may be open to services which are part of a much larger organisation, like public libraries, and are designed to cope with extremely large databases and/or allow wider access. In the early 1970s British Telecom (or The Post Office as it then was) developed a *viewdata* system called Prestel which enabled users to access thousands of pages of information on all sorts of topics via the medium of the telephone and specially adapted television sets (and later also PCs). The system has never quite lived up to its early promises but is still going strong. A number of public libraries were involved in the early trial of Prestel and recognized the potential of the system, if not of Prestel itself. Eventually, local authorities began to set up their own viewdata systems of information about council services and other local information. The public could access the system either directly from home or through terminals located in libraries and other public buildings. In some instances, the library service is responsible for maintaining the database, in others another department of the local authority. Viewdata systems offer the following:

— access to large amounts of continually updated information;
— use of graphics;
— public online access from home, workplace or publicly located terminals;
— centralized updating of information.

Some disadvantages are:

— they need dedicated teams to maintain the database;
— many clientele of community information services would not be able to afford equipment to access the database or would be afraid of using a computer;
— limitations on the amount of information that can reasonably be presented by the system.

Some public libraries, like Berkshire, are beginning to recognise the income-generating potential of viewdata, with electronic *Yellow pages,* teleshopping, rental pages, and closed user group facilities. Apart from running viewdata systems, mini- or mainframe computers can also be the hosts for community information databases using such software as IBM's STAIRS (Storage and Information Retrieval System). Some libraries set up their databases on a mainframe computer from the start; others, like my own, have transferred from a PC-based system. Some advantages of using a mainframe computer are:

— almost limitless power;
— speed of operation;
— updating from multi-access points;
— online access from other council departments, the public, etc.;
— possible links into computer issue systems;
— feedback from other departments/organisations using the system.

Disadvantages are:

— they are not particularly user-friendly - no use of graphics;
— it can be difficult to maintain consistency of input and updating with multi-access;
— they take second place to other council programmes, such as payroll.
— you need to 'log on' each time the system is used.

Reference was made above to possible links between mainframe-based community information files and library computerized issue systems. In fact, a number of these systems now offer add-on features for storing community information themselves. The advantages of these are:

— access to database through every library in the system;
— public access through OPACs (Online Public Access Terminals) or, in some cases, dial-in facilities;
— multi-access to inputting and updating database.

Disadvantages are:

— they can slow down issue system;
— they are not usually accessible by other council departments;
— with multi-access, it can be difficult to maintain consistency of inputting and updating;
— as with viewdata systems, information is usually limited.

Inevitably, with a technology that is developing so fast, there will be new systems for presenting information coming along. Glasgow has been experimenting with HyperCard, which allows the user to search through text, pictures, numbers and instructions to gain information about the city. Before long someone is bound to be using CD-ROM or interactive video.

Online searching

Another use for your PC might be to link into other remote databases such, as a local authority's viewdata system. To do this you will need' a *modem,* to link the PC to the telephone network, and communications software, which could be a separate package or part of a suite of software such as LotusWorks or Windows 3.

Most online databases, except for local viewdata, are not appropriate for community information services, but there is one that *is: Volnet UK,* operated jointly by The Volunteer Centre UK and the Community Development Foundation. Volnet UK is an online information service containing thousands of references to press items, journal articles, reports, books and current research projects on community development, voluntary action, youth affairs, child care and social policy issues, stored on an easy-to-use computer database. For a modest annual fee (00 local community/voluntary agency, £90 national/ regional voluntary agency, £150 central/local government department) you get unlimited access to the database (no charge per second or minute), a telephone helpline, plus a photocopy service for articles, for which a small charge is made. Details from Volnet UK, Community Development Foundation, 60 Highbury Grove, London N5 2AG.

Computer programs

Providing welfare benefits information and advice can be notoriously difficult because of the complex legislation, which is why some advice centres and public library community information services are harnessing the power of PCs to help them. These are usually designed for use by advisers although, over the years, some attempt has been made to develop client-operated systems, largely without success.

Welfare benefits programs contain the rules of the benefits system and present on the computer screen a series of questions. The adviser, in consultation with the client, types in the details and the computer works out whether the client is entitled to benefit and, if so, how much. The results can usually be printed out and given to the client to take away. The main benefits covered include Income Support, Housing Benefit, Family Credit and Community Charge Benefit. The advantages of these programs are:

— consistency;
— they do not let you forget little-used regulations or 'passport' benefits, where claiming one benefit automatically entitles the client to others;
— a novice worker can tackle more complex cases;
— 'what-if' calculations can be done speedily;
— printouts of results can be obtained;
— some clients like the computerized approach and are reassured by it.

Some disadvantages are:

— they are only as accurate as the information input;
— the benefits, system is so complex, programs are bound to have quirks;
– an experienced adviser can usually work faster than the program;
— they ran lead to over-confidence;
— some clients can be intimidated by a computer and find it intrusive;
— they are no substitute for experience.

The following chart lists the main welfare benefits programs available and their features. For more details, addresses etc., see the *Computanews* factsheet Welfare benefits programs (see Wow for details of all the factsheets in this series).

Other programs

There are other PC-based programs and databases available on such areas as debt advice calculations and sources of funding from charitable trusts. Resource Information Services, in conjunction with LASA's Computer Development Unit, is currently developing a database of advice agencies in London for piloting in autumn 1992. A good way of keeping up with the latest developments in programs for advice work is to take out a subscription to the excellent bimonthly periodical *Computanews*.

Statistics

Collating and manipulating statistics is one area where computers have a distinct advantage. They can do in seconds or minutes what would take hours of work manually. However, if all you want the computer to do is add up and produce totals in broad categories, then you might as well stick to pencil and calculator. But, for detailed analysis of enquiries and graphic representation of information by means of pie or bar charts, graphs, etc., you will need a computer program. There are two options: either devise your own system using a spreadsheet package or a relational database system linked with a spreadsheet package, or buy a specially designed program. A lot of the pioneer work in this field has been carried out by LASA's Computer Development Unit which, some years ago, developed CRESS (Client Records and Enquiry Statistics Service) and is currently engaged on developing a model recording system called STATS. Finally, there are many more uses to which a community information service might wish to put its computer, e.g. word processing, accounts, graphics, desktop publishing, but these aspects apply to many other organisations and it is beyond the scope of this book to cover them.

3

Information Base

Information is the life-blood of a community information service and the information file is at its heart. Unless the heart is sound and continually pumping a supply of regularly renewed and fresh information into the system, it will not function at its best. Therefore, it is important to give extra care and attention to planning the resources needed to set up a sound information base and a workable system for keeping it up to date.

Some basic things you will need to consider are as follows:

— How is the information to be collected?
— What method is to be used for processing and storing information?
— How is the information to be retrieved?
— What size is the file likely to be?
— What areas, geographical and subject, is the file to cover?

In addition, you will need to consider how the information is going to be disseminated, if it is not just for internal use; but that is the subject of the next chapter. The kind of system you choose and the degree of its sophistication will depend on the nature of your information service, the size and complexity of the information you need to store, the staff, and the financial resources available. When designing a system, make sure it is readily understandable to all those using it—volunteers and public included—and not just to professionals.

Coverage

In identifying the need for your community information service, you should have reached a decision already on the community to be served. This may be either a geographical community or a community of interest or both. Either way, you will still need to make a decision about the extent of your information base. For example, a neighbourhood information service must decide what information to collect on the wider area—town, county, region, nation—outside its local community. An information service aimed at a fairly wide area may need to limit its interests to a particular sector of the community or to a particular range of subjects, e.g. the low paid, those receiving income support, or those with debt problems. Even an information service in support of a local campaign may benefit from collecting information on similar campaigns or problems country-wide.

Types of information

The information base of your service is most likely to include the following types of information:

Soft information—details of clubs, societies, organizations and services; individuals; events, etc. Usually this information will not be available in a published form, or at least not in sufficient detail, and it will be necessary to make a conscious effort to collect it. This information may comprise the major part of the resources file.

Hard information—factual information on a specific subject e.g. benefit rates for single-parent families, how to get legal aid, how to change your name. This information will be available in a variety of Banns, some ephemeral such as leaflets, pamphlets, booklets, broadsheets, posters, periodical articles, etc. Such items are usually kept in a vertical file, in storage boxes or similar receptacles and accessed via some form of index or classification scheme. Other hard information may be in the form of books, multi-volumed reference works, law books, or even audiovisual forms. If there are many items of this type, they will need to be classified and shelved.

Supplementary information is information already produced in a particular format—directories, handbooks, diaries, annual reports, constitutions, newsletters—of organizations appearing in your information file.

'Soft' information

It is highly unlikely and undesirable that an information service should need to 'go it alone' in the collection of information. Such is the volume, complexity and variety of sources of information in present-day society that, unless your service has very narrow terms of reference, it will be virtually impossible for it to collect and keep up to date all the information that is required.

Therefore, it is important that you first of all identify the information providers, support services and 'gate-keepers' in your community and establish effective contacts with them. These links may already have been forged in the process of conducting a community profile. They now need to be fostered and strengthened, so that there can be a mutual exchange of information. These contacts will also be able to provide you with useful feedback from the community as to the success or otherwise of your service. The network of contacts can be maintained on a fairly casual basis as the need arises, or you might want to formalize the arrangement. Some ways of doing this include irregular 'get togethers', informal luncheon clubs, regular meetings with agendas and minutes, or the circulation of a newsletter or bulletin. Other activities that could develop out of such meetings are joint collection of information, shared publicity, compilation and publication of directories, information handbooks and leaflets, training, and general discussion of common problems. Collecting information is a time-consuming process and there is no one method of going about it. You will probably have to use a combination of several techniques to build up a satisfactory information base. One thing definitely to be avoided is duplicating work that has already been done. So first of all identify the following:

Existing information files. Contact all the other community information services, council departments and organizations who are likely to maintain information files and ask if they would be willing to share this information. Try to offer something in return, either an exchange of information or some other help you can provide.

Local directories. There are several types of directory that may be available in your area and which are useful sources of soft information: (a) local government authorities often produce directories or town guides of their area which contain a certain amount of local information or they may produce a guide to council services; (b) telephone directories, especially *Yellow pages* which have an alphabetical subject arrangement; (c) area directories, such as those produced by Thompson's Newspapers, which are similar to *Yellow pages* but also contain a section of community information—your local newspaper may produce a directory of local services, sometimes in conjunction with local information groups; (d) citizen's guides may also be produced by the local newspaper as a supplement to an existing newspaper; (e) CVSs or RCCs sometimes produce directories of voluntary organizations in their area or you may find these listed in your local CVS/RCC annual report; (f) directories covering a special subject, such as accommodation, halls for hire, etc.; (g) directories aimed at a particular interest group or groups e.g. people with disabilities or senior citizens.

National directories are useful not only for the wider network of services but also for identifying local offices of a national organization.

Other methods to use in building up your information base and maintaining its currency include:

Looking and listening. A lot of information can be gathered by simply walking around your community, looking at noticeboards, picking up leaflets, or attending open meetings, fairs, fetes and other community events. This method of collecting information is unpredictable and requires more than a 9-to-5, five-day week.

Contact with individuals. People are a major source of information in any community and there are always those to whom others naturally go for information. Try to identify such people and enlist their help, possibly by offering something in return—bartering is a time-honoured system! Direct contact with individuals in other information services and organizations is often a better way of eliciting information than impersonal methods and also paves the way for further cooperation. Pay regular visits to such centres.

Scanning newspapers, magazines, newsletters, etc. can turn up details of new organizations; changes of personnel, premises or hours of opening; new services introduced; and may highlight problem areas where information may be needed.

Other documents, including council minutes and agendas, planning regulations, annual reports (ask to be put on mailing lists for these), leaflets and manifestos.

Media publicity. Local press, radio and cable television stations may be prepared without charge to put out a call for organizations to contact your service. If not, then consider inserting an advert or, where there is, a local directory produced, have a tear-out slip included for organizations to fill in and return to you. As a result of these various methods, an amount of raw material will have been obtained which may be of use to your information service. How accurate, up to date and complete the data is will depend very much on the reliability of the source. In most cases, unless you have every confidence in the source, the information will have to be checked before it is entered in a more permanent form in your resource file. So, at this stage, simply record it onto say a scrap 5in × 3in card and put it into a temporary file.

The information you have obtained will be of several different kinds but the most common will probably be that relating to organizations, clubs and societies. This is the most difficult type of information to collect since it is ever changing and therefore unrelenting effort will be required to achieve even reasonable completeness or accuracy—100% will be impossible. However, with a good system for collecting and updating the information, you should be able to build up and maintain an acceptable file.

A lot of staff time will be needed to carry out this work, so first of all investigate whether there are other local information services that need this type of information and would be willing to help in its collection. It may be possible to collect the information through an umbrella group, where the work can be farmed out so that it is not too great a burden on any one organization. Alternatively, a joint approach can be made on behalf of a number of organizations.

Ideally, the most effective way to collect information of this kind is to pay a personal visit to each organization or service, but rarely will that be possible without extensive staff resources or a very small community. The cheapest and quickest way to collect this information is by telephoning. Prepare a standard list of questions to ask so that entries in your information file follow the same format.

Telephoning is only practicable if you have a reasonably small number of organizations to contact, say up to one hundred. If visits and telephoning are ruled out, then the information can be collected initially by postal questionnaire, with a request for up-to-date information sent at least once a year and also when it is known from other sources that changes have taken place. A covering letter should be sent with the questionnaire or update request, explaining why the information is needed and asking for cooperation. If the information is to be passed on to other organizations or commercial bodies, either free or for payment, this should be drawn to the attention of the recipient of the questionnaire, so that they have an opportunity to decline to give the information or insist that it is not so disseminated. If the information is to be stored in a computer, then you will need to meet the requirements of the Data Protection Act.

If it can be afforded, include with your questionnaire some means of returning it free of charge, as this will significantly improve the response rate. Separate forms may be required to collect different kinds of information. The following is a suggested list of headings which you might need to include on forms for collecting information from two of the most common types of organization.

Clubs and societies

— *Name:* the name by which the club is best known, plus the full name if different. Indicate relationship to larger body, i.e. branch, regiment, lodge, etc.

— *Secretary's name, address and telephone number* or those of a similar person if the organization has no secretary.

— *Place, day and time of meetings.*

— *Purpose of organization* if not self-evident from the name.

— *Eligibility:* any restrictions by age, sex, ethnic group, occupation, status (single, divorced, widowed) etc.

— *Subscription:* any charge to become a member or to attend meetings.

— *Annual general meeting:* the date of an organization's AGM can be a useful indication of when to send out update forms as this is when officers or policies are likely to change.

— *Other officers:* names, addresses, telephone numbers of treasurer, president, chairman, publicity officer, membership secretary, etc.

— *History of the organization* including special events or persons associated with it.

— *Publications:* newsletter, diary, commemorative brochures, annual report, etc.

— *Date* the information was obtained and/or last updated or checked.

Agencies and organizations providing a service

— *Name:* popular name and full name, e.g. CHAT (Come Here and Talk), SHAC (Shelter Housing Action Centre), plus relationship to parent body where necessary.

— *Address:* street address and postal address, Post Office, box number if used.

— *Telephone and fax number,* including—service number, administration number, after-hours or hotline numbers.

— *Contact person:* personal name, title and address, if different from above.

— *Hours of opening:* days and times; note if seasonal, e.g. holiday period, term time.

— *Services provided:* advice, counselling, practical help, etc.; types of enquiry the service would like to have referred to them.

— *Eligibility:* age, income, sex, residency, status.

— *Application procedures:* walk-in, appointment or waiting list; what papers or documents need to be brought.

— *Cost:* free, fees, means-tested, donations; any facilities for payments to be spread over a period; help available from local or central government, charities, etc.

— *Geographical area served:* neighbourhood, city, county, region, *ad hoc* area; no geographical restrictions.

— *Branch offices:* extension bureaux, mobiles, surgeries, etc.; include hours of opening, routes and times of stops.

— *Director,* administrator or executive director of the service; name and telephone or extension.

— *Volunteers:* does the service use volunteers and for what purposes? Method of recruitment.

— *Publications:* directories, handbooks, leaflets, annual report, etc.

— *Funding:* local government grant-aided, donations, etc.

— *Special facilities:* foreign languages spoken, access and facilities for people with disabilities, photocopying or fax service, escort, advocacy, etc.

— *Transportation:* how to get to the service, e.g. bus route numbers, underground line and station, etc.

— *Date* information was obtained and/or last updated or checked.

These two lists represent most of the facts that a community information service might need to know about an organization or service. In practice, depending on the scope of your service, it may not be necessary to include all the fields in the questionnaire. It is a good idea to get the person filling in the questionnaire to sign it, thereby giving the information service some protection against claims of giving out wrong information—a not uncommon occurrence, especially when the information is committed to print.

There are other types of 'soft' information that your service might need to collect, for example halls for hire, places of local worship, accommodation, 'What's-on' events, local industry. The procedure is much the same:

— Decide what information you need to know.

— Devise a standard format or list of questions to ask.

— Identify possible sources of information.

— Decide which method or methods to use to collect the information: telephone, personal visit, postal questionnaire, press advert, etc.

How to store 'soft' information

There are various methods that can be used for storing information:

A *list* is easy and quick to consult, can be photocopied for clients to take away and can be faxed, but has very little flexibility for inserting and updating information.

A *strip index* provides flexibility, can easily be photocopied, and is available in various forms: large binders holding many pages, smaller folders containing just a few pages, address books, wall-hung panels, rotunda units, etc. Strips are available in several colours, which allows for a simple categorization, and various widths. Even so, they are limited as to the amount of information that can be contained on them. It is also not quite as easy to insert new strips as the manufacturers claim.

Cards are still one of the most commonly used systems for storing information. They are infinitely flexible, easy to insert and update, can be sorted into any preferred order, and require very little technical know-how. The most popular sizes are 5in × 3in, used mainly for indexes or temporary information waiting to be checked, 6in × 4in, and 8in × 5in, which are large enough to contain sufficient information about most organizations or services and to be preprinted with a standard grid for recording the information. There are more superior types of card file available, such as the Rondofile or Rotadex systems which use custom-designed stationery and therefore tend to be more expensive. With systems that use standard cards, you can—if you are hard-up or want to save trees—use the reverse of scrap cards. Card files have a number of disadvantages: they are not so easy to carry around, they are not easily reproducible if someone Wants a copy of a particular section, multiple access (e.g. by name, subject, area, service, etc.) requires duplication of cards, and the updating process can be tedious.

You may still find around *edge-punched cards* which offer a primitive type of multi-access to the information on the card through the strategic use of knitting needles or rods. Personally, I would save up and get a computer.

Loose-leaf binders with one sheet for each entry, sometimes called 'sheaf' binders, have a similar flexibility to cards. They are slightly slower to add to and amend but are more portable. They are suited best for alphabetical arrangements as they are difficult to guide.

Microcomputers now have the capacity to handle immense information files that can be accessed by any number of predetermined variables or even free-text searching by keyword, depending on the software used. With a printer attached, all the information or sections of it can be printed out on demand or to provide a master for printing by conventional methods. Personal computers now begin at prices that bring them within the range of most community information services. However, there is danger in automatically seeing the computer as the best solution for maintaining your information file, as this may not always be the case. A lot depends on the size of your file and its complexity, what you want to do with the file, and to what other uses you want to put the computer. The importance of the computer in, information and advice work is such that it merits a chapter to itself, and you will find these and other aspects dealt with in more detail in Chapter Eight.

Filing system

Whichever method is chosen for physically storing the information, except for that by microcomputer, it will be necessary to decide the best way of arranging entries so that the information can be retrieved swiftly and accurately. In order to ensure that the total resources of your information service are used to the full when answering an enquiry, it will help if the system used to organize the information file can be integrated with that for the vertical file and the bookstock. This point needs to be borne in mind now, although it will be dealt with more fully later.

The bulk of the information file is likely to comprise 'soft' information which you have collected about organizations, clubs, societies and services and, to a lesser extent, about individuals who are a valuable source of information or advice, plus items of 'hard' information not available or conveniently available in printed form. There are several ways in which you might want to retrieve this information—by the names of the organizations, by subject (i.e. area of interest), by clientele, by the type of service (e.g. counselling), or by place. In practice, the 'clientele' and 'type of service' approaches are usually catered for through the subject file rather than as separate files.

Organizations file

The master file for the whole system will usually be an alphabetically arranged sequence of entries by name of organization. It is generally recommended that the full, official name of the organization is used, with references from other forms of the name. In practice, it does not really matter as long as there are references from the alternatives to whichever form is chosen. There is a good argument for putting the main entry for an organization under the form of name by which most people refer to it, even if this differs from or is an abbreviation of the official name. This is especially so where the file is to be used by the public.

In addition to details of organizations, each entry in the master file may also contain certain 'housekeeping' details relating to the maintenance of all the information files, plus references to appropriate headings in the subject file, where relevant information can be found, and a classification number.

Subject file

Most enquiries received by a community information service are likely to be about the need for a service or activity or for help with solving a problem, rather than for information on a specific named organization. So the information you have collected about organizations, services and individuals will also need to be accessible by the services and activities they provide. There are two ways this can be achieved, by either using a subject index or having a subject file of organizations. In both, you will need to choose or adopt a set of subject headings which will adequately describe the information on file or elsewhere in the system and the interests of your clientele.

If you are compiling your own list of subject headings, choose terms that are in common use by your clientele, especially if they will be consulting the files directly, rather than the 'official' term, e.g. OUT OF WORK or ON THE DOLE instead of REDUNDANT. Always refer from alternatives not used to the chosen term.

A *subject index is* rather like the index to a book. It is an alphabetically arranged file of subject heading cards on which reference is made to where information on that subject can be found. The cards themselves do not contain information. The subject index can contain references to organizations, individuals and other supplementary material such as pamphlets, periodical articles, audiovisual material, books, etc.

A *subject file* consists of an alphabetically arranged set of subject heading cards behind which are filed copies of the organization cards appropriate to that heading and possibly cards containing items of 'hard' information. An alternative is to arrange cards according to a classification system either devised by yourself or adopted from another service, such as the NACAB classification scheme.

Place file

Where an information service covers a number of distinct towns, villages or neighbourhoods, each having a similar range of organizations, it may be helpful to have a file that can be accessed by place. There are a number of options. You could sort the organizations file initially by place, especially if it contains few organizations whose responsibilities extend to the whole area covered by your service. Alternatively, if most of the organizations are prefixed with the name of the place (e.g. EXVILLE ATHLETIC CLUB, EXVILLE COUNCIL FOR THE DISABLED), the alphabetically arranged master file will automatically bring together those from the same location, provided inverted headings have not been used.

Some arrangements will have to be made for organizations which do not conform to the pattern, either because the place-name does not feature at the beginning or because it is not contained in the name of the organization at all. In these cases, an additional card can be made out with either an inverted heading (e.g. EXVILLE, ROTARY CLUB OF) or the place-name can be prefixed.

The third option is to have a separate file of organization cards arranged initially by place and then alphabetically by name of organization or by subject.

Filing alphabetically

Filing alphabetically is not quite as simple as ABC, as any librarian will tell you. There are two recognized methods, known as 'word by word' and 'letter by letter'. In word by word, entries are initially sorted by the first word in the heading, then headings that begin with the same word are sorted by the second word and so on. Another way to describe this method, which may be more helpful, is to treat spaces between words in a heading as an imaginary letter coming before 'a' in the alphabet, then sort letter by letter.

In letter by letter, you simply ignore any spaces in the heading and sort one letter at a time from left to right. Here is how a small group of headings would look sorted by the two methods:

Word by word	*Letter by letter*
DO SOMETHING! BOYS CLUB	'DOG AND BONE' DARTS TEAM
'DOG AND BONE' DARTS TEAM	DOGSBURY RESIDENTS' ASSOCIATION
DOG SNIFFERS ANONYMOUS	DOGS HOMES
DOGS HOMES	DOG SNIFFERS ANONYMOUS
DOGSBURY RESIDENTS' ASSOCIATION	DO SOMETHING! BOYS CLUB

There are several other niceties to do with filing alphabetically but we only need mention here that hyphens are treated as spaces in word-by-word sorting and numerals are spelt out as said, so that 1900 (the year) is considered for sorting as NINETEEN HUNDRED and 1,900 as ONE THOUSAND, NINE HUNDRED.

File 'housekeeping'

In addition to the information needed to answer enquiries, there are other items of information to do with the maintenance of the file which may usefully be included on each entry, such as the following:

— the date the information was obtained, last updated or last checked, which will indicate not only the degree of reliability to be placed on it but also when to update;

— the date a questionnaire or update letter was sent - a check for chasing up non-returned forms;

— additional contacts or other information which does not fit into the main part of the entry;

— subject headings used in the subject file;

— place headings used in the place file, if not obvious from the name of the organization;

— feedback—comments from users of the service;

— 'tracings', i.e. a list of other cards that refer to they can be traced and amended or withdrawn when necessary.

The amount of this 'housekeeping' information you need to include will depend on how sophisticated you need your file to be. The bigger the information service and the larger the file, then the more likely it is that you will need to introduce a systematic procedure for processing information. In such a case it is usual for the housekeeping information to go on the reverse of each entry, using a standard grid like the one illustrated here. It is arguable that if your information file requires this degree of sophistication, you ought seriously to consider keeping it on computer.

For a small community information service, it may be quite adequate just to note the date when the information was collected, checked or updated.

Updating

By their very nature the entries in your database will be changing continually. Hours of opening, meeting places, officers, membership fees, subscriptions, charges, etc. are all susceptible to frequent change. Therefore, it is important to have a system for regularly updating each entry in the database. There are several ways of achieving this but, whichever method you adopt, it must be regular and ongoing.

Interim updating

All the entries for organizations should be checked at least once a year to ensure they are still correct. In between times, however, new information will be brought to your attention by various means, including word of mouth, newspaper reports, organization newsletters, company reports and by direct contact with the organization itself. If the source of information is reliable, it can be substituted immediately for the out-of-date information in the database but, if not, it should be noted and a further check made to verify its accuracy. A simple way to add new information to an entry in a card file is to write it onto self-adhesive labels or slips (obtainable at most stationers) which can be stuck over the original information. Even though an entry has been updated in between times, it should still be checked formally once a year.

Annual updating

Once a year is probably a reasonable time-span for updating your database but a shorter interval may be necessary if the information content changes frequently. You will need to decide how the annual update is to be carried out. Some organizations like to update the entire file at the same time, so that they can say the file was as accurate as possible at a particular date. However, this does create a tremendous amount of extra work for a period of several weeks and you may feel it necessary to get extra paid, work-experience or volunteer help. Another disadvantage of this method is that it captures a picture of organizations at a set moment in time. Some organizations may be just about to make changes, and your records for these would be out of date for almost a year.

Alternatively, you may decide to update on a continuous basis by using either the date the record was added to the database or the organization's annual general meeting (AGM) date as a trigger. This is easy to do if your database is kept on a computer, since a date field can be used to produce a subset of records and, by linking the database with a word processing package, a personalized standard letter can be printed out for sending to each organization. It is less easy with a card or any other kind of file. You can get little coloured metal tags to clip on to the top edge of cards, a different colour for each month, or you could use an appropriate symbol on the heading of the card, such as a coloured dot, a letter or number. Tags can make the file look a bit messy and are easily knocked off if it is in constant use; symbols require the whole file to be checked through.

My preference is to update records shortly before or after each organization's AGM, since most organizations, if they are going to change their officers or constitution, generally do it once a year at the AGM. As many organizations do not know their AGM date a year in advance, it is enough just to indicate the month in which the AGM is usually held. For those organizations and services which do not have an AGM, you will need to use the date the information was added as the trigger.

When writing to organizations to update their information, it is better to send them a copy of their record with a request to indicate any changes, rather than sending a blank questionnaire. This saves the secretary unnecessary time in repeating information that has not altered.

An alternative to writing to each organization is to phone, but this is time-consuming and costly, and only feasible if the number of organizations to contact is fairly small. Avoid sending out updates at times when people are likely to be away, such as during the summer. There are certain times when it is more appropriate to update other kinds of information, e.g. social security benefit rates (which usually change in April and September), adult education classes or school, college and university courses which change termly.

When an updated entry is returned it should be checked to see if the subject or place headings still apply. Minor changes can be recorded on the master card and any other cards in subject or place files; major changes may require a new set of cards to be produced. For those with computerized databases the process is simpler as just the one record has to be updated. Don't forget to change the date the information was last checked or updated.

'Hard' information

As well as the database, most information services will need a certain amount of 'hard' information to answer enquiries. Short, unrecorded or inadequately recorded items of 'hard' information, as we have already seen, can be incorporated into the database. However, the majority of hard information will usually be found in one or more of the vast range of print forms, starting from locally produced free broadsheets to extremely expensive multi-volumed loose-leaf reference works.

Within the scope of this book, it is not possible to go into detail about the sources of this material, since they will vary considerably according to the type and subject range of the service you are operating. Community information dates rapidly so any printed sources should be treated with care. However, you might find useful a chapter on the sources of community information that I contributed to *Printed reference material and related sources of information*, 3rd edn, Library Association Publishing, 1990, which concentrated on organizations and on those items which are regularly updated.

The following framework for collecting community information was originally devised by Grainne Morby, who at the time was working for the Community Information Project, with some additions of my own:

Distinguish between subject areas

In other words, identify the main topics into which the subject scope of your information service naturally divides. Throughout this framework I will take as an example an information service for which the main area of interest is housing. It is sometimes useful to apply a consistent criterion when dividing up a subject, although obviously this would not be so easy for an information service whose scope covers as broad an area as, say, 'community information'.

However, taking housing as our example, you could decide to divide it by type of accommodation, e.g. owner-occupied, private-rented, council-rented, New Town, Housing Association, institutional accommodation, tied accommodation, mobile homes, etc. In most cases you would probably need an additional category for subjects that cut across all or more than one category. In the case of housing, this might be 'squatting' or 'homelessness'.

Since the material you want to collect will usually be written to meet a particular need or needs, it is advisable to collect information around those needs rather than for fitting into a theoretical framework. The kind of broad client groups that might be identified in the field of housing are landlords, tenants, owner-occupiers, squatters, transients, elderly people, people with disabilities, the homeless. Then, one could identify client groups who share a common problem or need associated with their particular type of accommodation, such as eviction, dampness, house repair, renovation, harassment, mortgages, rent arrears, planning permission, redevelopment, etc. Once these subject areas and client needs have been identified, it should give you clearer guidelines when you come to select material from the various sources identified in the next part of the framework.

Print sources

Official

(a) National

— Pre-legislation: political party manifestos and policy documents, speeches by Ministers, the Queen's Speech at opening of Parliament, White Papers, Green Papers.

— Legislation: Bills, Hansard reports of debates in both Houses of Parliament, Acts, Statutory Instruments.

— Guidance to local statutory bodies: circulars and letters from Ministers, guidance notes, reports of Inspectors.

— Reference books: collections of legislation, e.g. *Statutes in force, Legal aid handbook.*

— Periodicals from government departments and agencies, e.g. *Department for Employment gazette.*

— Guidance to the public: leaflets, posters, videos and other A/V material.

— Ombudsmen.

(b) Regional

— Health authorities, British Rail.

— Privatized utilities: gas, water, electricity, telephone.

— Consumer watchdog bodies: Post Office Users' National Council (POUNC), Office of Gas Supply (OFGAS), Office of Electricity Regulation (OFFER),

Office of Telecommunications (OfTel), Office of Water Services (OFWAT).

(c) Local

— Local authority policies and decisions: agendas, minutes, standing orders, by-laws and regulations.

— Guidance to the public: handbooks, leaflets, etc. from local authorities, area and district health authorities, Community Health Councils, local offices of government agencies.

2 Non-official

(a) National

— Reference books and handbooks from commercial publishers.

— Voluntary organizations.

— Pressure groups, self-help groups.

— 'Umbrella' organizations, e.g. National Council for Voluntary Organizations, Federation of Independent Advice Centres.

— Professional bodies, e.g. The Law Society.

— Trade associations, e.g. National Association of Retail Furnishers.

— Educational bodies, e.g. National Extension College, Open University.

— Trade unions.

— The media.

— Practitioners in the field who publish.

(b) Local

— Claimants' unions.

— Law centres, other specialist advice centres.

— Neighbourhood and generalist advice centres, resource centres.

— Local 'umbrella' groups.

— Pressure groups, campaigning groups, action centres. Voluntary organizations.

— Local media: newspapers, community newspapers, radio, cable television.

(c) New technology

— Videotext systems: Prestel, teletext, private viewdata.

— Online computer databases, e.g. Volnet.

— CD-ROM, videodiscs, etc.

This list is not intended to be exhaustive but will give you some idea of the range of sources in which to look for information. Howard Matthews, in his book *Community information* has drawn up a set of criteria for selecting community information materials. It is aimed particularly at library community information services but may be generally helpful for anyone setting up such a service.

1. Selection should be done by those who know the community best.
2. Material should relate to specific, local, identified needs.
3. All material should be current.
4. All material should be written at a level appropriate to its intended use.
5. Material should be concerned with the practicalities of problem solving.
6. All new material should either fill a gap, offer a new viewpoint, or promise something better.

7. Material should take into account the level of use the client will make of it.

Obtaining publications and other material

Once the material you require has been identified, you will need to obtain it. Some material will be priced, in which case you will need to order it, and some will be free.

Priced publications

The procedure for obtaining priced publications, particularly in the field of community information, is not as simple as you might suppose. Since a lot of the material may well be fairly cheap and from small or community publishers, booksellers and library suppliers are reluctant to obtain it as the profit margin is likely to be too low for the amount of effort involved. The alternative is to order direct but this also has its difficulties as many small publishers now insist on money with order, and this can cause problems for some organizations through the need to raise a cheque or limitations on the amount that can be spent from petty cash.

A few national voluntary organizations, e.g. Age Concern England, operate a standing-order system for their publications—this is one solution, although you may need to accept blanket coverage of the organization's output. In the larger cities, you may find a community or alternative bookseller who is prepared to supply this material to order. A directory of alternative bookshops is published annually by the magazine *Radical bookseller*. Whatever the method of ordering, it is important to keep a record of what has been placed on order and from whom to avoid duplication of titles and as a check on supply. For each title make out an order or slip—this can be either a scrap 5in × 3in card or one specially printed with a standard grid. The following indicates the kinds of information that need to be recorded:

— title of publication—more important than author for this kind of material, since authorship is often unclear;
— author—might be an individual or an organization;
— price, date of publication and, if a periodical, frequency;
— supplier—this may be a bookseller, library supplier or the address of the producing body;
— date of order;
— source of information about the item;
— location, if you are ordering for more than one centre.

You may find it helpful to use the order cards later as the basis of a catalogue of the publications in your information centre; in which case, leave space at the top of the card for either a subject heading, classification number or filing code. After an order has been placed with a supplier, the order cards are filed, preferably by title, in one alphabetical sequence known as the 'order file'. When a publication is received, the order card is removed from the file and accompanies the publication to the next stage if it is to be used later as the catalogue card. If not, you may find it useful to file the order card in a 'publications received' file, until such time as the publication is permanently recorded in the system, after which the card can be thrown away.

Periodicals

Publications which arrive at regular intervals—weekly, fortnightly, monthly, quarterly—will not require an order card but you will need to keep a record of each title taken. This should include the following items of information:

— title of periodical;
— frequency;
— supplier;
— when subscription is due for payment;
— a grid to record receipt of each issue;
— instructions for disposal of back copies.

For those using computers, there are software packages available for periodicals management but these are aimed at organizations who take an extensive range of periodicals and such packages are not cheap. If you have a database management package on your computer, you would do better to devise your own periodicals database.

Free material

This can vary from quite substantial loose-leaf binders plus updates to leaflets, posters and bookmarks and may be required in bulk for clients to take. Since this is likely to be a frequent type of request, it may be quicker and simpler to duplicate a standard letter to send to organizations, with space left to fill in address, title of item, format (leaflet, booklet, poster, etc.) and number of copies required. It is advisable to keep a record of what is requested, if only as a check on whether it has been received or not.

A lot of the sweat has been taken out of identifying free materials, and addresses from where they can be obtained, through the setting-up of Camden Libraries' Free Leaflets Information Service (FLIS). For an annual fee (£120 in 1992) subscribers receive a copy of the Frills directory of free information leaflet suppliers, a monthly batch of new and updated leaflets and amendments to the *Frills* directory, and details of a model system for organizing leaflets. Details of this service can be obtained from Community Information Services, Camden Leisure Services Department, St. Pancras Library, 100 Euston

Road, London NW1 2AJ. A similar, but not so extensive, service is provided by the NACAB as part of its Information Service, but you would need to have approval to subscribe to the full pack.

Organizing hard information

We have already seen that hard information can be found in a great variety of forms. For the benefit of organizing it, the following categories can be identified:

Material in book form for use by clientele or information workers will be best arranged on shelves in the broad subject groups identified when acquiring the material or according to a classification scheme.

Ephemeral material for use by information workers is best stored in a vertical file using the same subject headings as those in the subject sequence of the information file, though probably with more subdivisions, or using a classification scheme. Alternatively, the material could be kept in file boxes on shelves using broad subject headings.

Ephemeral material for use by clientele on the premises is best kept in file boxes, ring or display binders and ideally interfiled with books. Vertical files are not recommended for public use as they tend to be a deterrent. Another way of dealing with ephemeral materials is to gather them together in packs on particular topics and, for maximum impact, to display them face outwards on sloping shelves.

Ephemeral material for the public to take away can be displayed in special leaflet dispensers, on a sloping surface or on tables. Ideally, they should be displayed in broad subject groups or by originating organization, e.g. Benefits Agency, Department for Employment, but this is rarely possible because even within organizations leaflets are produced in varying sizes.

Supplementary information

Many organizations produce printed material in the course of their work or activities. The most common types of material are directories or address lists of members (individuals or constituent groups), newsletters, events sheets or cards, annual reports, constitutions, posters, leaflets, funding appeals, campaigning literature, advertising brochures, balance sheets and commemorative booklets (anniversaries, etc.). All this material is potentially useful as back-up information to the database but there is no sure way of obtaining it. When sending out the original questionnaire to organizations, you can ask to be put on their mailing list for this type of material, if one is maintained.

Some organizations that operate on a shoestring may make a small charge for their mailing list facility. Even when you are put on a mailing list, regular receipt of material may depend very much on the enthusiasm or efficiency of the secretary of an organization. Often the best solution to obtaining material is to maintain regular contact with organizations and to pester them continually. When material arrives, it should be dated, so that you know roughly how old it is, and carefully filed for future use. The simplest method is to have an envelope or folder for each organization. Write on the outside of the envelope the name of the organization as used in your database and arrange envelopes alphabetically in boxes or a vertical file. You should also add to this file any cuttings from newspapers or magazines concerning those organizations. The file should be checked regularly, at least once a year, to remove out-of-date material. When writing to organizations for updated information for your database, ask them for any new literature.

Before throwing away the withdrawn material, check to see if it would be of use to some other organization or section of your service which collects material on local history.

Classification

It is not my intention to go into any great detail about the classification of community information materials. For most small information services, it will be quite adequate to arrange material by broad subject groups subdivided according to the form in which the clientele's needs and problems are presented. For ease of labelling vertical files, book spines and boxes, a simple notation can be used based on the initial letter or letters of subjects. For example, Cambridgeshire Libraries' community information service covers 21 categories:

Ben	Benefits	Gov	Government
Bus	Business	Hea	Health
Car	Careers	Hou	Housing
Com	Community Law	Legal rights	
Con	Consumer Mon	Money	
CR	Community relations	SC	Senior citizens
Dis	Disability	Tra	Transport
Edu	Education	Ump	Unemployment
Emp	Employment	Wom	Women
Env	Environment	You	Youth
Fam	Family		

Some libraries also include as separate categories: Death, Equal opportunities, Fuel (or Energy), Gay rights, Leisure, and Trade union rights. These categories can then be broken down into smaller subcategories as necessary. Taking the earlier example of Housing, a possible range of subcategories with a mnemonic notation might be:

A	Agricultural accommodation	Re	Rented accommodation
H	Homelessness	ReC	Council housing
I	Institutional accommodation	ReH	Housing Association housing

M	Mobile homes	ReP	Private rented
O	Owner-occupied	S	Squatting

Numerals could be introduced for more detailed subdivisions, e.g. O1—Buying and selling a house; O2—Home insurance; O3—Planning applications; O4—Development; etc.

An effective method that can be used where you have only a small number of broad categories (no more than ten and preferably less) is colour coding. Allocate a colour to each subject and attach an appropriate coloured sticker or tape to the spine of each book or file box. Colour coding can be used in conjunction with notation to provide more detailed subdivision of a subject. When a community information service grows to a size where broad categories are not adequate to contain all the material and allow efficient retrieval, then it may be necessary to consider using a classification scheme.

Two choices are open to you, either using or adapting a ready-made scheme or constructing your own. There are a number of general classification schemes used in libraries, of which the most well known is the Dewey Decimal Classification. These schemes have been constructed to organize the whole of knowledge and subjects are usually arranged on philosophical or logical principles. Consequently, they may not be sufficiently detailed or treat subjects in the way your clientele express their information needs. Most schemes have a degree of flexibility and it might be possible to adapt them. The NACAB has its own scheme for arranging materials in the broad area of community information, but it hardly merits the description of a classification scheme. However, it is sufficiently detailed and client oriented to be worthy of consideration.

4

Networking and Telecommunications

The basic information services which are offered by research networks fall into three main categories: information exchange, file and document distribution and information services. *Information exchange* services allow individuals and groups to communicate with each other across time zones and geographical space much more quickly than postal delivery would allow, and has proved the most popular and heavily used end-user application on networks by linking together people who would otherwise find it hard to meet face to face.

Electronic mail facilities enable the exchange of messages and ideas on a one-to-one basis, whether more formally as in the sharing of notes and drafts of work-in-progress, or informally for general social contact. Discussion groups which use electronic mail in conjunction with mailing lists support the exchange of information and messages between all members of a group at the same time. This is popular for ongoing debates and the exchange of news items in discipline-specific areas, allowing members to share ideas and experiences in an informal setting, to 'meet' new contacts, and to follow and influence the development of new ideas in their field. Bulletin boards are used in discipline-specific settings, but require a positive action from the user in connecting to the service, and reading or downloading items of interest, rather than depending on the blanket distribution of material through mailing lists. Computer conferencing and interactive video-conferencing are still quite rare activities on such networks, but will become increasingly common as the technical infrastructure becomes capable of real-time interactive and multimedia services, and are likely to have substantial implications for distance learning education.

File and document distribution support the distribution of items such as text documents, image files, and software programs on an individual search and retrieve basis. File transfer is permitted by the use of standard protocols so that data files can quickly be moved from one machine to another under the control of the end-user. As more electronic material is becoming available within the public domain, certain computer network sites offer an 'archive' service, in which data files can be stored on open access for retrieval by all network users.

Mail servers are commonly used as primitive database systems, returning files in response to commands received within electronic mail messages, as an automatic process with no manual intervention. This is often the method used for distribution of the composite articles within an electronic journal, for example—the user will request a particular file by name by placing the appropriate commands and filename within a mail message addressed to the mail server.

Information services are available through remote log-in protocols, which allow the user to link to a remote system and use it as though there were a direct connection between the two, within the constraints set by the host system. The service may be on a different network, as long as both end systems (user and host) are able to run the same protocols, and the networks and gateway used will support this. Online public access catalogues available for remote searching from outside the library or campus site are a common use for this facility, as long as the OPAC allows for a remote connection. There is, of course, no common standard interface for the various online catalogues and so the user must know, or be able to learn, the functions and abilities of each different system. Non-bibliographic databases are increasingly becoming available across research networks, particularly those which contain information within the public domain, or government-sponsored public information.

The full range of academic and research networks worldwide includes both large- and small-scale networks at differing stages in their development, and is too numerous to list here. Most research networks are organised on a national basis, or as a cooperative endeavour between smaller countries, as for example in the Gulf states.

RARE

The European academic and research networks are brought together in RARE (Reseaux Associes pour la Recherche Europeenne), the association for European research networking organisations and their users. This aims to overcome national boundaries in research networking by creating a harmonised computer communications infrastructure for the whole European research community. Based in Amsterdam, RARE has over 40 national and international research networking organisations as members, which are listed and described in the RARE 'State of the union' report. The RARE association also sponsors a number of working groups which initiate and co-ordinate advances in network technology and services; these include, for example, work on user support issues, information retrieval across the networks, and developing multimedia services.

The academic network for the United Kingdom is called *JANET* (Joint Academic Network). Similar networks exist for nearly all the other European countries, including Eastern Europe, although the range of facilities which each is able to offer can vary widely; in some former Communist countries, such as Romania, access is very difficult and services are unreliable. Others are far more highly developed, with extensive experience and expertise, and are moving towards a strategic position of greater independence from government support and self-sufficiency.

The Dutch academic network, *SURFnet*, is an example within this category. SURFnet networks together institutes of higher education, and scientific and industrial research organisations in the Netherlands, and has maintained a close involvement with the Dutch bibliographic utilities, taking a pro-active approach to the development of information services. In 1989 SURFnet became a private company, with a 49% share held by the Dutch telecommunications company PTT Telecom, and was required to become self-supporting in the near future. This has led it into substantial development in services and user support, working on-site with institutions and with individual discipline-based groups of users between institutions, to encourage and develop new users and uses for the network. There are several other major influences and initiatives which affect the shape of European academic networking at a transnational level, both outside and within the EC. These include:

Organisations which are co-operative efforts between countries grouped together by geography. NORDUnet is a collaborative effort between the Scandinavian group of national research networks: Denmark, Finland, Norway, Sweden, and Iceland aiming to enable an efficient connection to the rest of Europe. A similar arrangement has been proposed for the countries in the area of the former Yugoslavia.

EUnet is a large subscription-funded network, which serves European users from Scandinavia and the CIS (former Soviet Union) to North Africa. Founded by the European Forum for Open Systems, EUnet connects 6000 individual sites and networks together as Unix system users.

International treaty organisations which are established as European-wide enterprises, with funding from a number of countries. The most influential of these is CERN, the European Laboratory for Particle Physics, which has constructed *HEPnet* as a dedicated network serving research centres in high energy physics.

Ebone is the European backbone network, which provides a neutral interconnection between the backbone research networks which form part of the global TCP/IP based Internet. The backbone provides a high capacity 'highway' between the major first-level nodes in Europe (Stockholm, Amsterdam, Geneva, Paris, and London) to which other sites connect.

EuropaNet has developed from an EC-funded project conducted by COSINE (Co-operation for Open Systems Interconnection Networking), intended to develop a co-ordinated approach to networking the European research community, and provide an international infrastructure accessible by academic organisations, research institutes, and organisations co-operating with EC research and development. A pilot International X.25 Infrastructure (IXI) network commenced in 1990, forming a backbone which linked research networks in many countries, both inside and outside the EC itself. This has now been replaced by EuropaNet as a high capacity multi-protocol backbone which will handle both OSI (open system) and TCP/IP Internet-style protocols.

The *EARN* (European Academic Research Networks) association provides networking services for researchers and academics in Europe, the Middle East and Africa, as a store and forward network based on IBM computers. EARN is closely ,integrated with the US-based BITNET network, and is in fact almost indistinguishable from this in use, effectively acting as its European arm. In some countries EARN forms the major research network, while in others there is a gateway connection between EARN and the national network.

Global internet network

The Internet originally developed as a military network from projects funded by the Advanced Research Projects Agency of the US Department of Defence from 1969 onwards, and was known originally as ARPANET. In 1989, ARPANET was finally completely decommissioned from military service, and devoted to educational and research purposes.

Along with other emerging state and national network elements, this began to become interlinked through a major data communications backbone established by the National Science Foundation between six new supercomputer sites in 1985. In the late 1980s, the National Science Foundation developed a high speed network backbone called *NSFnet* from the existing infrastructure, linking-some 16 main sites around the United States with data rates of 1.5 Mbits per second (known as the T1 standard). The NSFnet forms the main data highway for the Internet, providing links via the 16 main sites to regional networks, and thence onwards to local networks and individual organisations. These main nodes may also provide gateways through to many other national and international networks, such as Earn (the European counterpart of BITNET) and CA net in Canada. The regional networks cover broad geographical areas, although with some overlap as a result of recent growth, and are run by a variety of organisations from commercial enterprises to government funded groups.

Parts of the NSFnet backbone are also provided by commercial enterprise, and this mix of public and private characterises the Internet situation. In principle, an organisation which has an Internet connection, or 'feed', from a local or regional node, and which has the required equipment capacity, may itself provide any number of feeds to other organisations and individuals who are looking for an Internet account, relaying the network traffic back and forth on their behalf. In this way, the network is able to grow organically and, since one system user may have more than one feed available to it, can provide multiple communication pathways between sites, and therefore a more robust and reliable service.

In anticipation of serving a more widely expanded role, the NSFnet is currently being upgraded to support a much higher data transmission speed (45 Mbits per second, known as T3 standard), providing the bandwidth which will enable the development of a range of interactive services in multimedia telecommunications. This strengthened backbone is now referred to as a 'cloud' to emphasise its non-linear, interconnected, nature. The glue which binds all these diverse systems and machines together is the use of the TCP/IP communication protocols suite.

Most of the machines which constitute the Internet proper, and many of those which communicate with it, use this rather old, but widely used and constantly developing set of protocols; their widespread use in the

Internet is part of its inheritance from the ARPANET, and is a major reason why TCP/IP usage is seen as the main rival to the open-systems movement. Control of the network is distributed through various levels, with (at the moment) no overall control imposed from a central point.

The main backbone NSFnet is currently managed by a not-for-profit consortium consisting of IBM, MCI (an important commercial network provider), and the Merit organisation, based in Ann Arbor, Michigan. The network uses a Domain Name System, similar to that of JANET, so that IP address numbers (long strings of digits) can be replaced by more explanatory structured domain names; the main difference from the JANET method is that these names are structured in reverse order, progressing from the narrower to the broader domain: from organisation on the left to country on the right.

New system users register with regional co-ordinators, who have the responsibility for mapping connection points, in order to make their existence known to other network users. This gives the Internet a much more informal flavour compared with JANET, making it difficult to say exactly how many Internet users exist, since there is no one point at which they are all counted. There are agreed conventions on the use of the Internet to which all users are expected to conform: that it is intended for educational use and should not be used for purposes of commercial gain. This restriction is commonly quite broadly interpreted, and by no means all of the traffic between educational and other institutions is strictly educational in content; although it does preclude the offering of straightforward commercial services across the network, even though many organisations with Internet connections are commercial in nature. Some believe that this restriction will be relaxed in the near future.

Internet Society

The main decision-making body for the Internet is the Internet Society, a voluntary organisation which aims to promote Internet technology and developments. A sub-group of this, the Internet Architecture Board, is responsible for approving new and upgraded standards and for allocating resources such as IP addresses. The Internet Engineering Task Force (IETF) is another voluntary body with open membership, which represents the user voice in Internet debates.

The Internet depends to a large extent for its success on willing co-operation among its participants, and conformity to the spirit of network culture and etiquette. For example, an unwritten rule is that users who are established on the network through the benevolence of a host organisation supplying their feed are ethically bound to consider similar requests made to them in the future. The cost of these connections is normally born as a part of the network overhead; by this means the overall cost is spread among the participants, so that network use often appears to the individual user as free, or at least providing unlimited usage for minimal cost.

Internet provides electronic mail services based on the Simple Mail Transfer Protocol (SMTP) mail convention. Electronic mail has also given rise to a variety of alternative uses beyond the simple exchange of messages between individuals. A large number of news groups and discussion groups have grown up over the Internet based on the use of mail servers; within BITNET, which has become identical to the Internet for many practical purposes, these are known by the name of the listserv software used on IBM machines. These function as automatic distribution lists for subscribers interested in an individual topic, which rebroadcast messages from individuals to the entire group. The Usenet newsgroups are also distributed over the Internet, and are available in a similar way.

An example of one of the more active, for library and information workers, is PACS-L, dedicated to the discussion of public access computer systems; this has about 2000 members in several countries, and generates some 10-15 messages per day. Within the LIS field, there are groups centred around specific information service types, library systems suppliers, and broader social issues. There are estimated to be over 3500 conferences active, in addition to the Usenet newsgroups. Electronic mail is also used for the distribution of several electronic journals which are available over the Internet, most with free subscriptions.

Once edited and compiled by human intervention, the journal may be distributed either in its entirety as a long e-mail message, or in the more sophisticated cases only as a contents page; subscribers can then receive individual articles as an e-mail message by sending a command which is automatically processed. Over 100 electronic journals, newsletters, and digests exist in the Internet environment. In this case, the listserver can be seen to function as a primitive database system. This practice saves on the use of network bandwidth by not transmitting unwanted information in the shape of unused articles; but also allows users to gather the information in the format most appropriate to their needs. Journals may also include graphics files, and text files may be available as plain ASCII or Postscript (laser printable) versions.

For sites with a direct Internet connection, real-time interactive access with public online information systems is available to remote sites. As with JANET, a common use is for access to online library catalogues. Since most of the main educational sites in the US are connected, a wide variety of catalogues are available, some with major collections—for example the Melvyl catalogue at the University of California, and that of the New York Public Library. An estimated 337 library catalogues are available through use of the Telnet remote access protocol.

The Library of Congress files are accessible over the Internet, indicating the extent to which it is being used for formal purposes by library institutions. These files offer access to 28 million catalogue records included in the LCMARC files, together with copyright files, public policy citations and federal bill status files. The Library also allows Internet access to its technical processing and cataloguing system, and to its SCORPIO reference and retrieval system. A wide spectrum of non-library sources of information are also available. Many of the government agencies attached to Internet make information resources openly available; these include, for instance, databases mounted by NASA in space science and astronomy and the CIA World Factbook. This kind of access is likely to increase in the future as the Internet develops: recent legislation colloquially known as the GPO Access Bill.

Sites with direct Internet access have the ability to transfer files directly from one machine to another in their original format, using the FTP protocol. The practice of 'anonymous ftp' has arisen in the Internet community, by which ftp archives are established on a host machine at a particular network site, with named directories which contain archives of files available for transfer. Although computer system users would normally have to be registered with the site system administration in order to connect to a particular machine, these hosts have allowed free access to these specified ftp archives without the necessity to register a username or password beforehand; although it is normal practice to enter the caller's network address as the password information.

This practice of 'anonymous ftp' is widely used to transfer entire documents, saving on the time-consuming necessity to view and save on-screen copies, and retaining any original formatting included with the file. The file can then be downloaded to a user's own machine, and used in whatever way is appropriate; the archive is able to distribute image as well as text-based information. Many ftp sites allow remote users to deposit files in the archive for others to retrieve.

A recent OCLC report estimated that there are about 3 million such files at more than a thousand ftp sites on the network, although the 20 largest sites account for more than half of these. Much of the material is source code for public domain computer programs, although the method is increasingly being used for the distribution of text files between specific groups or more widely. A major problem is that, as the report states 'the ability for network users to share information surpasses by far their ability to discover information on the Internet'. As with JANET, a main problem with resources on the Internet lies in the difficulty of finding out what information is available. Since there is no central administration of the network which controls all uses of it, there is no central directory of resources, although distributed network information centres are emerging. The problem is of a much greater magnitude than that faced by JANET, however, due to the much larger number of individual connections, and consequently the larger number of services and resources potentially available. It is also the case that resources are often duplicated in different network sites, and may exist in varying and incomplete versions and formats.

A number of resource guides have been drawn up by enthusiasts, covering both library-based databases, and those offered by other organisations, as well as lists of discussion and news groups which are known to exis.

Long-term answers to the problem are the subject of debate, especially among some sections of the library community.

From 1992, the Internet is poised on the brink of a further phase of development. A concept sponsored by Vice-President Albert Gore for many years, and now enacted in the High Performance Computing Act of 1991, promises to continue national development in the existing interconnected array of networks to upgrade and expand the system, opening it out to more colleges, schools, and public libraries as a national research and educational resource. This 'information superhighway', to be known as the National Research and Education Network (NREN), will aim for the development of a national 3 gigabit per second (a gigabit = one thousand million bits of data) network capacity by 1996. This represents an increase of approximately 2000 times over the current bandwidth, and as a rough guide would make the network capable of carrying 100,000 pages of text or 1000 bit-mapped photographic images each second.

As with SuperJANET, this will support a vast expansion in the number and range of services possible, and make multimedia communications such as desktop video-conferencing feasible as an everyday reality. Another major goal for NREN is the standardisation of protocols across the existing patchwork of networks, and the integration of TCP/IP with OSI protocols to enable both to be used in parallel. This is not an isolated development, but is indicative of a number of initiatives within this vein in the United States. The Pacific Bell corporation, for example, is building a broadband network (CalREN) in California to link participating universities, research laboratories, major hospitals, and leading high technology firms in the Los Angeles and Bay Area to develop innovative applications for education, healthcare, and business. These include projects such as the use of tele-seminars for remote educational programmes, medical image processing, remote patient monitoring, and specialist diagnosis, and the development of collaborative precompetitive research with industry and commerce.

Proponents of the NREN argue that the United States is falling behind in economic competitiveness because government, business, industry, and education cannot access the information resources which it needs to maintain international competitiveness and economic strength. Another school of thought argues that such needs would be best met by market forces in the shape of existing commercial networks such as MCI, funded by charging market prices for services. This argument has raised serious issues on future policies for the NREN on the issue of charging of services, which at the moment appear as though free to many end-users; and the use of NREN by commercial service providers.

Campus wide information systems

Concepts such as the 'electronic library', in which larger proportions of educational support material are delivered in electronic form to users who are more geographically dispersed, have raised the profile of local networking as a means of integrating access to the diverse range and types of information available from all sources within the campus environment. In recent years, such developments have been carried out under the name of campus-wide information systems (CWIS), which are intended to bring together this variety of local information within a single framework. Access to this information should be simplified by an easy to use interface, which does not present barriers to the casual user, and is potentially available from all points of the local network. In many ways, this parallels some of the forms of community information systems which have emerged as civic facilities, but is more localised upon and targeted at a smaller and more easily identifiable community.

The concept of a CWIS as a broad umbrella encompassing diverse information types precludes too strict a set of conditions on the structure and format of the information; in this sense, the CWIS forms an information base of both structured and less structured information, rather than a database in the precise sense of the term. A typical CWIS might include:

— staff and student directory information, including telephone, postal and e-mail addresses;
— a diary of local events and university calendars;
— course information, administrative details and timetables;
— a listing of research projects and interests;
— university rules and regulations;
— newsletters related to the local campus;
— community and travel information;
— library catalogues and library service information;
— locally produced indexes and databases;
— links to other CWIS, catalogues etc., located at different campuses.

By bringing this information together in one access structure, a CWIS can help to integrate a campus community which is split between different sites or spread over a wide area and develop a sense of community. There is also some interest in developing this approach as a method for inter-university communication at the campus level to encourage collaborative endeavours and cooperation, rather than through formal administrative structures. The information system can be developed as an extension of a library online catalogue, and be included within the same framework as an available network resource, or be developed as a general computer-support facility.

The direction from which the impetus for development comes is likely to influence the shape of the outcome, and the underlying objectives it is intended to achieve. The CWIS may be centralised onto a single machine from which remote access is possible, or act as a gateway to other local systems, calling the information up as needed. Whether the CWIS takes a centralised or more distributed approach, the task of maintaining and updating the information is normally the responsibility of the information providers. This may be either by submitting updated files to the operators of a centralised system, or by directly maintaining the data in one of the nodes which constitute a distributed system, to which the CWIS offers gatewayed access.

The ubiquitous spread of network access and microcomputers have encouraged the development of more pro-active forms, under the aegis of local governments or local voluntary not-for-profit groups (particularly in the United States), which aim to provide the framework for community action which supports two-way networking, rather than the simple one-way passive consumption of display only systems. Viewdata systems have been installed in public libraries since the early 1980s, following the emergence of the British Telecom Prestel public information system. This is now a rather outdated and unsophisticated system, and is not amenable towards tailoring for local community information.

The late 1980s saw the growing use by public libraries of private viewdata systems which are developed and sometimes managed by commercial enterprises on behalf of their clients; these can be customised for individual applications and managed as a closed user group facility, offering specific information targeted at a well-defined user group. Added to the local focus in information content, there is also the advantage that some local authorities adopt private viewdata as an internal corporate information system, allowing the library to make use of any spare capacity.

The Electronic Public Information Network (previously the Local Authority Videotex Association) acts as a forum for channelling ideas and advice in videotex, investigating hardware and software issues, and developing applications for community information needs. This has some 46 local authority members and a number of other public sector and private organisations. In the context of local government authorities rather than just public libraries, a survey by the Society of Information Technology Managers in 1992 revealed that 19% of UK local authorities already have public access terminals installed, and that a further 14% planned to do so in the near future. These were installed in venues as diverse as libraries, council buildings, and shopping precincts, containing information on:

— local organisations and events;

— details of general practitioners;

— transport information;

— tourist information, including accommodation listings;

— information services aimed at local economic development, for example EC information on legislation, calls for tender, potential European business partners;

— one-stop enquiry shops, staffed by assistants able to make use of the local authority computer network to answer information enquiries on council services and activities.

An alternative to Integrated library system module is the use of a purpose-designed module within an integrated library system such as GEAC. This has the advantage of allowing the information to be directly controlled by the library authority itself, and to integrate it with the other activities and information services offered by the public library. Community information, for instance, may appear as one option on an Online Public Access Catalogue terminal, along with information relating to library holdings, updated and maintained in the same way.

The use of an integrated system gave the possibility of direct access to the information, rather than requiring the user to traverse the 'tree' structure of menus typical of viewdata systems, with the use of various access points; and offered the functionality to manipulate and print subsets of the information base as specialised products. Once again, maintenance of this system requires co-operation with neighbouring areas, since urban information requirements are not constrained by administrative borders. A recent development in the provision of community information has been the growth in co-operative host systems which, instead of building up a centralised bank of information for dissemination to users at terminal access points, concentrate rather on building a facilitating infrastructure which offers a framework for diverse groups to build and maintain their own information systems and services.

Host systems offer general facilities for creating local information files, the exchange of information between specific small user groups, and the creation of developmental projects and workshops, as well as more traditional services such as access to external databases. The Manchester Host system uses an internationally available communications software system more widely known as Geo-net, which is installed in some 40 countries around the world; Manchester Host is directly linked to several of these other Hosts in Europe (including Eastern and Central Europe), Russia and the USA through the international telecommunications networks.

The Host is accessible to its subscribers through use of a phone line, PC and modem. The Host approach assumes that users are potential information providers as well as consumers of information, encouraging an active participation in creating new applications and making contributions to existing ones. This led the Host initiative to borrow the idea of electronic village halls from the telecottages movement, and establish these in localised areas of Manchester, offering new technology facilities and training for particular groups, organised and managed by these groups themselves: for example electronic village halls have been established by women's groups, for small local business, and for the local Bangladeshi community.

As well as supporting greater participation for the individual in the information age through a philosophy of low-cost access and distributed processing, the Host approach has been to promote private and public sector partnership for the development of specific project initiatives for closed user groups. This involves cooperation between local government, employers and businesses, higher education institutes, trade unions, and non-governmental organisations, working on projects to extend the ISDN network and the consequent development of broadband information services, the extension of electronic data interchange (EDI) to smaller enterprises, and the development of a communications park for business. A number of closed user groups built around specific cooperative needs have evolved including:

— the Manchester Chinese Information Centre, supporting document exchange in Chinese script to the local ethnic community;

— the Manchester Business School, which uses the system to communicate with similar institutions on an international footing;

— the Manchester Asian Trading Network to improve trading links between local Asian business and suppliers in Bangladesh;

— the Manchester Design Community, in which smaller enter prises co-operate on bidding for larger contracts as a consortium.

On a wider geographic level, links with other European cities allow for greater co-operation in trans-regional development initiatives. The European and international linkages are likely to develop more strongly in the longer term, encouraged by the recent bid by Manchester to host the Olympic Games. The Host system brings together a diversity of community issues and related information activities focused on a locality. A range of networks have also sprung up to link together groups and organisations working in similar Areas, though geographically dispersed.

The 'networking' term is sometimes used rather freely in this context; some examples of these are closer to centralised database systems which offer remote access to users. Volnet, for example, is a central database host, providing a route to information for workers in the voluntary and community sectors at low-cost. The database offers online access to a bibliographic database, backed up by a photocopy-based document supply service, and to information on research projects and the details of UK parliamentary candidates. GreenNet provides a similar service for non-governmental organisations and individuals working with ecological and environmental issues, giving access to a range of computer conferences and resources, with a common structure to the location of information files in the network.

APC GreenNet links together progressive organisations with an interest in the development of information communication for social change, such as Amnesty International. A range of similar networking initiatives exist, some short- and some longer lived. These can operate at a purely national level, or work on an international scale. While many of the existing community networks in the USA have evolved from local initiatives, stemming either from citizen groups or public authority organisations, recent years have seen the emergence of commercial organisations piloting or operating information networks directed at local users on a for-profit basis. These organisations make information produced by, others available whilst profiting from advertising through the network facilities. *American CitiNet* operates this service bureau arrangement, with particular customer bases in Omaha and Boston.

The *regional Bell operating companies,* the US regional telecommunication suppliers, are beginning to offer gateway facilities to information providers who are then able to recover their costs from information users through the normal billing arrangements of the Bell companies. A number of local government agencies are providing information and services in this way. As well as communicating with clients of their services, local government authorities have used information networking as a means of co-ordinating and delivering the services for which they are responsible.

There is an increasing recognition for the need to integrate and consolidate the single-focus information sets that are incomplete and incompatible, or fragmented across departmental and administrative boundaries, in order to deliver services effectively and support local development. The networking of databases and administrative systems increases access to information and forms a platform for the development of more powerful and sophisticated integrated systems. Local access to council services and information is effected by networking local branch offices and the creation of information points at which the public can find out about a range of council services, such as housing, employment, transport, and trading standards, together in one place; and can make specific enquiries about their individual progress, in areas such as payment of council tax or council house repairs.

Information access points such as these can be queried by telephone, and in some areas have taken the form of mobile services linked to a central computer system. This growth in the integration of information systems is linked to the development of new forms of service based on emerging information technology. Geographical information systems are a prime example of this, since much of the work of local authorities is spatially related. Different information bases, for example, may contain mapping data on the location of gas, electricity, and water utility pipes, property ownership and land use, and demographic information for strategic planning. Although these may be distributed over different locations and agencies, their integration across a network offers the opportunity for more advanced services: for example, transport information management systems which link traffic flows with highway maintenance and emergency services; or demographic planning with library development and community analysis to determine information needs.

Local authorities are increasingly providing information services linked to local economic development. While the Manchester Host is one important example of a far-reaching approach to this, more traditional information services include access to European databases for information on European Commission tenders and contracts, EC legislation, and searching for business partners in other EC countries. A similar requirement encourages the integration of information access between different service delivery agencies. The Child Protection Register maintained by social service departments, for example, is in some cases available to accident and emergency departments of local hospitals in electronic form. The recent Care in the Community Act presupposes the exchange of information between social service departments and community health authorities.

The National Disability Information Project, formed under the auspices of the Department of Health, is a further influence developing this role for public service agencies. One of the pilot projects is the GUiDe system under development in Gloucestershire between the Gloucester and Cheltenham Health Authorities and the County Social Services Department. This deals with information for elderly and disabled people, and gives networked access to health professionals in hospitals, voluntary organisations, health centres, and social services offices. Another project is based at Gateshead Libraries and Arts Service, well known for its innovative viewdata-based home shopping experiment. The Gateshead Disability Information project aims to make information from the council on disability available in various complementary forms—sound, text and video—

of the user's own choosing, and through a variety of delivery mechanisms.

There is a similar requirement for local government and local agencies to interwork with central government in an online networked environment, dealing with electronic information, often driven by central government directly. The Department for Education, for instance, uses electronic data interchange (EDI) to communicate with school educators on statistics and teachers' pensions matters, and similar arrangements for transport and trading standards are likely to emerge. Quasi-governmental organisations also have information exchange requirements with local areas, and as these bodies automate their information resources and archives they are developing online access arrangements to replace manual administration for remote users. Increasingly, these applications demand more sophisticated information exchange facilities and broadband network links to accommodate heavy data transfer loads and multimedia information types. A recent example is the MONARCH system developed by the Royal Commission on Historical Monuments of England, an electronic version of the National Monuments Record. The online version of this gives remote access for about 200 users to some 6 million items of information on ancient monuments, including graphic images with hypertext linkages as well as text-based searching.

The information is used by local government for planning purposes, by English Nature for conservation decisions, and by the National Trust for property management, and will in the future be linked to geographical information systems for map-based searching and retrieval. Local authorities have traditionally been involved in the direct provision of services, including information services and information related to other activities.

As information becomes more and more important as a basic commodity for daily life, many see local government as having a role in the planning and development of a local information infrastructure, aimed at facilitating the integration and sharing of information from many sources and encouraging a policy of common access and citizen participation as well as enabling local economic and community development.

As changes in society, and in the structure and nature of organisations create changes in work patterns and habits for those who work in them or use their products and services, the change towards client-focused rather than organisation-focused services may offer opportunities for a new role for local government in this area. Perhaps the first developments in this area can be seen in the recent creation of 'One stop shops' providing information, counselling, and advice support services for local businesses, established under the auspices of the Department for Trade and Industry. These are mostly based on joint arrangements between Training and Enterprise Councils, chambers of commerce and local authorities, taking different forms in different areas.

Several of the development programmes started by the Commission for the European Community programmes are aimed at the development of networking as a supportive means for social and community development. The STAR programme, aimed at the less developed areas of the EC, has been used to develop the telecommunications infrastructure for rural areas to stimulate the use of information networking for employment and skills development. The ACE-HI scheme, administered by the Association of Community Enterprises in the Highland and Islands of Scotland is an example of this type of activity (with additional funding from BT), resulting in a £16 million investment in ISDN networks, and their successful use for the delivering of training and the development of enterprises which conduct their business through such networks, in remote islands and isolated parts of the mainland. Other EC social programmes have made extensive use of networking and telecommunications. The COMETT programme has used networking to promote transnational co-operation between commercial enterprises and universities for the delivery of training in technical skills. The HORIZON programme is establishing a disabled people's network through Europe, while the New Opportunities for Women programme is funding the partnership of Athens, Manchester, and Seville in building a telematics development network for the exchange of skills, information, and experience on women's training, employment, and enterprise. The European Community established the ROME (Reseau Observatoires Metropolitains en Europe) network in 1989 to advise the Commission on research and information development activities for urban areas.

European Urban Observatory

A three-year project known as the European Urban Observatory was initiated in 1992 linking ten European cities in a European-wide network to support strategic decision-making and the common interpretation of information on a European-wide basis. The aim of this project is to monitor urban trends through the sharing of urban management information, the transfer of experience and comparative evaluation of policy. Information is structured into three levels, dealing with basic indicators for policy decision-making, with quantitative comparative data, and with individual city data stored locally; these levels are linked together through the use of X. 25 private networks, and the BT Tymnet wide area network employed to form a closed user group. This networking of public management information contributes to the development of pan-European urban policy issues, and gives a comparative background resource at the local level. Information networking in the health service sector in the United Kingdom has become a vital activity in recent years, stimulated by a growing movement for the improvement of health information services, following the work of the Korner Group on information systems, and stimulated by the radical organisational changes creating an 'internal market' for purchasers and providers of health services. These tendencies have created a pressure for the harmonisation and integration of all forms of information within the sector, and a demand for wider accessibility and sharing through computer networks and other applications of information technology.

The distinction between traditional bibliographic information services and other information sources has lessened with 'information' and 'intelligence' being taken to include, sometimes primarily, statistical and demographical information. Within this context, networks are used to link the office automation and service environment with information providers across many administrative levels. Management information in this framework would include:

— literature in the form of written or audiovisual material: published books and journals, etc., as well as unpublished material in the form of correspondence, internal reports, and committee minutes;
— quantitative information, in the form of data relating to the activities and context of the organisation; statistical returns, demographic analysis, performance indicators, trends analysis.

Within the health sector, an integrated delivery of information services more often requires sharing and exchange between fragmented units, now within a more competitive context. Library units, for example, may include within the same region headquarters libraries, departmental libraries, small service points in branch hospitals, postgraduate medical centre and research information points, and nursing libraries; each with varying degrees of autonomy. With a growing amount of information available in electronic form, user requirements are likely to involve the retrieval of information from remote sources across a network, as much or more than from a local collection, and to varying forms and types of data.

A medical researcher, for example, could require not only bibliographic references, and full text source material, but also images and the ability to process images, datasets of published social and epidemiological statistics, and so on. At the international level, medical information services are developing strengthened links through the use of networks. The HealthNet system, for example, provides access for health professionals in developing countries to medical literature and databases and to colleagues elsewhere, through the use of low-cost packet satellite technology. HealthNet is initially targeted at Africa, and includes access to British and North American gateways which allow medical libraries and information units in these areas to 'twin' with similar organisations in Africa.

Generic facilities such as electronic mail and file transfer through computer networks open up the possibility of more extensive contact between health professionals in the context of an electronic community. The increasing depth of special knowledge possessed by a widening spectrum of health professionals, located geographically separate from each other, and the interdisciplinary nature of health science, point towards a need for networked and integrated solutions to information needs. At the same time as information management has assumed a higher profile within the health sector, there is a growing interaction with external agencies fuelled by information interchange.

Some instances of co-operative networking with local authorities have been mentioned earlier—a common interest in demographic analysis for strategic planning is another obvious example—and the same trend emerges in health service relations with other public service organisations. The range and volume of data involved can be quite significant: a medium-sized hospital can send some 300-400 pathology and radiology reports per day to several dozen local general practitioner centres, and up to 100 discharge letters; a large general medical practice may make some 40 referrals per day to hospitals, and perhaps 7000 registrations per year to Family Health Service Authorities. Each of these activities involves the transmission of information and storage within the receiving systems, with the desirability of enabling the direct capture by the receiving application, and avoiding a need to re-key data which is already in electronic format.

The data needs to be exchanged between autonomous sites, loosely coupled in systems with a local focus. Externally, information flows will move from the National Health Service to product suppliers, service providers, government agencies, local authorities, European and international organisations, the insurance and banking sectors, private health care agencies, and other national health services. To achieve an electronic data integration across the whole health service delivery chain, and with organisations in its environment, the development and application of standard forms of information interchange is required.

The standard provides for the definition of data elements, syntax rules, and the structure of messages built from these data elements in a way that can be adapted for various applications; EDIFACT is managed by the United Nations as a cross-sector global communications standard, and is also defined within GOSIP. The NHS Information Management Executive has initiated many projects intended to contribute towards the development of a common infrastructure through the use of information systems strategy. A major plank within this strategy is the desire to create a unique NHS number for individual patients, enabling the creation of a population register designed for sharing across the sector, and forming a natural integration of basic administrative activities. This will underpin NHS-wide electronic networking, and together with agreed standards for information interchange, lead towards a shared language for health care throughout the sector.

A number of these projects are aimed at general practitioners, and their links with other health agencies, involving the identification of a basic information structure common to all GP practices, and the development of compatible systems.

More broadly, projects are developing standards which apply across the sector, for:

— the development of a common basic specification as an extension of the NHS Data Model, to cover data exchange standards, minimum datasets, clinical information for resource management; and the information demands of hospital and regional decision support systems;

— the development of an NHS Administrative Register to act as a shared register of basic administrative details meeting the requirements of District Health authorities, Family Health Service authorities, general practitioners, and hospitals;

— a Community Information Systems Project to facilitate the exchange of information to support contracting, and the development of datasets for ambulatory care in hospital and community settings, for use by community health services.

The National Health Service in the United Kingdom has seen a vast increase in the importance of information management, with information networking forming a vital part of this. It is certain that the importance of networking activities will continue to grow as a strategic element in the construction of integrated information and intelligence.

Open systems

The concepts of open systems are now widely accepted in principle, with many believing that the OSI model forms the underlying solution to connectivity problems. In practice, however, the actual take-up of OSI in terms of working products has been slower than at first anticipated. The slow pace of standards development tends to prolong uncertainty amongst end-users, and discourages suppliers from manufacturing OSI products on a large scale due to the lack of a mass market. The lower network-dependent levels of the OSI model are well established in both local and wide area networks; the upper levels are much less well supported with few general or specialised products in most areas.

The second problem facing OSI products is that of conformance testing, to ensure that inter-operability standards are met. These are relatively new, and although normally carried out by an independent third party, do not necessarily guarantee full compatibility; variations within the paper standard mean that compliant products will not always work with each other, still further undermining user confidence and acceptance. The interchange technology should allow a user working on one system to use an application on another system, without concern with data formats; the long-term goal is to allow network users to co-operate seamlessly with each other, regardless of physical location or equipment.

A common framework for networked information interchange must incorporate generic application problems, such as remote database access, file transfer and interpersonal messaging, in a way that separates the local form of the application from the interchange aspects, enabling flexible variations in the former while standardising on the latter.

De facto and de jure standards may emerge from two main sources. De facto standards are those which derive from the use and popularity of easily available products, through a process in which the most successful become widely accepted as industry standards. Proprietary standards from single computer manufacturers fall into this group; while having the advantage of the backing of a major interest group, their future development is unpredictable, and they are 'closed' systems in that the full specification for the standard is not published but kept as a trade secret. De facto standards may also emerge through adoption by a number of different product developers, and have the general support of a wider range of users who may also participate in the standards making process itself. This type of process is likely to be founded on widespread availability, and may be stimulated by an initial development, or adoption, of the standard in government administration projects. This has been the case with the TCP/IP communications protocols, which are widely used in industry, government and education (particularly in the United States) and form one approach to the 'opening' of computer systems to each other. De jure standards are those which emerge from an organised, usually public, programme sponsored by governmental or international initiative, emerging from an open debate over several years; by their nature, these developments are more speculative in nature, formulating paper specifications rather than products.

The successful take-up of the standard may depend on the willingness of private manufacturers to build conformable products, or on the degree to which the standard can be imposed by regulation. The CCITT recommendations for telecommunications, for example, can be reinforced by regulations governing approval of equipment for connection to public networks. Standards for software in computer systems cannot be regulated in this way, but can be encouraged by making them mandatory in private tenders for substantial government information system projects.

The main international efforts towards the specification of a framework for open, intercommunicating, systems has been the work done under the aegis of the International Standards Organisation (ISO) and known as Open Systems Interconnection. Although this is a long-term programme intended to take effect slowly, at the present time the ISO Open Systems model has had more influence in Europe than elsewhere.

Open systems interconnection (OSI) aims to develop a framework for the development and approval of computer networking standards that provides communications-based user services which support inter-working with computer systems from different manufacturers, in different geographical locations. This framework defines a conceptual and functional model for supporting multi vendor, multimedia and multi-software networking by formalising and delineating the problems involved in sustaining it, and structuring them within an open architecture. The basic idea of OSI is not to invent a completely new set of protocols where adequate ones already exist, or to impose any one single approach or technology, but instead to acknowledge existing protocols by placing them within the framework of the model according to open architecture principles. In this way, OSI functions as a focus for co-ordinating standards development, and depends on achieving a consensus view from all interested parties.

The organisation progresses its work through a web of committees, subcommittees and working groups, developing and adapting standards through lengthy consultation processes. Before being formally adopted as an International Standard, a specification will pass through working paper, draft proposal and draft international standard phases, with public comment and feedback at each stage; ten years is a not untypical timespan for this process.

The basic OSI reference model was formally adopted in 1983, and has since been elaborated for particular task types and application areas. The mission of OSI is described as:

— to specify a universally applicable logical communications structure;

— to encourage different users to communicate with each other by compatible implementation of communication features;

— to serve as a reference point in the development of new communication services;

— to enable the steady evolution of applications through the flexible incorporation of technical advances and the expansion of user requirements.

The open systems interconnection model does not

impose a single standard, but incorporates a collection of existing standards, placing them in the context of an abstract model of the communications process. Compliance with the model is intended to ensure functional equivalence between computer systems. The term system is here used to denote a collection of computers, software, peripherals, and human operators which have information transfer capabilities as an autonomous whole—that is, a tightly linked computer network as much as a single computer installation.

OSI is therefore a standard for network-to-network communications. Given the tremendous diversity of needs and options in this area, a single universal protocol is not possible. The OSI approach is to group functionally similar protocols into a set of layers, each of which represents a particular class of service available in open systems. The basic reference model defines each of these layers by specifying both the *functionality* of each layer and the *interface* between adjacent layers.

The specification of the functionality within any particular layer defines what is to be done rather than *how* it should be done. The way in which these functions are implemented in software programs therefore can vary between different products, although the outcomes should remain compatible. The specification of the interface between layers ensures that the information which is received and passed on between software modules is in a standard form. The functional layers are stacked in a pre-defined order to form organised and structured communication tasks. Each layer provides a set of services to the next highest layer in the stack on demand; to be able to provide these it receives a set of services from the next lowest layer in the stack. Since each layer is providing its own set of specialised tasks (specified as the functionality of the layer), it acts as a user in relation to the layer beneath, requesting services from it but knowing nothing about how they are achieved.

Data passes up and down the stack using the standard interfaces as a conduit, with each layer adding control information relevant to its own specialised tasks in the overall communication process, and passing the package on. An analogy might be a set of Russian dolls, in which the larger doll encapsulates a smaller one. In OSI terms the original nugget of data is passed down and encapsulated by larger control messages as it passes through each layer on the transmitting system; on receipt the process is reversed, and the larger containers are stripped off as the message passes back up the stack of equivalent layers on the receiving system. The model deals only with the logical structure of the communications process and says nothing about how this is to be physically implemented. Since each layer is acting as a self-contained module within its own boundaries, an individual implementation of layer tasks in any particular system can change without having an overall effect on the communication strategy, as long as it conforms to the logical requirements.

Software modules can then be changed in individual systems to accommodate changes in user needs and network technology, as long as the new version continues to provide the same set of services through a standard interface. In the OSI model the overall communications tasks are partitioned into seven layers, with no overlap between them. Each layer communicates with to equivalent 'peer' layer on the remote system by exchanging messages on matters for which it alone is responsible. This is actually achieved through using the services provided by subordinate layers, but each individual layer works as though it were speaking directly with its peer in the remote system. This peer-to-peer communication is made possible by the standard boundaries between layers which are the same on both linked systems. The seven layers in the model fall into two main sections. The three uppermost layers are primarily concerned with the applications communicating via the linked systems, and with organising the provision of services to human users.

The three lowest layers are concerned with the technical transmission problems of sending data across networks; the fourth layer (the transport layer) acts as an interface between these two broad tasks. The three lower layers are supported in both the end systems and the network mediating between them; the upper layers are in the end systems only. The physical layer controls the actual physical connection between the two systems, the hardware standards used, and the method of data transmission, working at the level of the individual data bit.

The data link layer provides error handling and flow control, and works at the level of the data frame. The network layer controls both routing decisions and the relaying of data packets through intermediate systems, concealing from the upper layers the particular path through the network which is being used. The transport layer is the first to be primarily concerned with end-to-end operation, concerned with quality of service and ensuring a reliable connection for the upper layers. There are five different classes of service available from the transport layer, including connection-oriented and connectionless services. The end systems must agree which class is in use for the session before exchange of data can commence.

The session layer is responsible for setting up an individual session between two systems, and managing the inter-system dialogue on behalf of the higher layers; for instance, synchronising the information flows between the applications, and allowing activities to be started, abandoned, paused, and restarted correctly. The presentation layer negotiates how data is to be presented to the application, dealing with character sets and codes, agreeing to exchange data in a shared common format. End systems which use different information coding sets (such as ASCII or EBCDIC) can use a special open transfer syntax notation called Abstract Syntax Notation 1 (ASN. 1). The application layer, the topmost layer of the OSI stack, is responsible for interfacing with the local end system and ultimately for supplying direct network services to the user. In an open systems environment, all lower level OSI functions can only be accessed through the application layer, and not directly.

The application layer is not a user application in its own right, but rather handles the semantics of the communication process in the same way that the presentation layer handles the syntax. It has specialised elements for different generic applications, such as file transfer and electronic mail, which interface with proprietary packages for these applications installed on the local end system. For example, a person would send and receive electronic mail through the same package which they normally use on their own system; this local package translates the mail into terms acceptable to the OSI e-mail application layer element, which in turn initiates the setting up and management of the appropriate communication characteristics by the next layers, and so on down the stack. For the transfer to be successful, the receiving system must be able to support the same kinds of action, in reverse.

5

Computers in Schools

Instrumental uses of the computer to help people think have been dramatized in science fiction. Many cultural barriers impede children from making scientific knowledge their own. Among these barriers the most visible are the physically brutal effects of deprivation and isolation. Other barriers are more political. Many children who grow up in our cities are surrounded by the artifacts of science but have good reason to see them as belonging to "the others"; in many cases they are perceived as belonging to the social enemy. Still other obstacles are more abstract, though ultimately of the same nature.

Most branches of the most sophisticated modern culture of Europe and the us are so deeply "mathophobic" that many privileged children are as effectively (if more gently) kept from appropriating science as their own. Space-age objects, in the form of small computers, will cross these cultural barriers to enter the private worlds of children everywhere. They will do so not as mere physical objects. This chapter is about how computers can be carriers of powerful ideas and of the seeds of cultural change, how they can help people form new relationships with knowledge that cut across the traditional lines separating humanities from sciences and knowledge of the self from both of these. It is about using computers to challenge current beliefs about who can understand what and at what age. It is about using computers to question standard assumptions in developmental psychology and in the psychology of aptitudes and attitudes. It is about whether personal computers and the cultures in which they are used will continue to be the creatures of "engineers" alone or whether we can construct intellectual environments in which people who today think of themselves as "humanists" will feel part of, not alienated from, the process of constructing computational cultures.

But there is a world of difference between what computers can do and what society will choose to do with them. Society has many ways to resist fundamental and threatening change. Thus, this hook is about facing choices that are ultimately political. It looks at some of the forces of change and of reaction to those forces that are called into play as the computer presence begins to enter the politically charged world of education.

In many schools today, the phrase "computer-aided instruction" means making the computer teach the child. One might say the computer is being used to program the child. The child programs the computer and, in doing so, both acquires a sense of mastery over a piece of the most modern and powerful technology and establishes an intimate contact with some of the deepest ideas from science, from mathematics, and from the art of intellectual model-building.

The learning paths that have led hundreds of children to becoming quite sophisticated programmers. Once programming is seen in the proper perspective, there is nothing very surprising about the fact that this should happen. Programming a computer means nothing more or less than communicating to it in a language that it and the human user can both "understand." And learning languages is one of the things children do best. Every normal child learns to talk. Why then should a child not learn to "talk" to a computer? There are many reasons why someone might expect it to be difficult. For example, although babies learn to speak their native language with spectacular ease, most children have great difficulty learning foreign languages in schools and, indeed, often learn the written version of their own language none too successfully. Isn't learning a computer language more like the difficult process of learning a foreign written language than the easy one of learning to speak one's own language? And isn't the problem further compounded by all the difficulties most people encounter learning mathematics?

Two fundamental ideas run through this chapter. The first is that it is possible to design computers so that learning to communicate with them can be a natural process, more like learning French by living in France than like trying to learn it through the unnatural process of American foreign-language instruction in classrooms. Second, learning to communicate with a computer may change the way other learning takes place. The computer can be a mathematics-speaking and an alphabetic-speaking entity. We are learning how to make computers with which children love to communicate. When this communication occurs, children learn mathematics as a living language.

Moreover, mathematical communication and alphabetic communication are thereby both transformed from the alien and therefore difficult things they are for most children into natural and therefore easy ones. The idea of "talking mathematics" to a computer can be generalized to a view of learning mathematics in "Mathland"; that is to say, in a context which is to learning mathematics what living in France is to learning French.

It is generally assumed that children cannot learn

formal geometry until well into their school years and that most cannot learn it too well even then. But we can quickly see that these assumptions are based on extremely weak evidence by asking analogous questions about the ability of children to learn French. If we had to base our opinions on observation of how poorly children learned French in American schools, we would have to conclude that most people were incapable of mastering it. But we know that all normal children would learn it very easily if they lived in France. Much of what we now see as too "formal" or "too mathematical" will be learned just as easily when children grow up in the computer-rich world of the very near future. We use the examination of our relationship with mathematics as a thematic example of how technological and social processes interact in the construction of ideas about human capacities. And mathematical examples will also help to describe a theory of how learning works and of how it goes wrong. Take from jean Piaget a model of children as builders of their own intellectual structures. Children seem to be innately gifted learners, acquiring long before they go to school a vast quantity of knowledge by a process call "Piagetian learning," or "learning without being taught." For example, children learn to speak, learn the intuitive geometry needed to get around in space, and learn enough of logic and rhetorics to get around parents-all this without being "taught". We must ask why some learning takes place so early and spontaneously while some is delayed many years or does not happen at all without deliberately imposed formal instruction.

Child as builder

If we really look at the "child as builder" we are on our way to an answer. All builders need materials to build with. Where we are at variance with Piaget is in the role we attribute to the surrounding cultures as a source of these materials. In some cases the culture supplies them in abundance, thus facilitating constructive Piagetian learning. For example, the fact that so many important things (knives and forks, mothers and fathers, shoes and socks) come in pairs is a "material" for the construction of an intuitive sense of number.

But in many cases where Piaget would explain the slower development of a particular concept by its greater complexity or formality, we see the critical factor as the relative poverty of the culture in those materials that would make the concept simple and concrete. In yet other cases the culture may provide materials but block their use. In the case of formal mathematics, there is both a shortage of' formal materials and a cultural block. The mathophobia endemic in contemporary culture blocks many people from learning anything they recognize as "math," although they may have no trouble with mathematical knowledge they do not perceive as such.

We shall see again and again that the consequences of mathophobia go far beyond obstructing the learning of mathematics and science. They interact with other endemic "cultural toxins," for example, with popular theories of aptitudes, to contaminate people's images of themselves as learners. Difficulty with school math is often the first step of an invasive intellectual process that leads us all to define ourselves as bundles of aptitudes and ineptitudes, as being "mathematical" or "not mathematical," "artistic" or "not artistic," "musical" or "not musical," "profound" or "superficial," "intelligent" or "dumb."

Deficiency becomes identity and learning is transformed from the early child's free exploration of the world to a chore beset by insecurities and self-imposed restrictions. Two major themes—that children can learn to use computers in a masterful way, and that learning to use computers can change the way they learn everything else—have shaped research agenda on computers and education. The metaphor of imitating the way the child learns to talk has been constantly with us in this work and has led to a vision of education and of education research very different from the traditional ones. For people in the teaching professions, the word "education" tends to evoke "teaching," particularly classroom teaching. The goal of education research tends therefore to be focused on how to improve classroom teaching. But if, the model of successful learning is the way a child learns to talk, a process that takes place without deliberate and organized teaching, the goal set is very different.

The classroom as an artificial and inefficient learning environment that society has been forced to invent because its informal environments fail in certain essential learning domains, such as writing or grammar or school math. The computer presence will enable us to so modify the learning environment outside the classrooms that much if not all the knowledge that schools presently try to teach with such pain and expense and such limited success will be learned, as the child learns to talk, painlessly, successfully, and without organized instruction. This obviously implies that schools as we know them today will have no place in the future. But it is an open question whether they will adapt by transforming themselves into something new or will wither away and be replaced.

Although technology will play an essential role in the realization of our vision of the future of education, our central focus is not on the machine but on the mind, and particularly on the way in which intellectual movements and cultures define themselves and grow. Indeed, the role we give to the computer is that of a carrier of cultural "germs" or "seeds" whose intellectual products will not need technological support once they take root in an actively growing mind. Many if not all the children who grow up with a love and aptitude for mathematics owe this feeling, at least in part, to the fact that they happened to acquire "germs" of the "math culture" from adults, who, one might say, knew how to speak mathematics, even if only in the way that Moliere had M. Jourdain speak prose without knowing it. These "math-speaking" adults do not necessarily know how to solve equations; rather, they are marked by a turn of mind that shows up in the logic of their arguments and in the fact that for them to play is often to play with such things as puzzles, puns, and paradoxes. Those children who prove recalcitrant to math and science education include many whose environments happened to be relatively poor in math-speaking adults. Such children come to school lacking elements necessary for the easy learning of school math.

School has been unable to supply these missing elements, and, by forcing the children into learning situations doomed in advance, it generates powerful negative feelings about mathematics and perhaps about learning in general. Thus is set up a vicious self-perpetuating cycle. For these same children will one day be parents and will not only fail to pass on mathematical germs but will almost certainly infect their children with the opposing and intellectually destructive germs of mathophobia. Fortunately, it is sufficient to break the self-perpetuating cycle at one point for it to remain broken forever.

The Turtle is a computer-controlled cybernetic animal. It exists within the cognitive minicultures of the "LOGO environment," LOGO being the computer language in which communication with the Turtle takes place. The Turtle serves no other purpose than of being good to program and good to think with. Some Turtles are abstract objects that live on computer screens. Others, like the floor Turtles shown in the frontispiece, are physical objects that can be picked up like any mechanical toy. A first encounter often begins by showing the child how a Turtle can be made to move by typing commands at a keyboard. FORWARD 100 makes the Turtle move in a straight line a distance of 100 Turtle steps of about a millimeter each. Typing RIGHT 90 causes the Turtle to pivot in place through 90 degrees. Typing PENDOWN causes the Turtle to lower a pen so as to leave a visible trace of its path, while PENUP instructs it to raise the pen. Of course, the child needs to explore a great deal before gaining mastery of what the numbers mean. But the task is engaging enough to carry most children through this learning process.

The idea of programming is introduced through the metaphor of teaching the Turtle a new word. This is simply done, and children often begin their programming experience by programming the Turtle to respond to new commands invented by the child such as SQUARE or TRIANGLE or SQ or TRI or whatever the child wishes, by drawing the appropriate shapes. New commands, once defined, can be used to define others. For example, just as the house in figure 5.1 is built out of a triangle and a square, the program for drawing it is built out of the commands for drawing a square and a triangle.

The figure shows four steps in the evolution of this program. From these simple drawings the young programmer can go on in many different directions. Some work on more complex drawings, either figural or abstract. Some abandon the use of the Turtle as a drawing instrument and learn to use its touch sensors to program it to seek out or avoid objects. Later children learn that the computer can be programmed to make music as well as move Turtles and combine the two activities by programming Turtles to dance. Or they can move on from floor Turtles to "screen Turtles," which they program to draw moving pictures in bright colours. The examples are infinitely varied, but in each the child is learning how to exercise control over an exceptionally rich and sophisticated "micro-world."

Readers who have never seen an interactive computer display might find it hard to imagine where this can lead. As a mental exercise they might like to imagine an electronic sketchpad, a computer graphics display of the not-too-distant future. This is a television screen that can display moving pictures in colour. You can also "draw" on it, giving it instructions, perhaps by typing, perhaps by speaking, or perhaps by pointing with a wand.

On request, a palette of colours could appear on the screen. You can choose a colour by pointing at it with the wand. Until you change your choice, the wand draws in that colour. Up to this point the distinction from traditional art materials may seem slight, but the distinction becomes very real when you begin to think about editing the drawing. You can "talk to your drawing" in computer language. You can "tell" it to replace this colour with that. Or set a drawing in motion. Or make two copies and set them in counter-rotating motion. Or replace the colour palette with a sound palette and "draw" a piece of music.

You can file your work in computer memory and retrieve it at your pleasure, or have it delivered into the memory of any of the many millions of other computers linked to the central communication network for the pleasure of your friends. That all this would be fun needs no argument. But it is more than fun. Very powerful kinds of learning are taking place. Children working with an electronic sketchpad are learning a language for talking about shapes and fluxes of shapes, about velocities and rates of change, about processes and procedures. They are learning to speak mathematics, and are acquiring a new image of themselves as mathematicians.

Some of the children were highly successful in school, some were diagnosed as emotionally or cognitively disabled. Some of the children were so severely afflicted by cerebral palsy that they had never purposefully manipulated physical objects. Some of them had expressed their talents in "mathematical" forms, some in "verbal" forms, and some in artistically "visual" or in "musical" forms. Of course, these children did not achieve a fluency in programming that came close to matching their use of spoken language. If we take the Mathland metaphor seriously, their computer experience was more like learning French by spending a week or two on vacation in France than like living there. But like children who have spent a vacation with foreign-speaking cousins, they were clearly on their way to "speaking computer."

When we have thought about what these studies mean we are left with two clear impressions. First, that all children will, under the right conditions, acquire a proficiency with programming that will make it one of their more advanced intellectual accomplishments. Second, that the "right conditions" are very different from the kind of access to computers that is now becoming established as the norm in schools.

The conditions necessary for the kind of relationships with a computer that we will be writing about in this book require more and freer access to the computer than educational planners currently anticipate. And they require a kind of computer language and a learning environment around that language very different from those the schools are now providing. They even require a kind of computer rather different from those that the schools are currently buying. It will take most of this chapter to convey some sense of the choices among computers, computer languages, and, more generally, among computer cultures, that influence how well children will learn from working with computation and what benefits they will get from doing so. But the question of the *economic* feasibility of free access to computers for every child can be dealt with immediately.

Our vision of a new kind of learning environment demands free contact between children and computers. This could happen because the child's family buys one or a child's friends have one. For purposes of discussion here (and to extend our discussion to all social groups) let us assume that it happens because schools give every one of their students his or her own powerful personal computer. Most "practical" people (including parents, teachers, school principals, and foundation administrators) react to this idea in much the same way: "Even if computers could have all the effects, you talk about, it would still be impossible to put your ideas into action. Where would the money come from?" What these people are saying needs to be faced squarely. They are wrong. Let's consider the cohort of children who will enter kindergarten in the year 1987, the "Class of 2000," and let's do some arithmetic. The direct public cost of schooling a child for thirteen years, from kindergarten through twelfth grade, is over $20,000 today (and for the class of 2000, it may be closer to $30,000).

A conservatively high estimate of the cost of supplying each of these children with a personal computer with enough power for it to serve the kinds of educational ends described in this book, and of upgrading, repairing, and replacing it when necessary would be about $1000 per student, distributed over 13 years in school. Thus, "computer costs" for the class of 2000 would represent only about 5 percent of the total public expenditure on education, and this would be the case even if nothing else in the structure of educational costs changed because of the computer presence.

But in fact computers in education stand a good chance of making other aspects of education cheaper. Schools might be able to reduce their cycle from 13 years to 12 years; they might be able to take advantage of the greater autonomy the computer gives students and increase the size of classes by one or two students without decreasing the personal attention each student is given. Either of these two moves would "recuperate" the computer cost. Our goal is not educational economies: it is not to use computation to shave a year off the time a child spends in an otherwise unchanged school or to push an extra child into an elementary school classroom.

George Mamunes, 14, a gangling ninth-grader dressed in flannel shirt, blue jeans and hiking boots, knits his thick, dark eyebrows while putting the finishing touches on a computer program, already nearly 300 lines long. For those uninitiated in the special languages of the computer age, it looks like a hopeless mess of numerical gibberish. But when completed, these arcane instructions should produce a computer image of the heart detailed enough to show every major artery and vein, as well as valves and chambers.

The electronic heart is part of a teaching tool George is putting together for eighth-grade biology classes. A few feet away sits Pam Miller, 14, a ninth-grader with long, brown hair draped far down her back. She is operating a computer program—or software—that simulates the workings of a nuclear reactor. Today she is fine-tuning the section that governs the control rods, those regulators of the reactor's nuclear fires. Tapping away at the keyboard, Pam explains: "You have to maximize the power output without destroying the reactor." Suddenly, flashing numbers burst upon the screen. "There," says Pam, her face lighting up. "Reactor overheated. Power output low. Reactor core damaged. Melt-down!" A disaster that she has brought on intentionally, just to show how it could happen.

Other disciples, seated at terminals scattered around the room, are no less absorbed. Meilin Wong, 15, chic in blue velour blouse, jeans and Bass moccasins, is trying to figure out what went wrong with her business data management program. She is an old hand at such troubleshooting, having spent much of last semester "debugging" a program that, when printed-out, stretches over 30 ft. Jim McGuire, 13, is creating a video game called Spaceship, which will let electronic star warriors zap a boxy-looking orbital intruder.

A more mundane program is emerging from 15-year -old Dave McCann's terminal: a verb test for seventh- and eighth-grade Spanish classes. Off in a corner two youngsters are putting the impish face of Mad magazine's cartoon hero, Alfred E. Neuman, onto the computer screen. Says Muller, as he presides proudly over these after-hours computer converts: "No one told them they have to be here. They're not usually doing assignments. They're experimenting. They're letting their imaginations run free." *t*-Muller's disciples are not all math whizzes. Or straight-A students. Or particularly precocious. They are reasonably normal youngsters who have grown up with computers. For them, in ways that few people over 30 can understand, manipulating these complex machines is as natural as riding a bike, playing baseball or even solving Rubik's cube. Like thousands of others across the country, they are part of a revolutionary vanguard: the computer generation. Not only is this generation propelling traditional education down promising avenues, it is tugging at the entire social fabric, foreshadowing changes at least as startling and momentous as those ushered in by a new generation of automobile users more than a half-century ago.

In the classroom, where youngsters are being introduced to the machines as early as kindergarten, they astound—and often outpace—their teachers with their computer skills. After school they gather at the mushrooming number of computer stores (more than 1500 at last count) or join the computer clubs that are becoming a regular part of the youthful landscape. Huddling around any available machine, they argue over their programs, thresh out computer problems and swap software as intensely as kids once haggled over baseball cards.

In the summer, they may even go off to computer camps, another growth industry, and if they are Boy Scouts, they may try for a computer merit badge. During mischievous moments, they may tinker with one another's programs, writing in steps that will flash an unexpected insult or obscenity across a buddy's video screen. Some try to pick the encoded electronic locks on copyrighted software, taking glee in outwitting their elders, or spin fanciful plots to break into computer networks.

A few turn their skills to profit by showing baffled businessmen how to get idle, new computers to run, or by establishing Delaware-based corporations to market their own software creations. To the bafflement of their parents, they talk in a jargon of their own ("Hey, Charlie, you should have POKED instead of PEEKED"). As with so many other changes in contemporary life, the spark for this revolution is technological: a bit of silicon sophistication variously known as the personal, home or microcomputer. No larger than an attache case, apart from its video screen, this mighty mite packs the computing power of machines that two decades ago occupied a full room. Yet the micros, as they are affectionately called, are a relative bargain to buy and are becoming steadily cheaper.

Many models cost under $1000, bringing them within reach of schools, parents or the children themselves. Last week, in the sharpest price break yet, Timex announced it will begin selling a small home computer for a suggested retail price of $99.95. But size and price cannot explain why computers have taken such a strong hold on so many youngsters. Certainly their interest has been stirred by a related rage, video games, whose computer-generated flashes, zaps, and pings have not only all the appeal pinball machines had for their elders but go a significant step further: they pique young minds to learn more about all that electronic prestidigitation. But many experts, and most of the young operatives, agree that the overwhelming attraction of the machines is the lure of control, the pleasure of being able to think out and then make something happen, a satisfaction all too often denied children.

Recognized by students and teachers alike as his school's best computer programmer, Lewis works afternoons as an instructor for a computer consulting firm, introducing younger children to the machines. Last year his employers sent him to Chicago, where he displayed his special teaching gifts before a meeting of educators. As Lewis told *Time* correspondent Peter Stoler, "we love these machines. I've got all this power at my fingertips. Without computers, we don't know what do be. With them, I'm somebody."

Perhaps because of the faintly macho side of computers, the bug seems to strike many more boys than girls in the pre-adolescent years. Says Steve Siegelbaum, Lewis's teacher: "Maybe it's because boys are pushed more toward math and logic than girls are. Maybe it's because boys are just more aggressive." Paradoxically, the computer passion is often stirred in youngsters who seem least likely to be interested in high tech. Jay Harstad, 12, of Minnetonka, Minn., litters his house with poems and sketches but will do almost anything to avoid doing his math homework. Yet Jay is one of the Gatewood Elementary School's premier computerniks and regularly helps teachers introduce fourth-graders to the machines. At West High School in Wausau, Wis., Chris Schumann, 16, a junior, has made a name for himself by translating musical notes into digital form and getting a computer to play Bach and Vivaldi through its loudspeaker. Originally, Chris regarded computers as remote and forbidding, but that changed when he was introduced to his first micro. "It looked real friendly," he says. "It didn't overpower you. It wasn't this ominous thing but something you could get close to."

The closeness can be contagious. Explains Nick Newman, 15, Muller's chief disciple at Ridgewood: "The more you do on the machine, the more enjoyable it gets. It becomes habit-forming." In Alpena, Mich., youngsters who had learned computer skills in junior high were devastated when they got to senior high school and found too few machines to go around. Says Alpena Elementary School principal Burt Wright: "I've got high school kids begging to come in after school and use our machine." The truly addicted—known half scornfully, half admiringly as computer nerds—may drop out almost entirely from the everyday world. In Lexington, Mass., one legendary 16-year-old nerd got so deeply immersed in computers that he talked to no one, headed straight to his terminal after school and barely sat down for meals.

The only way his father could get him away from the terminal was to go down to the cellar and throw the house's main power switch, cutting off all electricity.

Barry Porter, 14, of San Francisco, is a computer-age truant, so attached to the machine that he often skips school, rarely reads anything other than computer manuals and hangs out with his pals in the Market Street computer store, often plotting some new electronic scam. Barry (not his real name) currently boasts an illicit library of about 1000 pirated (*i.e.* illegally copied) programs worth about $50,000 at retail prices, including such software gems as VisiCalc, the popular business management and planning program. Before security was tightened up, he regularly plugged his computer into such distant databanks as the Source (which provides news bulletins, stock prices, etc.) via telephone without paying a cent.

Computer generation

No one can say exactly when the computer generation began—certainly not earlier than the 1960s, when computers began appearing in schools. But even computer whizzes in their twenties are acutely aware of how soon they are likely to be outstripped by today's grade schoolers. Says Steven jobs, 27, the multimillionaire co-founder of Apple Computer Inc.: "These kids know more about the new software than we do." New York computer executive Charles Lecht goes further: "If you were born before 1965, boy, you're going to be out of it." Where their parents fear to tread, the microkids plunge right in, no more worried about pushing incorrect buttons or making errors than adults are about dialling a wrong telephone number. Says mathematician Louis Robinson, IBM's resident computer sage: "They know what computers can and cannot do, while adults still regard them as omnipotent." Says Hughes Aircraft Chairman Allen Puckett, who shares an Apple with son Jim, 12: "A lot of adults grew up in a slide-rule world and still reject computers. But computers are as natural to kids as milk and cookies."

More and more members of the computer generation are tasting the heady pleasure of teaching their own teachers how to use the machines and, if they are lucky enough to have computers at home, instructing their parents as well. Says Ridgewood's Newman, a regular teacher of teachers: "It's a sort of mutual doorway. The barriers between adult and child, between teacher and student, are broken, and it's person to person. Nobody's looking down on anyone; they're looking each other right in the eye." Often adults find it easier to ask a child how to do something than to ask another adult. Says University of Kansas education professor Mary Kay Corbitt: "One adult student of mine brought her son to computer class, and we discovered that he was doing her assignment while she watched. Two weeks later she overcame her anxieties and was participating fully." Confronted with the strange and unsettling world of the computer, teachers can get a useful perspective on what it is like to be a student again. After taking part in an elementary course in programming, Lois Brown, 54, a Wausau grade-school teacher, is thoroughly chastened. "Now we realize how little kids feel when there's a concept they don't understand. We sat in that course not wanting anyone to know all the things we didn't understand." Despite their obvious wariness of computers, parents are taking the lead in getting them into the schools. In Florida, communities have staged cake and candy sales, carnivals and tree plantings, weekend car washes, even a bike-a-thon to raise funds to buy computers. Says Marilyn Neff of Miami: "We feel computers will be the new paper and pencil." Of the 250 computers in the schools of Utica, Mich., more than two-thirds have been purchased by parent-sponsored fund drives. Says Utica Principal Paul Yelinsky: "Moms and dads are coming in and telling the counsellors they have to get their kids in computer classes because it's the wave of the future." So important is computer literacy that the Alfred P. Sloan Foundation is beginning a major program to get even such traditional liberal arts schools as St John's College in Maryland to begin giving courses in it. Though many schools began purchasing computers with federal aid budget cutbacks are drying up that well. Apple's jobs points out that other nations, especially Britain, France and the Soviet Union—though surprisingly not the electronics-minded Japanese—are paying far more attention to computer education than is the US. Earlier this year, jobs persuaded California Congressman Pete Stark and Missouri Senator John Danforth to introduce bills in Congress that would allow computer manufacturers to take a hefty tax write-off for any machines they donate to elementary and high schools. Under the present law, full deductions for such scientific equipment are allowed only if it is given to colleges and universities.

Jobs originally spoke of giving an Apple to every public elementary and secondary school in the country, more than 80,000 computers worth as much as $200 million retail. Now he thinks private schools should be included and is encouraging other manufacturers to join in the program as well. Meanwhile, Apple's archrival, the Tandy Corp., maker of the Radio Shack computer line, is taking a different tack: it has pledged $500,000 in equipment to spur development of educational programming, or courseware, for the classroom. Many of the approximately 100,000 computers now in US schools—roughly one for every 400 students—are in affluent suburbs like Ridgewood, a national leader in computer education. But the machines are also found in the unlikeliest of places. On a Chippewa Indian reservation in Wisconsin, computers are being used by young members of the tribe to learn their ancient and nearly forgotten language. Alaska's small rural schools have been ordering computers to meet a special need: they allow students of different ages and abilities in the same small classrooms to learn at their own pace. Dubuque, Iowa, where the *New Yorker* founding editor Harold Ross disdainfully located his provincial old lady, has 13 machines and another 20 on order. Bill Holloway, a professor of computer education at the University of Kansas, calls the spread of small computers in the classroom nothing less than an avalanche. According to various industry studies, there may be from 300,000 to 650,000 computers in the schools by 1985.

So far, the most common, and least interesting, way to use school computers is in direct drill and review. The machine simply quizzes, prods and grades the student, very much like a robot teacher. Hundreds of programs of this type are available for popular computers like the Apple II Plus, Radio Shack's TRS-80 and the Commodore PET. But many of these programs are little more than computerized rehashes of the old classroom flash cards that go back to the days of McGuffey's readers. One notable difference: today when the student answers correctly, the screen will light up with WOWS, HOORAYS or smiling animals. Wrong answers may produce sad or scowling faces, perhaps accompanied by a falling tear. Partly because of teachers' fears—of the machines and for their jobs—and partly because of the poor quality of software, the frequently heralded electronic revolution in the classroom has been slow to occur. Now, however, it is being pushed along by steady improvements in teaching programs, thanks to imaginative enterprises like the Minnesota Educational Computing Consortium.

One of its more refreshing drills: a program called Wrong Note, which helps teach sight reading of musical scores. As a simple tune emanates from the computer's loudspeaker, matching notes appear on the screen, but sometimes the quiz intentionally errs and obliges students to find the false note. In order to do so, they can order up a repetition of the tune as often as Bogie and company did in *Casablanca.* Says Kenneth Brumbaugh, director of the consortium's instructional services: "Imagine asking a teacher to play it again and again!" Even very young children can profit from such exercises. At the Nordstom Elementary School in Morgan Hill, Calif., a suburb of San Jose, Colin Devenish, 7, is working with a classmate on the arithmetic drill, honing his skills in addition and subtraction. Unlike youngsters doing such drilling in the past, Colin seems to be enjoying himself enormously. Why? "Because," he replies mischievously within earshot of his teacher, "the computer doesn't yell."

Computers, operated only by touching a few buttons, are also remarkably effective devices for educating the handicapped. At the California School for the Deaf in Fremont, Rhonda Revera, 16, has worked with computers for five years, studying every subject from fractions to spelling. Rhonda offers a paean to the machine in sign language: "Computer makes me remember. It is fast, easy and better than writing on paper." Still another important use of computers is as a remedial tool. One is a spelling drill with a special incentive built into it: if all the answers are correct, a video game pops onto the screen as a reward. When one youngster worked his way through the drill, even classroom hecklers were impressed. Said one: "Hey, Old Wentworth's getting better." More entertaining and demanding are think tank-type strategy games like Geography Search, which launches competing teams on a Columbus-like voyage of exploration. They must make their way across the Atlantic, taking into account currents and winds, finding their longitude and latitude by means of star patterns and the length of a shadow thrown by a stick at high noon (methods that worked for Columbus, after all), and coping with such unforeseen perils as an outbreak of scurvy, an attack by pirates and a tropical storm. Only shrewd planning, wise choices and cooperative action ensure survival. The simulated voyage becomes uncannily real to the participants. Says the game's creator, Thomas Snyder, 31, who heads Computer Learning Connection, Inc., of Cambridge, Mass.: "When they get near the end and the computer finally shows them another ship near by, they act as if they had actually spotted a ship at sea."

Until a few years ago, the few computers available in secondary schools were essentially "dumb" terminals linked by telephone lines to a large, centrally located machine that served a variety of users through an arrangement called time-sharing. All the courseware was stored in the big computer's powerful memory, which could be tapped at will by students and teachers. The most successful example of such a system—and the one still used by Wisconsin's Chippewa Indians—is PLATO (for Programmed Logic for Automatic Teaching Operations).

Developed in the 1960s by the University of Illinois and Control Data Corp., PLATO is an exemplary teacher containing more than 8000 hours of courseware, much of it in a continuous curriculum. Thus, if a youngster forgets a point from an earlier lesson, PLATO will search its prodigious memory and patiently recapitulate. But such time-sharing schemes are extremely expensive, since they require open lines to the central computer. They also can become backed up at peak hours, and do not always lend themselves readily to what is the most intellectually demanding use of the computer: learning how to program it. For this, the inexpensive, easy-to-operate personal computer, entirely self-contained and relying on equipment immediately at the student's side, is an ideal instrument—much more "user-friendly," as manufacturers like to say, than big machines. Yet even with a handy micro, programming can overwhelm the uninitiated. The programmer and computer must "speak" a common language. In the early days of the digital computer, this was extremely difficult.

The machine reduces all the information it receives, whether it arrives as letters, numbers or graphic symbols, into the simplest possible electronic statements: either a yes or a no, represented by pulses of high or low voltage. To command the machine in its own internal language meant writing out endless strings of one or zeros, called bits and bytes, symbolizing those yes or no statements. But scientists soon began creating alternate languages for communicating with the machines that vaguely resemble everyday speech. The most popular of these computer tongues is BASIC (for Beginner's All-purpose Symbolic Instruction Code).

Developed at Dartmouth by mathematician John Kemeny and his colleague Thomas Kurtz to let even the least mathematically gifted student converse with the university's computers, it is "understood" by virtually all of today's personal computers. To show just how easy the language is, Kemeny offers this extremely simple lesson in programming: tell the computer to find the square roots (i.e., the numbers that, when multiplied by themselves, yield the original numbers) of eleven successive values, say 20 through 30.

The entire operation can be accomplished for a program of just four steps:

```
1  FOR N = 20 TO 30
2  PRINT N, SQR(N)
3  NEXT N
4  END
```

Translated into everyday language, the first line tells the computer to let N stand successively for 20 through 30. The second instructs the machine to print the first value of N (that is, the number 20), compute its square root (SQR) and print out the result. The third tells the computer to go on to each of the succeeding values all the way through 30. Finally, the program tells the computer to call it a day, its job having been done. Even the smallest machine can do such calculations in a flash, compared with the hours of work they might require of human computers. To preserve their creativity, the students can readily store their programs on magnetic tape or on a small, 45 rpm-size plastic record called a floppy disc—which is not, as some parents believe, a new form of back injury. Then when the occasion arises for using the program again, the computer operator merely loads the instructions back into the machine and punches in some new values for N.

The same broad principles apply to the creation of all software, even complex simulations like Geography Search. Literal-minded brutes that they are, computers do exactly what they are told. No more and no less. But youngsters of even the most tender age are surprising educators by showing they can master the beasts with startling ease. Computer software expert Leona Schauble of the Children's Television Workshop (producers of *Sesame Street)* recalls getting an eight-year-old boy at Manhattan's Little Red School House started on a simple computer game.

The game generated an image of a frog that would leap up and catch a butterfly, provided the right buttons were hit. After a few minutes, she checked back and found the frog jumping in slow motion. When she asked the youngster what happened, he replied, "Well, we wanted to make the frog catch more butterflies. So we got a listing of the variables and slowed him down." In other words, the youngster had broken into the game's program and changed it to suit himself.

To instruct very young children, even Kemeny's BASIC is much too mathematical. Instead, more and more schools are turning to an innovative computer language called LOGO (from the Greek word for reason), developed by Seymour Papert and his colleagues at MIT. A mathematician who studied with the Swiss psychologist jean Piaget, Papert has become something of a guru of the computer generation, predicting that the machines will revolutionize learning by taking much of the mystery out of mathematics, science and technology. Says he: "The computer can make the most abstract things concrete."

With a deceptively simple set of commands, LOGO enables youngsters who know nothing of geometry and algebra, and barely know how to read, to manipulate a triangular figure, dubbed the Turtle, on a computer screen and trace all manner of shapes with it. At the Lamplighter School in Dallas, teachers using LOGO get youngsters of three or four to write simple computer instructions. In one game, they maneuver "cars" and "garages" on the computer screen in such a way that the cars are parked inside the garages. While playing with LOGO, the youngsters learn simple words, the difference between left and right, and geometric concepts that they would not ordinarily encounter until junior high.

The machines crop up in the lives of youngsters even before they enter school—and sometimes before they learn to walk or talk—in the guise of such siliconised gadgetry as Little Professor and Speak & Spell. With a few presses of the button, these computerized games produce flashing lights, squealing sounds and disembodied voices that inculcate the rudiments of spelling and calculating. A record of sorts may have been set by Corey Schou, a computer scientist at the University of Central Florida in Orlando: he rigged up a home computer so his five-month-old daughter could operate it by pressing buttons in her crib and changing the designs on a nearby screen. Says the proud papa: "Basically, it's an electronic kaleidoscope, another diversion, another learning device." Whatever it is, it prepares youngsters for all those buttons they will encounter soon enough in and out of school. Parents and teachers may shudder at the thought, but it is only a short hop from skilful operation of a video game to learning fundamentals of programming. Says MIT Sociologist Sherry Turkle, 33, who has been studying the youthful computer culture for five years: "The line between game playing and programming is very thin. Programming takes what is powerful about games—this articulation of knowledge, this learning about strategy—and carries it to a higher level of power." By the time the youthful programmers reach the eighth or ninth grade, their skills may reach a marketable level. In Chicago, Jonathan Dubman, 14, and Kay Borzsony, 13, have formed a company called Aristotle Software to sell their own computer games and graphics programs. Says Kay: "The nice thing about the computer business is that there is no real bias against children. In the computer magazines, you read articles by 12- and 13-year-olds." Laura Hyatt, 15, of Ridgewood, helps a stymied local insurance office figure out how to use its software. Says she: "It's better than babysitting." And, at $3.50 an hour, somewhat more profitable.

The prodigy of prodigies may be Eugene Volokh, 14, of Los Angeles. A Russian emigre, he earns $480 each week by doing 24 hours of programming for 20th Century-Fox, while carrying a full load of courses as a junior at UCLA. This year Greg Christensen, 18, of Anaheim, Calif., could make $100,000 in royalties from a video game he developed that was bought by Atari. Other youngsters are waiting at the sidelines in hopes of catching up with these young entrepreneurs. Every Tuesday night, Scott Whitfield, 13, and his brother Shawn, 11, appear at the Menlo Park, Calif., public library to get computer instruction. Says Scott: "We'll probably never get a job if we don't learn how to use a computer." Not all youngsters take equally to the machines. In a typical computer class, only about one in five students becomes seriously involved. Says Steven Scott, 16, of Wausau's West High: "Either you get the hang of it or you don't." Even so dedicated a computernik as Ridgewood's Nick Newman finds programming interesting only for a purpose. His own goal is to apply his computer knowledge to a career in science or medicine. Whatever these youngsters make of their computer experiences, they will surely confront the world differently from their parents.

The precise, orderly steps of logic required to use and program the machines promise to shape—and sharpen—the thought processes of the computer generation. Indeed, the youngsters playing all those strategy games are doing precisely what corporations do when they plan to launch a new product, or what military leaders do when they devise strategies to confront a potential foe.

Whether such abilities will change the world for the better is another matter. Princeton psychologist George Miller, for one, has doubts that "a few years of thinking like a computer can change patterns of irrational thought that have persisted throughout recorded history."

Other social critics ask if clear thinking is enough—if, in fact, there might not be a danger in raising a generation to believe that it has the analytical tools to contemplate any problem. Says MIT computer science professor Joseph Weizenbaum: "There's a whole world of real problems, of human problems, which is essentially being ignored." It is still impossible, after all, to reduce a human relationship to a printout or to solve a moral question by bits and bytes.

6

Computers in Manufacturing

In Japan manufacturing productivity is currently growing at the rate of 4.1 per cent a year. France and Germany have manufacturing productivity growth rates of 4.9 and 5.0 per cent a year, respectively. Meanwhile, in the US the rate of growth in manufacturing productivity has fallen sharply. From 1969 to 1973, output per man-hour increased at a compound rate of 2.9 percent. From 1973 to 1979, the gains dwindled to 1.6 percent a year. In the US the program to reverse this productivity pattern significantly must rely on the continued development of advanced technology and its application.

Perhaps the most important element in this reliance on innovation is increased factory automation and a growing use of computers and microprocessor technology in manufacturing. Today, we are on the technological and sociological edge of a dramatic increase in the use of computers in our factories. This will have a profound impact on the nation's productivity growth in the next decade. Within the next 10 to 15 years, four evolutionary trends will meet on the factory floor: (1) the increasing power and simplification of computers, (2) a widespread appreciation of the practicality of computerized manufacturing and robotic applications, (3) a new realization of the impact of computers on people and of people on computers, and (4) a growing awareness of the urgent need for manufacturing innovation in our society.

Many computerized factory systems exist today as islands of automation. The immediate task of the scientific and technical communities is to use the increased power and simplicity of computers to link these elements into an integrated system. Making use of low-cost computer hardware to perform more and more jobs will make such an integrated factory system economically viable. Some difficult technical problems remain. We must develop generally accepted, standardized interfaces between computerized design engineering and computerized manufacturing, between individual machines and machining centers, and between computers and the people using them.

We must also refine the present state of application technology and reduce the cost of the factory automated system through the increased use of computers. Advances in factory automation are dependent on advances in computer technology.

Computer evolution

The technological changes in the computer field during the past several years clearly equal any technological change that has occurred in our society over the past 100 years. The introduction of high-performance, low-cost microprocessor and storage technology has dramatically improved and enhanced the functions and capabilities of computer software and hardware. With today's increased power, manufacturing computer systems can be made more adaptable to the manufacturing environment, thus cutting systems engineering costs and time per installation. The cost of computer hardware itself has been steadily declining. This trend will continue with the introduction of new technologies such as very high-performance microprocessor chips based on very large scale integration (VLSI). On the other hand, the cost of the human and software resources for systems engineering and programming has gone up. In 1955, 85 percent of the total cost for processing information was hardware; it is estimated that by 1985 hardware will account for only 15 percent of this total cost. To improve manufacturing productivity we must reverse this trend by optimizing the use of our human resources and taking advantage of the increased computer power and reduced hardware Costs. The need to make increased use of available computer power is heightened by the decline in available technical manpower.

The National Science Foundation found the annual growth rate of scientific and R&D personnel between 1954 and 1969 to be 5.9 percent. Some 556,000 employees were involved in technical work in 1969, but the number fell to 517,000 in 1973 and then grew to only 610,000 by last year—a rate of only 2.8 percent annually. The increased capability of computer technology and broad availability of application software packages, including the expanded use of problem-oriented languages and database software, can reduce the cost of program development and maintenance by a factor of 10.

The graphics capabilities of engineering computers can link integrated design and drafting systems to manufacturing systems. With these "user-friendly" approaches to provide a bridge between man and computer, the user can interact directly with the manufacturing system without traditional interfaces and jargon-heavy manuals. Computers and the applications they support can now be considered for functions or activities that only recently were impractical. The opportunity for the application of this technology, for all practical purposes, is unlimited.

Manufacturing automation

Advances in the two primary elements of factory computerization—computer-aided design (CAD) and computer-aided manufacturing (CAM)—will create a new industrial revolution. By integrating design with manufacturing, we can not only turn out new product designs much faster, but also program the computer to make sure the designs provide quality and reliability as well as the lowest possible manufacturing costs. CAD/CAM is the integrated use of advanced computer technology in engineering and manufacturing. It is a common database of part and product geometry and related information which makes it easier to translate a creative idea into a final product at a reduced cost. With CAD, a user can define a part shape, analyse stresses and other factors, check mechanical actions, and automatically produce engineering drawings from a graphics terminal. When CAD is combined with the CAM system, the user can also manipulate nongraphic data such as bills of material, shop information, and cost factors.

The end result is greater design flexibility and what is referred to as designing to cost. The CAD functions can be grouped in four categories: design and geometric modelling, engineering analysis, kinematics, and drafting.

— In design and geometric modelling, the designer describes the shape of a structure with a geometric model constructed graphically on a cathode-ray tube. The computer converts this picture into a mathematical model, which is stored in the computer database for later use. Many other design functions depend heavily on the model. It can, for example, be used to create a finite-element model for stress analysis, serve as input for automated drafting to make a drawing, or be used to create numerical control tapes for the factory.

— After the geometric model has been created, the engineer can easily calculate such things as weight, volume, surface area, moment of inertia, or center of gravity of a part. But the most powerful method of analysing a structure is probably finite-element analysis. In this technique, the structure is broken down into a network of simple elements that the computer uses to determine stresses, deflections, and other structural characteristics. The designer can see how the structure will behave before it is built and can modify it without building costly physical models and prototypes. This procedure can be expanded to a complete systems model, and the operation of a product can be simulated.

— With computer kinematics, the user can examine the effects of moving parts on other parts of the structure or design and can analyse more complex mechanisms.

— Finally, the CAD system automatically drafts drawings for use in manufacturing.

Computer-aided design is a good example of the transition of expensive, state-of-the-art computer technology to a commercial, economically justifiable system. Recent advances in CAD technology have increased the productivity and effectiveness of design engineering groups. Such systems will be even more common in the next five to ten years. Manufacturing groups can draw on the geometric and numerically coded description produced by CAD to create numerical control tapes, which allow direct computer control of shop machines, determine process plans and scheduling, instruct robots, computerize testing, and in general improve the management of plant operations.

Computer-aided manufacturing has five main functions: tool design, machine control, process and materials planning, robotics, and factory management.

— Manufacturing engineering and tool design deals with the machines and fixtures needed to make a new product. In effect, the set of machines, tooling, and fixtures is a new product, and all the techniques of CAD are used in fashioning it. The CAD techniques are then used to simulate plant operation and the integration of machines and materials handling.

— Machine automation consists of a chain of increasingly sophisticated control techniques. At the lower end of the spectrum are fixed automation with relays or cams and programmable controllers, where relays have been replaced by electronics. Moving up the spectrum, numerical control (NC) refers to controlling a machine with prerecorded, numerically coded information to fabricate a part. In this case, the machine is hardwired and not readily reprogrammed. In computer numerical control (CNC) the machine is directly controlled by a mini-computer, which stores the machining instructions as software that is relatively easy to reprogram. Because of the computer control, CNC has the advantages of much higher storage capability and increased flexibility. Virtually all numerical control is computer-based, yet only ten years ago CNC was an expensive exception.

— Process planning considers the detailed sequence of production steps from start to finish. The process plan describes the state of the workpiece at each work station. An important element in process planning is group technology, in which similar parts are organized into families to allow standardized fabrication steps; this permits significant savings by avoiding duplicate tooling and systems engineering. Most automated process-planning systems use a retrieval technique based on part families and existing databases for standard tooling and fabrication processes. Materials planning or manufacturing resource planning is concerned with the precise flow and timing of manpower, materials, and processes; it is a detailed look at how everything comes together. The ultimate goal is to have continuous use of all production equipment, no bottlenecks, and a minimum inventory.

— Because they are widely applicable, robots have a distinct advantage over specialized, highly engineered manufacturing systems. The economic advantage of a mass-produced, readily adaptable robot over a one-of-a-kind system with a great deal of engineering content is obvious. Robots are now being used to perform materials-handling functions in CAM systems. They can select and position tools and workpieces for NC or CNC tools, operate tools such as drills and welders, or perform test and inspection functions. Through visual or tactile sensors, the robot can manipulate objects. Through its computer intelligence, it can inspect the object and provide the machine with corrective feedback or actually reprogram the machine or change the tooling.

— Factory management coordinates the operations of an entire plant. Factory management systems tie together individual machine tools, test stations, robots, and materials-handling systems into manufacturing cells and the cells into an integrated whole. An integrated CAM system of this sort is usually hierarchical, with microprocessors handling specific machining functions or robot operation, middle-level computers controlling the operation and work scheduling of one or more manufacturing cells, and a large central computer controlling the overall system.

Reliability is greatly improved by structuring the control system correctly. Local, distributed control (with defined responsibilities) reports up to a supervisory control that, in turn, is linked to a managerial computer. This parallels the structure of the typical industrial organization.

Ultimately, the digital output from the CAD computer will be simply plugged into the CAM system to reprogram the plant's manufacturing computers. In such an integrated system, the databases will be organized in a way that avoids redundancy and reformatting of information. And any change in one part of the system will automatically revise dependent or related information in other parts of the system. Bridging the CAM and CAD systems will be one of our major jobs in the future. A fundamental difference that has to be reconciled is that CAD makes use of a pictorial, graphics-oriented computer database while CAM involves a great deal of text-oriented information. In other words, we need to find a way for the computer doing the drawing to speak the same language as the computer directing the manufacturing plant. Layering is one way to link these systems.

Layering is a particular technique for structuring the CAD and CAM databases. It enables various people to input data without losing control of the overall design and manufacturing process. Equally important, it enables shop people to see information that is meaningful to them without having to sort through and understand the rest of the information that is normally included in a drawing. To do this, all information is organized in an arrangement resembling layers, or slices, inside the database. The engineer or users in other departments of an organization can provide pertinent information or examine any or all layers of information according to their particular needs. As an example, a printed circuit board may have 250 to 300 layers of information.

A manufacturing engineer inputs layers of information that deal with fabrication and assembly. In turn, machine operators concerned with the details of the drilling and cutting configuration may access layers dealing with this part of the drawing. Other layers provide information pertinent to the needs of the purchasing department or component assemblers. Another major effort to integrate computer systems is an Air Force program called ICAM (integrated computer-aided manufacturing). This is a practical attempt to greatly shorten the time span for the implementation of compatible and standardized computer-manufacturing techniques and to provide a unified direction for industry.

The ICAM program provides seed money for the establishment, within private industry, of modular subsystems designed to computerize and tie together various phases of design, fabrication, and distribution processes and their associated management hierarchy. As appropriate, these mutually compatible modules will be combined to demonstrate a comprehensive control and management package capable of continual adjustment as production needs and the state of the art change.

The ICAM program is divided into five major parts.

— Defining the manufacturing architecture. This permits a concentration on problems of generic scope and wide applicability as the basis for later projects in integration, support, and application systems and demonstrations.

— Developing integration methodology. This activity provides a bridge between industry and ICAM for the transfer of ICAM technology for the integrated factory of tomorrow. The projects addressed include establishing factory simulation techniques, ICAM implementation techniques, configuration management, modelling tools, software integration simulation, automated systems engineering methodology, and various system analysis and design capabilities.

— Establishing support systems. This is concerned with

the portion of the ICAM system involving computer operations, including both software and hardware and both operational and managerial aspects of computerized manufacturing.

— Establishing application systems. This includes such items as manufacturing cost and design guides, the design-manufacturing interface, manufacturing standards, group technology concepts, and scheduling and process planning. Under an ICAM contract, the National Bureau of Standards considered standards in computer communications, languages, and networks to identify potential conflicts within an integrated manufacturing environment. Other areas of concern include robotics, prototype integrated production cells, integrated materials-handling and storage systems, and integrated manufacturing control and material management.

— Demonstrating the ICAM program. The ultimate goal in ICAM is the use of totally integrated manufacturing systems by industry in the completely automated factory.

Robotics

The problems encountered in trying to integrate advanced computer concepts, new manufacturing technologies, and the shop floor are clearly evident in the evolution of robotics. Robots are classified according to the way we provide them with information and the amount of self-adaptability they possess. The most comprehensive categorization of robots is provided by Japan's Industrial Robot Association:

— Manual manipulators are worked by an operator.

— A fixed-sequence robot has a manipulator that repetitively performs successive steps of an operation according to a predetermined sequence which cannot be easily changed.

— A variable-sequence robot is similar to the fixed-sequence robot except that the set information can be easily changed.

— Playback robot reproduces, from its computer memory, operations that were originally executed under human control.

— An Nc robot is a manipulator whose tasks are programmed by using numerical control tapes or cards.

— An intelligent robot, using sensory perception, detects changes in the work environment and proceeds accordingly, using its decision-making capability.

Industry today is focusing on the development of NC and intelligent robots. There has been a growth in the number of firms that manufacture and sell such robots which is reminiscent of the proliferation of minicomputer companies in the 1960s.

Basically, robots are microprocessor-controlled mechanical devices that perform a function or provide an intelligent interface between machines and processes. They can be intelligent enough to make on-the-spot manufacturing "decisions." But for robots to become practical, we must reduce their size, mechanical complexity, and installed cost—primarily through the expanded use of computer and control technology.

Robots can duplicate human manipulative skills with accuracy and precision. Their flexibility and versatility, as opposed to hard automation, make robots ideally suited to the kinds of small batch jobs that constitute the bulk of industry's manufacturing activity. Today, robots, are freeing people from jobs that present serious health hazards, are mundane, or are highly repetitive. In most cases their use is justified for non-economic reason In the US industry has been slow to adopt robotics. This reluctance appears to be due primarily to the large initial investment and the general availability of relatively inexpensive manual labour. Why install a $100,000 or $150,000 robot to perform a $25,000-a-year job? Also, the majority of today's robots are monsters: bulky, unwieldy mixtures of hydraulic and mechanical contraptions with a machine tool heritage.

This situation is changing. Robots are becoming more streamlined, and, when they are manufactured in large quantities, will rapidly decline in cost. Many technologically innovative firms are entering the business. Equally important, system engineering, which represents as much as two-thirds of the cost of a robotic application, is being greatly reduced. It is not difficult to imagine that in a short time the cost of a typical robotic system will be paid back in one or two years.

In the next decade the cost of a robot is likely to be down to $10,000 to $20,000, while skilled labour costs might easily be $25 or $30 an hour. When this economic threshold is reached, there will be a virtual flood of robotic applications. When this happens, robots will play an important part in the totally integrated factory of the future. Most of our plants will have a direct numerical control supervisory computer that coordinates the activities of several NC and CNC machines or hardwired machining centers and robots and connects all the machines into a system. The robot interface will handle the transfer of material and, with newly developed sensory capabilities, will also perform the in-line inspection of parts. For the near future, however, our factories will be some particular mix of machines, robots, and people that makes the most economic sense. Eventually—in a decade or so—robots will fill a void in the supply of skilled labour. There has been a shift in the labour force from blue-collar to white-collar workers and from production jobs to service jobs. Currently, about two-thirds of our work force and 85 percent of all college graduates are employed in a service-related activity.

The total service-oriented labour force is expected to increase by 20 percent in the 1980s—to about 85 million people. This shift to a service economy, coupled with the slowdown in the growth of the US population, suggests that many businesses will find factory labour in short supply: this is already the case in Sweden today. At a leading university in Japan, there is a robot with human-type hands and legs, TV-camera eyes, artificial ears and mouth, and touch and joint sensing. These technologies are combined to provide the robot with some of the capabilities of a two- or three-year-old child.

For example, when ordered to fetch an item in the room, the robot looks around the room and finds the article, walks to it, picks it up, and brings it back. If the robot does not understand a command, it speaks up. Such robots are essentially showcase examples: they are not appropriate for the majority of industrial applications. In fact, a universal person-like robot would make little sense except for very limited, specialized applications. At present, the major applications for robotics are in arc welding and material transfer. In the future, the major application will be in assembly. Artificial intelligence is a worthwhile goal, but for the moment industry has more than enough applications for "dumb" robots. Employment of robots in these applications is actually limited by the extensive engineering required to put them to use. It is estimated that by 1990 two-thirds of the robots sold to industry will be off-the-shelf, modular units rather than specially designed systems. Looking at automated systems generally, by the end of the decade, 30 percent of our systems will consist of hard automation, about 20 percent will be adaptive control, and the remaining 50 percent will be systems of a universal programmable nature.

Respondents to a study conducted by the Society of Manufacturing Engineers ranked the technical and performance barriers constraining the rapid utilization of robots in US industry.

The leading technical barriers were mechanical manipulation, vision systems, tactile systems, sensory systems, programming, and control systems. The primary performance barriers included accuracy, speed, and the ratio of capacity to size. Robots will have a much greater impact in manufacturing when their total installed cost is reduced and they are more easily programmed. As with CAD and CAM systems, the most difficult thing about putting in a robot is interfacing it with the factory—both the machines and the people.

Research today is focused on the development of (1) equipment that will make greater use of computer technology to cut the cost of systems engineering and power electronics, improve servo-motor technology, and rapidly move from hydraulics to electrics; and (2) sensors that will enable robots to perform more reliably and with greater precision and adaptability.

A good overview of sensor types has been provided by Bejczy:

> The nonvisual sensor information is used in controlling the physical contact or near-contact of the mechanical arm/hand with objects in the environment. It is obtained from proximity, force-torque, and touch-slip sensors integrated with the mechanical hand. These sensors provide the information needed to perform terminal orientation and dynamic compliance control with fine manipulator motions ...
>
> Terminal orientation and dynamic compliance control are essential and intricate elements of manipulation. Soft and adaptive grasp of objects,

> gentle load transfer in emplacing objects, assembling or disassembling parts with narrow tolerances, and performing geometrically and dynamically constrained motions (like opening or closing a latch or fitting two parts together) are typical examples of manipulator control problems that challenge both sensor and control engineering . . .

Vision systems close the control loop and allow the robot to interact in a dynamic, changing environment. A second use of vision will be for the critical inspection of the batch-produced parts. The position and orientation of the part can be used in advanced automation systems to direct a robot manipulator to pick up the part for an assembly or transfer operation.

The Robotics Laboratory at Westinghouse is working on state-of-the-art applications in many of these areas. Systems and development engineers are working on the integration of controls, tooling, processes, computer, and other elements of the automated factory. Specialists in robotics are concentrating on developing and applying high-speed vision systems, tactile and force feedback sensors, high-performance electric servo systems, adaptable programmable assembly techniques and computer control, and artificial intelligence.

One of these projects is called APAS (automated programmable assembly system). Funded in part by the National Science Foundation, APAS is a pilot program in which robots are used to assemble components into the end bells of the Westinghouse line of fractional-horsepower motors. It is a development project intended to transfer newly developed technology to the factory. The fractional-horse power motors are currently assembled in batches averaging 600 units at a time. There is a 20-second assembly time per motor to put together 30 different parts, and there are 13 changeovers a day to handle 450 different motor styles. The first section of the line puts parts on the motor end bells. To start the 15-second subassembly operation, a vision system in conjunction with a five-axis PUMA (programmable universal machine for assembly) robot inspects the end bells to make sure they are the style currently being assembled.

The end bell is then oriented and placed on a pallet. The next step in the assembly is the insertion of the uppermost components: a thrust washer, a bearing cap, and a felt washer. An auto-place robot picks up the parts and loads them onto an anvil. The end bell is moved into the station, and the parts are passed on. At the same time a semisolid lubricant is injected. At the next station, four screws, a plastic plug, and a contact point are inserted. Following this there is a complicated assembly procedure. In order to assemble all the different styles of end bells, several styles of certain parts are required. More precisely, six styles of mounting rings and three styles of dust caps are needed. Programmable feeders are used to accomplish the feeding and orienting of all these parts. At this station, a PUMA robot picks up a mounting ring, dust cap, and felt washer on an oil finger from the programmable feeder and places them on an insertion device, where they are fitted onto the end bell.

At the final station, a vision system and a PUMA robot are used to perform the final inspection of the end bell, pick it up from the pallet, and remove it from the system. The computer control and sensory parts of APAS are the most revolutionary elements of the application. A distributed microprocessor system is needed to handle many simultaneous tasks in the short 15-second assembly time, and a visual sensory system is required to provide orientation and feedback.

One master microprocessor controls the entire system. Under its control are three types of smaller microprocessors for vision control, local process control, and robot path control. All these controllers work in conjunction with the master computer to coordinate the inspection and assembly procedures. The vision system on this project recognizes randomly oriented parts on an assembly line after a multipass learning cycle controlled by an operator. It can also be used to rotate the part to any given angle.

Fostering innovation

The technology exists in many parts of the world to achieve significant advances in many areas of factory automation. Many European countries are working on numerical control, process planning, and group technology approaches rather than the graphics approach emphasized in the US. They are well advanced in integrating CAD and CAM systems. In Japan, major advances are achieved through the efforts of the Ministry of International Trade and Industry (MITI). For example, hundreds of millions of dollars and some of the finest minds in business and universities are being applied to the task of developing a fifth-generation computer.

Another example is a $60 million government-funded project to develop a flexible machine system. This system will use high-energy lasers to manufacture small batches of machined parts with assembly line efficiency. The project involves more than 500 engineers from 20 Japanese companies, and it could revolutionize much of manufacturing. MITI makes use of Japan's homogeneity and organizational milieu. It would be inappropriate for the US to adopt the same methods to foster manufacturing innovation.

However, we must recognize the urgency of the problem. The US is one of the few major industrialized nations in the world without a significant coordinated industry-government-university program directed at improving manufacturing technology. We need a national strategy for productivity improvement that brings together government, business, labour, and academia in a cooperative, rather than adversary, relationship. We will have to remove many of the disincentives to innovation and find new ways to capitalize on our diversity and our proven creative and inventive abilities. Just as MITI capitalizes on Japan's homogeneity, we must find new ways to foster, encourage, and channel our innovative diversity.

At present, Westinghouse is working with the National Science Foundation and the universities of Rhode Island, Florida, and Wisconsin on technology development programs. Along with the Robotics Institute of Carnegie-Mellon University, we are developing "seeing," "feeling," and "thinking" robotic systems for several of our factories. We are also very interested in the Air Force's ICAM program to coordinate sophisticated design and manufacturing techniques now used by industry on a piecemeal basis. This program attempts to integrate design, analysis, fabrication, materials handling, and inspection and to develop hardware and software demonstration manufacturing cells in selected aerospace plants.

Sociological impact of automation

The easier it is for people to use computers, the broader will be their applications in manufacturing. We are moving away from the airplane cockpit approach, with rows of complex devices, to create simple computer tools. Compare the ease with which we use personal computers today with the way we approached computers in the early 1970s.

The same changes will occur in manufacturing. The computer has three language levels: machine language, programming language such as COBOL or FORTRAN, and user interface or problem-oriented language. Designing the computer so that it can be quickly used by someone familiar with a problem—but not with computers—is the most difficult of all programming tasks. Today, computers "converse" with users in pictures, in ladder diagrams, or in the secretarial language of word processing.

Voice recognition systems will free workers' hands to perform other tasks and make it even easier for them to use computers. In the future, when research efforts begin to pay off in systems with some understanding of natural language and with "common sense," communications with computers may become as simple as talking to a three-year-old. An important area of concern in manufacturing is worker safety. Automated systems and robots must be able to work side by side with humans.

Major developments are taking place in the sensor area, particularly with proximity detectors and ultrasonic sensors, to make robots more suitable for inclusion in existing factories. The application of automated systems in manufacturing will have several major affects on the people involved in production. It will make our jobs more interesting and challenging; it will enhance job security; and it will multiply the productivity increases. Workers today are looking for greater job satisfaction through greater involvement and increased sophistication. New technologies provide this added dimension to the workplace. For instance, draftsmen use CAD today to perform work that was normally performed by engineers just five or ten years ago. Engineers, in turn, are freed to delve into even more technically sophisticated areas. As a peripheral advantage, the critical need for technical manpower is partially satisfied.

To manage technological change, we must manage our human resources better. For example, we must commit ourselves to ensuring that none of our workers is laid off because of technological changes, as long as they are willing to be retrained and accept new job assignments. Our experience at Westinghouse has been that employees displaced by robots normally move up to better, more challenging work. We should also rethink who can do what job.

For instance, there is a tremendous potential for productivity improvement if the person who knows the machine better than anyone else also has the skills to program the machine while it is working on another job and the skills to debug the programs on the spot. In Westinghouse, by putting the programs for people first, we expect to multiply the productivity improvements that are gained through technology and capital investments. With participative management, for instance, employees welcome advanced technology because they feel in charge of it. Only when these programs are in place will we emerge from the showcase and token automation phase that manufacturing is presently in.

Today, scientific work in the application of computers to factory automation is in the embryonic stage. We are on the verge of seeing the cost of NC, CNC, and robotics become low enough for these systems to be economically justifiable for many more applications. The cost will continue to decline as application problems are resolved and the computer becomes an understood and respected partner in the manufacturing environment.

First came numerically controlled machine tools, which performed their operations automatically according to coded instructions on paper or Mylar tape. Then came computer-aided manufacturing, or CAD/CAM, which replaced the drafting board with the CRT screen and the numerical control tape with the computer. The new systems integrate all these elements. They consist of computer-controlled machining centers that sculpt complicated metal parts at high speed and with great reliability, robots that handle the parts, and remotely guided carts that deliver materials.

The components are linked by electronic controls that dictate what will happen at each stage of the manufacturing sequence, even automatically replacing worn-out or broken drill bits and other implements. Measured against some of the machinery they replace, flexible manufacturing systems seem expensive. A full-scale system, encompassing computer controls, five or more machining centers, and the accompanying transfer robots, can cost $25 million. Even a rudimentary system built around a single machine tool—say, a computer-controlled turning center—might cost about $325,000, while a conventional numerically-controlled turning tool would cost only about $175,000.

But the direct comparison is a poor guide to the economies flexible automation offers, even taking into account the phenomenal productivity gains and asset utilization rates that come with virtually unmanned round-the-clock operation. Because an FMS can be instantly reprogrammed to make new, parts or products, a single system can replace several different conventional machining lines, yielding huge savings in capital investment and plant size. Flexible automation's greatest potential for radical change lies in its capacity to manufacture goods cheaply in small volumes.

Since the era of Henry Ford, the unchallenged low-cost production system has been Detroitstyle "hard" automation that stamps out look-alike parts in huge volume. There is little flexibility in hard automation's transfer lines, which get their name from the transfer of the product being worked on via a conveyor from one metalworking machine to another. But such mass production is shrinking in importance compared with "batch production" in lots of anywhere from several thousand to one. Seventy-five percent of all machined parts today are produced in batches of 50 or fewer.

Many assembled products too, ranging from airplanes and tractors to office desks and large computers, are made in batches. Even such stalwarts of inflexible mass production as the automakers are developing systems to produce more low-volume models for small market segments. In the past, batch manufacturing required machines dedicated to a single task. These machines had to be either rebuilt or replaced at the time of product change. Flexible manufacturing brings a degree of diversity to manufacturing never before available. Different products can be made on the same line at will. General Electric, for instance, uses flexible automation to make 2000 different versions of its basic electric meter at its Somersworth, New Hampshire, plant with total output of more than 1 million meters a year. The strategic implications for the manufacturer are truly staggering. Under hard automation the greatest economies were realized only at the most massive scales. But flexible automation makes similar economies available at a wide range of scales.

A flexible automation system can turn out a small batch or even a single copy of a product as efficiently as a production line designed to turn out a million identical items. Enthusiasts of flexible automation refer to this capability as "economy of scope." Economy of scope shatters the tenets of conventional manufacturing. There is no long trip down the learning curve on the factory floor, thanks to the unprecedented precision the system brings to each step of the manufacturing process, from machining to inspection.

The manufacturer will be able to meet a far greater

array of market needs, including quick-changing one—seven the needs of markets the company is not in now. He can keep up with changing fashions in the market-place—or set them himself by updating his product or launching a new one. He has many more options for building a new plant: FMS frees manufacturers from the tyranny of large-scale investments in hard automation, allowing construction of smaller plants closer to markets. Flexible manufacturing is the ultimate entrepreneurial system: it will allow fast-thinking manufacturers to move swiftly into brand-new fields and to leave them just as swiftly if need be—at the expense of less agile older producers. As the new tools come increasingly into use, "some companies will find themselves blind-sided by competitors they never imagined existed," says Joseph D. Romano, a vice-president at A. T. Kearney Inc., management consultants. Flexible manufacturing systems were developed in the US more than ten years ago by Cincinnati Milacron, Kearney and Trecker, and White Consolidated. The US remains a world leader in the technology: the major machine tool builders are being joined by new suppliers with great financial resources and technical abilities, such as GE, Westinghouse, and Bendix.

The joint venture will bring together GM's considerable capabilities in design and software and Fanuc's expertise in building and applying robot systems. GMF plans to start building products next year. However, most of the action in flexible automation is now in Japan, and both American and European manufacturers will soon start feeling the pressure. Like many other manufacturing technologies conceived in the US—among them numerically-controlled machine tools and industrial robots—the FMS was greeted with a yawn by US manufacturers.

The Japanese have become the implementers par

excellence of this new type of factory automation, not because they are great technical innovators, which they admit they are not, but because they have moved fast in putting the new systems into their factories. Once again, the path to success in a new manufacturing method leads through those Japanese factories set up as spotless little towns with flower beds and tree-lined streets. A visitor to Japan these days finds the new manufacturing system turning out parts for machine tools in Nagoya, electric motors near Mount Fuji, diesel cylinder blocks in Niigata, and many other products elsewhere. In most cases these plants run on three shifts. During the day skeleton crews work with the machines. At night the robots and the machines work alone.

In Fanuc Ltd's cavernous, bumblebee-yellow buildings in a pine forest near Mount Fuji, automatic machining centers and robots typically toil unattended through the night, with only subdued blue warning lights flashing as unmanned delivery carts move like ghostly messengers through the eerie semidarkness. This plant, one of two in the Fuji complex, makes parts for robots and machine tools (which are assembled manually, however). The machining operation, occupying 54,000 square feet, is supervised at night by a single controller, who watches the machines on close-circuit TV. If something goes wrong, he can shut down that particular part of the operation and reroute the work around it. Some Americans think that Fanuc's Fuji complex is just a showcase. Some showcase.

The total cost of the plant was about $32 million, including the cost of 30 machining cells, which consist of computer-controlled machine tools loaded and unloaded by robots, along with materials-handling robots, monitors, and a programmable controller to orchestrate the operation. Fanuc estimates that it probably would have needed ten times the capital investment for the same output with conventional manufacturing. It also would have needed ten times its labour force of about 100. In this plant one employee supervised ten machining cells; the others act as maintenance men and perform assembly. All in all, the plant is about five times as productive as its conventional counterpart would be.

Across the street, 60 machining cells and 101 robots toil in a big two-storey facility automatically machining parts and assembling them into 10,000 electric motors a month. There is nothing else like it in the world. Men perform maintenance functions here in the daytime. The robots work through the night, in silence marred only by hydraulic sighs and the sibilance of those automatic carts. The first floor of the plant contains the machining cells and 52 robots. Machining is carried out on about 900 types and sizes of motor parts, in lots ranging from 20 to 1000 units.

Machined parts are temporarily stored in an automatic warehouse; they are automatically retrieved when they are scheduled for assembly on the second floor. Yamazaki Machinery Works Ltd operates a flexible automation plant near Nagoya that makes parts of computerized numerically-controlled lathes and machining centers; the latter combine several metal-working machines and incorporate automatic tool changers. In the daytime 12 workers man the $20 million plant. At night only a lone watchman with a flashlight is on duty while the machines keep on working. A conventional machining system with similar production volume, according to Yamazaki, would require 215 workers and nearly four times as many machines, and would take three months to turn out the parts the new plant makes in three days.

The company estimates that over five years of

operation its plant will produce after-tax profits of $12 million, compared with $800,000 for a conventional plant that size. Yamazaki is now transferring this technology to its machine-tool-making plant in Florence, Kentucky—bad news for Yamazaki's American competitors. But the most astonishing Japanese automated factory will be started up next month by Yamazaki about 20 miles from its headquarters near Nagoya. This will be what Tsunehiko "Tony" Yamazaki, the personable senior executive managing director, describes as his company's twenty-first-century factory. The new plant's 65 computer-controlled machine tools and 34 robots will be linked via a fiber-optic cable with the computerized design center back in headquarters. From there the flexible factory can be directed to manufacture the required types of parts—as well as to make the tools and fixtures to produce the parts—by entering into the computer's memory names of various machine tool models scheduled to be produced and pressing a few buttons to get production going.

The Yamazaki plant will be the world's first automated factory to be run by telephone from corporate headquarters. The plant will have workmen, to be sure: 215 men helping produce what would take 2500 in a conventional factory. At maximum capacity the plant will be able to turn out about $230 million of machine tools a year. But production is so organized that sales can be reduced to $80 million a year, if need be, without laying off workers.

The Yamazaki plant illustrates yet another aspect of economy of scope: with flexible automation, a manufacturer can economically shrink production capacity to match lower market demand. Though Japanese machine tool makers are the most ambitious installers of flexible automation, they are by no means alone. FMS is spreading throughout Japanese manufacturing, with Panasonic, Mitsubishi, and other consumer and industrial goods producers installing the new systems. So far, nothing even remotely comparable is happening in manufacturing in the US or anywhere else in the world. Disturbingly, all of US industry can boast only about 30 flexible manufacturing systems in place; in Japan one large industrial company, Toyoda Machine Tool Co., has more than 30. Frets David Nitzan, director of industrial robotics at the research and consulting firm SRI International, "We are facing another sputnik—a Japanese sputnik."

The growing Japanese lead underscores frequently heard charges that US managers are too remote from technical disciplines to appreciate the potential of such new technologies, and too engrossed with short-run financial results to invest in them. More often than not, machine tool makers report, executives of US manufacturing companies look at something like a flexible machining system only in relation to the narrowly defined functions of the conventional tools it might replace—not for its potential to provide a different, and far more efficient, organization of the manufacturing process. "Cost accounting is a very poor language to communicate new ideas in," observes Paul R. Haas, vice president of Kearney and Trecker's special-products division. One consequence of this myopia is apparent in the ageing of the US machine tool stock. "Many American factories are barrier reefs—one old, tired technology piled on top of another," says James A. Baker, the executive vice president in charge of GE's drive to develop automated systems. "Even when they build new factories, Americans tend to use the same old machines, shipping them from the old plant to the new plant."

Uncle Sam is the Methuselah of machine tools: more than 34 percent of US tools are 20 or more years old, the highest proportion in any major industrialized nation. Even England is better off; only 24 percent of its machine tools are similarly ancient. In Japan, only 18 percent of machine tools are 20 or more years old; 61 percent are less than 10 years old, against 31 percent in the us. In fact, fewer than 4 percent of machine tools installed in the US are numerically controlled—though the concept has been commercially available for a quarter of a century.

The art of managing the factory is no less antiquated. Fixated by the short run, managers have pursued all sorts of piecemeal efforts to hold down costs without stopping to map out systematic ways of organizing the factory floor for more efficiency. Too often production procedures in US factories appear to be little more than accretions of *ad hoc* solutions to problems ranging from space shortages to union-dictated work rules.

Managers focus obsessively on chipping away at direct labour costs rather than exploring better ways to organize the work force—or investigating the extent to which new technologies are making direct labour costs less important. Japanese corporate leaders, by contrast, tend to be sympathetic with technical disciplines—a far greater proportion of them are engineers—and they have more freedom to incur short-run costs in pursuit of long-run strategic objectives. Perhaps most important of all, a technology like flexible automation is a logical extension of a manufacturing philosophy that views the production of goods as a seamless activity that starts with product design and ends with support in the field—a philosophy, as the Japanese put it, of "making the goods flow like water."

"Japanese management takes a holistic view of manufacturing," says James F. Lardner, a Deere and Co. vice-president who supervised a major restructuring of the farm equipment company's manufacturing operation. "They apply logic and common sense to their problems rather than laboratory investigations and discounted cash-flow calculations."

Even before they began to adopt flexible automation, Japanese plants typically employed far fewer people for a given output than American and European plants. The Japanese were able to do that by reorganizing production—including the placement of machine tools on factory floors. In the US and Europe machine tools are usually grouped by type, and parts are directed to them as required.

The Japanese instead place different types of machines together so that each given part can be processed in one place. Much quicker than anyone else, too, the Japanese have taken to such important concepts as "group technology"—the grouping of similar parts into families for easier manufacture and better inventory control. Like so many other Japanese manufacturing methods, group technology isn't new; the idea evolved in the 1920s in Germany. A central element of the Japanese manufacturing philosophy is the famous just-in-time concept, the system in which materials and components are delivered as required on the shop floor, not accumulated and stored for future use.

Since one-third of factory space is usually employed for storage, the savings are substantial. But there is much more. By reducing inventories to the lowest level at which operations can be sustained, the Japanese force their manufacturing organizations to deal with problems previously hidden. For example, the Japanese already practised preventive maintenance on their machine tools to a degree unknown in the US. Just-in-time has forced them to do even better, because the flow-through of products requires every single machine to function perfectly all the time. Yet the Japanese do nothing that Westerners can't—if they only decide to do it. Marvellously efficient factories using the latest automated equipment exist in the US and Europe, towering like islands of excellence in a sea of stagnation and yielding remarkable benefits to their owners. Take Deere and Co.'s giant new tractor assembly plant in Waterloo, Iowa, which need not take a back seat to any plant in any industry anywhere. In the past few years, Deere has restructured the Waterloo complex from a gigantic, somewhat chaotic job shop into a world-class producer. Deere has poured $500 million into the complex, $150 million of it into the 2.1 million square foot assembly plant. Chassis and engines received from sister plants are joined with tractor cabs and bodies made at Waterloo into gleaming mechanical behemoths. Almost all the materials handling at Waterloo is under computer control. Each part or subassembly—engine, transmission, wheels, and so on—is automatically assigned to a specific customized tractor ordered by a dealer; it is retrieved from storage and delivered automatically to the assembly line just when it is needed. Putting just-in-time to work, Deere has cut inventory in some areas by as much as 50 percent, saving millions of dollars.

Flexible automation allows Deere to build a tractor at least twice as fast as before. And it has given the company a new agility: Deere can now successfully compete not only against other big manufacturers but also against "short-liners" that make only one farm implement in higher volumes. What's more, the company is right now is bidding on a defence contract worth hundreds of millions of dollars. If it wins the contract, it will start making bulldozers, graders, and other heavy construction equipment on its new flexible automation lines—putting new pressure on such established manufacturers as Caterpillar and Case.

But if manufacturers think that they have to pour hundreds of minions of dollars into flexible automation to reap its rewards, they are mistaken. They can begin by acquiring smaller machining centers to modernize portions of their operations. Clifford R. Meyer, president and chief operating officer of Cincinnati Milacron, recalls his delight at recently visiting one of his client companies, which occupies a garage at the end of an alley in a Los Angeles suburb. Inside, a father-son entrepreneurial team mans $450,000 worth of the latest computerized machine tools—successfully competing as a parts supplier to aerospace companies against much larger firms with older production equipment. Furthermore, not all plants that install flexible automation have to be started from scratch. GE, Ford, and GM are among the manufacturers that have successfully revitalized old plants by installing new machinery.

Like many other American companies, GE had for years lagged in automating its own factories. Some old GE plants, James Baker notes, "make Santa's workshop look like the factory of the future." Today, however, GE can boast notable successes in converting some of its old plants into what it calls "factories with a future"—a marketing slogan the company uses to impress upon potential customers that they need not build entirely new factories of the future. Its meter plant in New Hampshire, modernized at a cost of $25 million, is the epitome of an antiquated multistorey mill building.

Another ancient GE plant, the Erie, Pennsylvania, locomotive facility, is being transformed with a $300 million investment into an ultramodern automated factory—inside if not on the outside. Building a batch of locomotive frames formerly took about 70 skilled machine operators 16 days; the newly automated factory will turn out these frames in a day—untouched by human hands. The displaced workers are being retrained for other, more sophisticated jobs. As a general matter, in fact, flexible automation threatens employment less than might be supposed.

The US faces a shortage of skilled machinists for the rest of the decade, and automation of assembly, where semiskilled jobs predominate, will proceed much more slowly than automation of machining. GM is also advancing. Last October it installed its first flexible automation system, an Italian-built Comau system with three machining centers, at the Chevrolet Gear and Axle Division in Detroit. Almost immediately GM discovered just how valuable the new manufacturing flexibility can be. When an outside supplier failed to deliver a front-axle component up to quality standards, GM brought the job in-house. It designed and built the tooling for the component on the FMS in ten weeks—a job that normally would have taken up to a year. As yet, such examples are rare exceptions.

The majority of US manufacturers either do not yet grasp the significance of the new technologies, or do not want to invest while money is still expensive and future markets uncertain. Moreover, there are still no turnkey flexible manufacturing systems available. Installation of big systems requires skilled people not all companies may have on hand. But as GE's Baker argues: "We're running out of time and excuses." The price of delay may be disaster, as the experience of some American machine tool manufacturers show.

During the 1970s the Japanese became the world's first mass producers of computerized machine tools. While the majority of US machine tool makers—small companies, in the main—plodded along using old technologies and methods, the Japanese redesigned their tools for easier manufacturing with flexible automation and equipped these tools with advanced yet simple electronic controls that the humblest job shop could understand. Then, in the late 1970s, the Japanese caught the US toolmakers napping in the midst of the capacity crunch, with delivery times stretched up to two years.

The Japanese, to be sure, played an additional trump. Their machine tool industry had been mobilized by Japan's Ministry of International Trade and Industry (MITI) into a cartel and bolstered with millions of dollars in government funds, as shown in documents obtained in Japan by lawyers for Houdaille Industries, the US machine tool maker that has asked President Reagan to deny investment tax credits for some Japanese tools sold in the US. This double-barrelled assault left US makers of numerically controlled machining centers and lathes in shambles. By the end of last year the agile Japanese had captured more than 50 percent of the US market for those machines.

The US machine tool industry has lost its erstwhile position as the world's leading producer to competitors not only in Japan but also in Europe and even Taiwan. The National Academy of Engineering, usually not given to alarmist statements, in a report soon to be issued calls the Japanese and other foreign inroads "a very threatening development that could seriously endanger the future economic security of the American industry."

The reason for concern is simple: the machine tool industry is central to the growth of all manufacturing. There will be more Japanese surprises in the years to come. This October, for instance, the Japanese government's mechanical engineering laboratory near Tokyo will unveil a small prototype factory of the future where novel, laser-equipped machine tools will take production automation a big step beyond where it is now. The new machines will perform metalworking processes now done separately—such as turning, drilling, and milling—all at once, cutting batch production time of metal parts in half and reducing the number of production processes by 60 percent.

7

Information Service

There are a number of functions which can be performed by a community information service, of which the following are the main ones:

Self-help, as the name suggests, requires that users find the answers to their own problems. The community information service input is directed towards selecting appropriate materials, reprocessing information in a form that can be readily understood, packaging information, and arranging all these materials in a way that is easier for the customer to use. This kind of service is most suitable where there is insufficient staff or lack of trained staff to operate a personal enquiry service, such as a small branch or mobile library, or for deposit in an unmanned centre. It is usual for materials to be assembled, produced or packaged by a district or central office. *Support* for other information services or for groups of professional workers, etc. Where there are adequate information services for the public, the greater need may be for an information service to support the work of other agencies and workers in the field. This could take one or several of the following forms:

— selective dissemination of information (SDI) which, in essence, involves channelling information to meet the expressed subject interests of groups or individuals;

— current awareness services;
— press cuttings service;
— provision of loan collections of reference books;
— provision of publicity and educational materials;
— provision of local information.

Information giving, which can range from simple directional information to the complex, such as eligibility for housing benefit, and may involve *steering* an enquirer to an agency from whom further help or advice can be obtained, without the service making contact with that source of help or advice.

Referral, on the other hand, is a more active form of steering in which contact or an appointment is made for the enquirer with an agency who can help. In some cases, it may be necessary to *escort* the client to the agency if it is felt that they do not have sufficient confidence to make contact, may be intimidated by officials, or are likely to have difficulties in explaining their case.

Advice is information tailored to individual need. Giving advice can be a fairly neutral activity, such as setting out options from which the enquirer must make his or her choice, or it can involve evaluation of options with recommendations as to the best course of action.

Practical help with writing letters, form filling or making telephone calls.

Advocacy is needed where a client is not capable of obtaining the information, services, benefits or justice to which he or she is entitled. A positive identification is made with the client's case, which is then argued in front of officials, tribunals or courts on the client's behalf.

Community education, in the context of information and advice work, is a process of increasing the self-sufficiency of individuals or groups to manage their own affairs, obtain their rights, etc. or to improve their awareness and understanding of issues that affect them.

Community action involves the information service in playing an active role in precipitating change either by acting itself or by alerting other individuals and groups to campaign. Such action can arise out of an analysis of enquiries received, where it becomes apparent that there is a lack of a service or facility in the community or where a situation exists that is causing injustice or disadvantage to people.

Outreach is a means of providing information or a service to a clientele wider than that usually served by the community information service, in either geographical or sociological terms. It covers the use of extension bureaux, mobiles and deposit collections as well as the use of media, e.g. newspaper or magazine articles, radio, television, advertising or viewdata.

Counselling requires a greater commitment of time and level of training to help individuals with problems. At one extreme it can involve simply lending a sympathetic ear to clients who, in externalizing their problems, may thus be better able to face them and arrive at a solution. On the other hand, counselling can lead on to diagnosis and analysis, with ultimate referral of clients to clinics for treatment. Counselling should not be undertaken without specialized training.

Not all these activities will be appropriate to your organisation or the community it is intended to serve. Some organisations, for example, have to be impartial, and therefore are precluded from activities which might be construed as 'political' or partisan or from taking sides in a dispute.

Although for the purposes of this book the different

functions of an information service have been treated separately, in practice such clear distinctions can rarely be made. The process of information-advice-advocacy is often referred to as a 'continuum'. Boundaries are blurred and not generally recognized by users, even though, in setting up a service, limits have to be placed on its actions. Someone seeking information or help with a problem is not really interested in the philosophy of your organisation but in obtaining a satisfactory answer, or solution, irrespective of the means used to obtain it.

Consequently, some people have argued that it is wrong to set up an information service and attempt to limit its functions to just giving information or advice but not advocacy, since users' expectations may be raised but not completely satisfied. On the other hand, it can be argued that something is better than nothing. The decision must be yours but, in setting up a service, you must have a clear idea of what you expect it to achieve and, if it is necessary to set limits, how to deal satisfactorily with cases that need to be taken beyond those limits.

Structure

The next decision to be made concerns the structure of your service. Is it going to operate from one central point or from a number of outlets? From a static centre or a mobile unit? Obviously, the decision will depend to a great extent on the nature of your community. If it is a rural one, with small, scattered pockets of population, then you may want to consider either using a mobile service point or operating through a network of individuals, e.g. village contacts. If your community is a 'closed' one, such as a school or an organisation, then one static centre is likely to be more appropriate.

The structure of an information service whose community covers a large geographical area—nation—

wide for instance—may need to reflect a greater usage by telephone or post, rather than face-to-face contact with clientele. A general rule, already mentioned but worth repeating, is to start modestly and then expand from a secure base, rather than to overcommit at the start and then have to retract.

Management

An information service is set up to meet the needs of a given community and one of the best ways to ensure that the service meets its objectives is for the community to be represented on its management. A fairly common pattern is for a management committee to be made up of representatives from statutory bodies, the service itself, and from individuals and groups in the community. No one group should dominate the management committee and its chairperson should preferably be neutral. An independent committee is particularly necessary where an information service works in the voluntary sector but receives most of its finding from a statutory body. This is in order to guarantee that undue pressure may not be exerted by the funding bodies on the way the service operates. It may be more difficult for a community information service belonging to a statutory organisation to have an independent management committee and, in those circumstances, an alternative would be to set up some form of advisory group representing users.

The responsibilities of a management committee or advisory group might include some or all of the following:

— laying down rules for the use of the service;
— monitoring use and recommending changes;
— suggesting new strategies or areas of work;
— ironing-out trouble spots;
— taking community action where lack of provision or malpractice is identified by the information service;

— lobbying for funds or improved facilities;

— giving specialist advice and help on such matters as budgeting, publicity, law, etc.

What is needed to start an information service?

Establishing and operating a community information service requires certain resources:

— *finance:* capital and revenue;

— *facilities:* premises and equipment;

— *staff:* paid/voluntary, training, health and safety, etc.

– *a system:* for the collection, processing, storage, retrieval and dissemination of information.

Financial resources

Whether you are setting up a community information service from scratch or simply adding another function to an existing service, there are bound to be financial implications. Capital expenditure will most probably be required to provide premises, furniture and equipment. Revenue will be required to pay for such considerations as:

— staff salaries and travelling expenses;
— rent and rates;
— heating, lighting, water and telephones;
— insurances;
— stationery;
— publicity and promotion.

This is by no means a comprehensive list but it is essential that a budget or business plan is drawn up, setting out as accurately as possible the costs involved, so that expenses and sources of finance can be identified. A non-statutory organisation setting up an information service for the first time has a number of possible sources of funding:

Local authorities. Counties, district councils, parish councils are all empowered to make grants for this purpose. They will be the most likely source of substantial continuous finding and the most problematical. Local authority funding is usually given in the form of a grant which usually has to be Applied for and agreed each year. Often the decision is made close to the end of the financial year and so an information service may find itself always existing on a financial knife-edge. Changes in the political control of a council can often spark off a reappraisal of support for services.

Moreover, there is sometimes covert pressure by local authorities to influence the policies of organisations they fund, particularly those policies of which the authority disapproves. Local authorities can also give grants for capital expenditure—premises, furniture and equipment. Some will use their lotteries fund for this kind of grant, but not for revenue funding. In recent years, the introduction of rate-capping and standard spending assessments (SSAs) has severely curtailed the amount of money that local authorities are able to commit to the support of non-statutory services.

At the same time, other government legislation on, for example, compulsory competitive tendering is aimed at forcing local authorities to divest themselves of services that can, in the government's view, be better provided by the private or voluntary sectors. This may include local authority-run information and advice services. Where services are operated or taken over by voluntary organisations, there is a growing practice amongst local authorities to set down what is expected of the voluntary organisation in a contract which is signed by both parties and monitored.

If you cannot get funding from the local authority, it may be prepared to give support in kind, such as the provision of premises (short-term accommodation) or shared accommodation in one of its own buildings, e.g. the library, or community centre. The most likely local authority departments to approach are social services, leisure and amenities, libraries or education. Look out too for officers with titles like 'Community Development Officer', 'Youth and Community Officer', or 'Community Services Librarian', who may be able to advise you on what kinds of financial or other help are available. Your local Council for Voluntary Service (CVS) or Rural Community Council (RCC) may be able to advise you on the right approach to local authorities.

In the London area responsibility for grant-aiding voluntary organisations has been vested in a separate body known as the London Boroughs Grants Scheme. They can be contacted at 5th Floor, Regal House, London Road, Twickenham TW1 3QS.

Government departments and agencies. There is no doubt that the voluntary sector's prospects of funding from central government are not rosy at this present time, particularly for new projects. Funds available are contracting and many of the government departments are now channelling their grants through other agencies, such as Training and Enterprise Councils (see below). It would be advisable to consult your local Council for Voluntary Service or any of the books listed at the end of this section for the latest position regarding grants.

The following sources currently available may be of particular interest for a voluntary organisation wishing to set up an information or advice service.

The Public Library Development Incentive Scheme (PLDIS) funded by the Department of National Heritage and administered by the British Library Research & Development Department is also available to voluntary organisations.

Training and Enterprise Councils (TECs) are an important local source of funding, much of it coming from the Department for Employment. They will be particularly interested in projects that stimulate local employment, provide help for the unemployed. Or offer educational guidance. From 1992/3, TECs are administering an Ethnic Minority Grant which forms part of Section 11 funds but projects will almost certainly need to involve training, employment and/or enterprise. Unlike local government bids for Section 11 funding which can only cover revenue costs, TECs will be able to cover project costs.

Rural Development Commission is concerned to alleviate economic and social problems in rural England. Its Rural Social Partnership Fund supports voluntary organisations in partnership with other agencies which aim to tackle problems of rural disadvantage. This fund was set up for three years, starting in 1989, so you will need to contact them to see if it is continuing.

Local and national trusts are increasingly a useful source of funding for capital expenditure items but are less likely to provide revenue funding, except for innovative or experimental projects. Charities and trusts often have rules concerning what kind of project they can support. It is useful if you can find out what these are before applying since a little redrafting of your proposal could make it more acceptable. District Councils are supposed to keep a list of local charitable trusts and their terms of reference, but failing that the local CVS or RCC will usually be able to advise on possible sources of local funding. National trusts and their areas of interest are listed in *The directory* of *grant-making trusts,* an annual publication from the Charities Aid Foundation. You should find a copy in the reference section of most major public libraries. A similar type of trust administration that has appeared in recent years is the 'community trust'. Community trusts are independent bodies who receive money from a variety of sources—trusts, industry, local government—and give grants to voluntary projects. Applications may have to be siphoned first through the local CVS or RCC.

Directory of Social Change also publishes a magazine, *Trust monitor,* which contains information on new trusts, changes in policies, facts and figures, feature articles, etc.; three issues a year, subscription £20.00.

Commercial organisations are unlikely to provide funding for the day-to-day running costs of an information service but may be a useful source of capital funding for equipment, furniture or special projects. They may also give help in kind—donations of redundant equipment, training, etc.- or offer sponsorship deals for fundraising events and publicity.

Directory of Social Change also publishes a quarterly magazine, *Corporate citizen,* which gives up-to-date facts and help with understanding the corporate viewpoint; this costs £30.00 a year for voluntary organisations, £55.00 for others.

European Community, in certain circumstances makes grants to local authorities and to voluntary organisations for schemes which seek to alleviate deprivation or inequality. The European Social Fund is open to organisations that arrange training aimed at providing the skills needed for specific kinds of jobs. Applicants need to have agreement from central or local government to fund at least half (35% in Northern Ireland) of the costs of the training. The allocation of ESF grants has been decentralized and, as far as the voluntary sector is concerned, applications are handled and placed in priority order by the National Council for Voluntary Organisations. Final decisions are taken by the Department of the Environment. The European Community also administers many small schemes for making grants. These small schemes very rarely have more than a few thousand pounds available for any one project and rarely make more than one grant for the same activity. Grants must also be used in the year they are made. They are thus not much use for core funding but may contribute to set-up costs. Areas covered by schemes include employment, families, older people, disabled people, human rights education, women and combating racism and xenophobia.

There are numerous guides to obtaining grants and fundraising which cover all the sources of funding listed above and many others. Some of these guides are general in extent, others cover particular areas of concern or geographical areas.

Directory of Social Change also produces a set of 8- and 12-page Fundraising leaflets on Setting up; Planning a capital project; Drawing lip a budget; Raising money locally; Earning money; Organising an appeal; Doing research; Writing an application; Social sponsorship; Developing a strategy; Organising an event; Fundraising sources.

If a statutory organisation, such as a library, wants to set up a community information service then, in addition to whatever funding can be provided from within its own budget, the following are the most likely sources of funding:

The Public Library Development Scheme (PLDIS) was set up in 1988 to encourage new enterprises designed to extend or improve public library services in England. Activities likely to promote cooperation between public libraries and other libraries or organisations in the public or private sector are of particular interest. The Scheme is funded by the Department of National Heritage and administered by the British Library Research &

Development Department. It was originally funded for three years, but in September 1990 the Minister for the Arts set aside up to £250,000 per year for the three financial years 1992/3-1994/5. The Scheme provides up to 40% of the funding for projects, the remainder to be found by the library authority or other organisation and its partners. Applications can be made by such as the following:

— English local library authorities or their co-operative agencies, such as regional library bureaux;

— any public or private organisation (including those in the voluntary sector) able to demonstrate that the proposed development will contribute to the quality and cost-effectiveness of public library services in England or in a particular region; applicants are normally expected to involve one or more public libraries in the project.

Types of project in the community information field that have been helped through this Scheme include a feasibility study and implementation of a Training Shop in Peterborough Central Library, and Camden's Free Leaflets Information Service.

At the time of writing, it is not known whether PLDIS funding will be available for a further three years. Details may be obtained from Christine Burden, Public Library Development Incentive Scheme, The British Library Research & Development Department, 2 Sheraton Street, London W1V 4BH.

The British Library, Research & Development Department has given support over the years to innovative community information services such as South Hackney School 'Right to Know' project and South Molton Community Information project. If your proposed information service intends to break new ground then you may be able to interest the British Library (BL) in a research proposal. It would, however, need to cover the research element of the work. Only in exceptional circumstances has the BL provided financial help towards the setting-up and running costs of projects.

The Department has a five-year plan for priorities in research of which the broad areas of concern are the applications and implications of information technology, information as a tradable commodity, and the effects of economic and social constraints on services. Further details of current priorities are contained in their booklet, *Priorities for research* 1989-1994, available from The British Library Research and Development Department, 2 Sheraton Street, London WIV 4BH. Although most of the possible sources of funding listed above are for either capital items or relatively short-term running costs and do not solve the question of how to keep the service going in the long term, nevertheless they do make it possible to get services off the ground, to establish them on a sound footing and to demonstrate their worth to the community. Hopefully, this will then attract more secure and lasting financial support.

Many services provided by local authorities are encouraged to pursue income generation as a means of supplementing or making up a shortfall in budgets. There does not appear to be much scope in the field of community information for income-generation activities, other than marginal activities such as the sale of mailing lists to commercial organisations (a dubious practice at best). The one exception is in the provision of support activities, such as Camden's Free Leaflet Information Service, which is attracting support from libraries and other organisations nation-wide through a subscription system. Other organisations like the National Association of Citizens' Advice Bureaux successfully market their information service but this does not represent a major proportion of their funding. A community information service that is intended to be simply an extension of an existing statutory service will still need to be costed and the effect on other parts of the service assessed. It is highly unlikely that there will be spare capacity—either finance, staff or accommodation—lying around waiting to be used.

A sufficiently well thought out and argued scheme might attract additional funding from the authority or via other sources of finance, but the most likely scenario is that it will have to be provided out of the existing budget. This then means that some kind of re-assessment of current services must take place, in order that priority be given to the proposed service, and resources diverted to support it. It hardly needs to be said that for such a process to take place and be successful, both senior management and staff in the workplace need to be convinced of the value of the new service and to be committed to its development. The climate for developing such services in public libraries in the mid-1990s is not of the best.

Government legislation has focused attention on the 'core' services—lending books and providing reference and study facilities—and other services are expected to be self-financing. Pressure on local authority budgets as a result of rate-capping or the threat of it has meant a retraction of staff involved in outreach services, such as community information. Nevertheless, public libraries are still managing to come forward with innovative schemes, but the watchwords now are 'partnership' and 'income generation'.

Facilities

The choice of a suitable location for your information service will depend to a certain extent on what can be afforded and on the community you will be serving. If you already have suitable premises with spare capacity which can be used, this will help keep costs to a minimum but, if not, you will need to look elsewhere. It is always a good principle to try to locate an information service where it will be most accessible for its users. Even in a 'closed' community, such as a school or organisation, there may be parts of the building that are natural congregating points, e.g. hall, refectory, social/ recreational rooms, by the drinks machine. Obviously, the location of an information service which does not deal face-to-face with clients, but mainly via the telephone and post, is less crucial.

Research into the use of advice centres indicates that most people use them because they are familiar and very local. They also tend to use those which are near their homes in preference to those which are near their workplaces. So the ideal location for an information centre that is to serve the public is likely to be in the neighbourhood shopping area. This will not only make it accessible for the purposive user but should also encourage casual use, especially if it has windows that can be used to promote the service, Such locations, however, can rarely be afforded by one agency alone and you might need to consider sharing with other agencies.

Currently, with the recession at its height, there are vast numbers of shop premises lying empty which landlords Might consider letting on a short-term basis for a reduced rent. Sometimes district councils have empty property available for short-term lets. And short terms have a habit of being extended...

If obtaining your own prominently sited premises, either alone or shared, is out of the question, then consider the possibility of being housed by another organisation that already has premises in a suitable location, such as a library, community centre, council offices, nearly-new shop or even a commercial concern. Failing that, then the next best thing is to seek for premises where there is a significant traffic flow, even though it may not be with shops—for example near a popular bus stop, a school or clinic, on the way to a shopping centre, or in premises which regularly attract a large number of people, e.g. a community centre, library, health or day centre.

An information service that is intended to help those with special needs, such as people with disabilities or elderly people, might be best located in a place where they already meet for other purposes—a day centre or workshop for the handicapped, for example.

The following are some other features to look out for in locating a community information service:

- ground-floor accommodation for ease of access, especially for elderly and disabled people;
- prominent location—not tucked away in a back room or having rear access;
- facilities for display, such as a large picture-window;
- informal atmosphere—some buildings can look too official or have unpleasant associations which may constitute a deterrent to users;
- drop-in facility so that potential users, especially the more timid, have a legitimate reason for going into the centre for the first time to 'suss it out' without being challenged.

Space

The space requirements for your community information service will depend very much on the type of activities it will be undertaking. A *self-help service* makes little demand on office accommodation and does not require an enquiry desk, but will need a prominent location near the major traffic flow in the building and space for noticeboards and leaflet/display racks. A *support service or* one that does not deal face-to-face with clientele may only need an office in any habitable location with space for processing materials.

A purely *information-giving service* dealing face-to-face with the public may need a waiting/browsing area that is welcoming and relaxing, space for leaflet display and noticeboards, an enquiry desk prominently sited near to major traffic flow, and an office/workroom for the staff. An *advice/counselling service,* in addition to the above, will need an interview room(s) for those clients who need privacy. Some advice services put more emphasis on informality and seek collective solutions to problems through group discussion, rather than through a one-to-one approach. Here, the centre becomes more a social facility, encouraging people to drop in for a cup of tea or coffee and a chat, out of which information needs can arise incidentally. This style of operation calls for a kitchen or at least, space where drinks can be made, and a comfortable lounge-type area. An interview room may still be necessary for those clients who prefer privacy.

Furniture and equipment

Desks, tables and chairs. The importance of the enquiry desk being located near the main traffic flow has already been stated. It should be immediately visible on entering the building/room and clearly signed. Where the location is unfavourable, this can be overcome to some extent by good directional signs. The desk should be low and form the least possible barrier between the information seeker and the staff. It will need to have a fairly large surface to accommodate such things as card files and/or computer, telephone, frequently used quick-reference books, etc.

Drawers will be needed for pens, stationery, frequently used information files and cash (where the service has items for sale). A chair will be required for the use of staff, preferably one that is adjustable if more than one person is going to use it, and with a swivel where the staff need to turn round frequently to consult shelves or a noticeboard. There should also be a comfortable chair for clients at the enquiry desk and others nearby for those waiting to use the service, with possibly a low coffee table and some magazines for browsing while they wait.

An information service that handles a high volume of very quick enquiries, like a tourist information centre, might find it more convenient to have a higher bar-type counter with enquirers and staff either standing or using barstools.

Telephone. This is likely to be the most important item of equipment for the staff and the public in your information service. Some information services conduct most of their business with clients over the telephone. In such cases, where it is desirable to link a telephone enquirer immediately with another service, this can be achieved by means of a three-way or conference-line facility. The most useful location for the telephone is on the enquiry desk, although further lines or extensions may be required in interview rooms or offices. Opinions differ as to the desirability of having telephones in interview rooms. In some instances, when seeking information or trying to sort out a problem with another organisation on behalf of a client, it can be helpful to have the client by the phone so that points can be clarified as soon as they arise.

On the other hand, there will be occasions when you will want to talk frankly to another organisation without the client overhearing; in which case it is better if the telephone is located in a private office. Ideally, both options should be available but if this is not possible, then you will have to decide on the basis of which will cause the least inconvenience.

Where possible, your information service should have its own separate telephone line so that clients can make contact direct without having to go through a switchboard or waiting for lines to become available. If that is not possible, then an extension exclusively for the information service is the next best thing. It is helpful if you can obtain a telephone number that is easily remembered by users.

There are several instances where people living in more remote areas have been provided with free telephone access to a central information service through the installation of a direct line from a public building, e.g. a branch library. This has been used as an alternative to providing an extension bureau or to compensate for the withdrawal of local offices. The main space requirements would be for a soundproof booth or office.

A number of information and advice services have made it easier for clients to contact them by operating a Freefone service or using an 0800 number. Some information services, who need to recover the costs of providing information, are using pay lines, whereby the customer pays not only the cost of the call but also a fee for accessing the information. In these cases, the information is usually provided by means of recorded tape(s). Details of free telephone access services and pay lines can be obtained from your local British Telecom office. You may consider that it is important for your information service to be able to offer help outside its normal opening hours. In this case you will need to install a telephone answering machine, so that at any hour of the day or night when the service is closed, enquirers can leave messages. Some answering machines also enable you to record a message or information which is played back to callers when they ring the service. The kinds of information which might be appropriate to record in this way are contacts for emergency help, hotel vacancies, 'what's-on' events, bus or train times, etc.

British Telecom produce a useful free booklet, *Telephone helplines: guidelines for good practice,* which gives practical advice on setting up and running telephone helplines. Copies are available from your local BT office.

Computer. Now that microcomputers are within the reach of most information services, they are looked on as being a necessity rather than a luxury. However, if the computer is needed solely for the organisation of information, then it may only be of value where you have a particularly large database or need to access the information through a variety of search terms, Otherwise a card index system could be cheaper, quicker to consult and more user-friendly. Generally, a computer is needed for a variety of functions, e.g. maintaining client records, keeping statistics, correspondence, accessing online databases, designing publicity, etc.

Card files. If you are not using a- computer for storing your information, it is most likely that your information file will be kept on cards, the most popular sizes being 5in × 3in (127mm × 76mm), 6in × 4in (152mm × 102mm) or 8in × 5in (203mm × 127mm). These cards will need to be housed either in drawers in a wooden or metal cabinet or in open boxes/drawers (wooden or cardboard). Open cardboard boxes designed for card filing are fairly cheap and can be found at most office equipment suppliers. If you are really desperate, shoe boxes make a good substitute. Open wooden boxes are much more expensive but anyone with a smattering of carpentry should be able to knock up some from offcuts of wood. They don't need to be very sophisticated or load-bearing. Open boxes are easy to access and, with appropriate guiding, display the information clearly, but they also have some disadvantages: it is not convenient to stack one on top of the other; they are open to dust, drips from coffee cups, discarded chewing-gum and other unmentionable objects; and, if knocked over, the cards spill out and you have the tiresome job of re-filing them.

Card drawers overcome these problems, even if the information is slightly less accessible. Again, you can get cheap drawers made of cardboard or expensive ones in wood but the most common type is the two- and four-drawer metal filing cabinet. Each drawer holds approximately 1,000 cards and, if you need greater capacity now or later, units can be stacked one on top of the other. Some drawers have a rod which holds the cards in place but this can be a nuisance if you need to take cards out frequently for updating or have information on the back of cards. For even greater storage capacity you will need to consider a free-standing metal or wooden cabinet, but these can be expensive items. With more and more public libraries going over to microfiche or computer catalogues, there may well be an opportunity to pick up such a cabinet at a knock-down price. Enquire at your local public library—but don't mention my name!

There are on the market other more sophisticated files which usually have their own specially shaped cards. If you decide to buy one of these, you will need to take account not only of the cost of the equipment but also of the continuing cost of the specialized stationery. The systems described previously use standard sizes, so that it is possible to use scrap cards or print your own with a predetermined grid to save costs. One card unit that does have some useful features is the Rondofile which, as the name suggests, works on a turntable system, enabling the user to consult a large number of cards from one sitting position. Cards are easily removed for amendment and are available in a variety of colours, so it is possible to introduce an elementary colour-coding of information, say by area, subject or type of organisation.

A Rondofile is compact enough to be housed on the enquiry desk and thus can also be accessible to the public, if desired. One file holds 1,000 cards and, if more capacity is required, a second unit can be stacked on top. For details and up-to-date prices of Rondofiles contact M Myers & Sons Ltd, PO Box 16, Vicarage Street, Langley Green, Oldbury, Warley, West Midlands B68 8HF. The same firm has other card filing systems, including the Rondex, a rotating desktop file that holds up to 1,000 cards, available in three versions to take any of the standard card sizes referred to above.

A similar card filing system using a vertical rotary action is made by Rotadex Systems Ltd, 3/5 Fortnum Close, Kitts Green, Birmingham B33 0JL. There are 24 models in the range suitable for five different card sizes, the largest housing 9,000 cards.

Many office equipment suppliers have these systems in stock.

Filing cabinets. Filing cabinets and dividers will be needed for keeping flimsy publications such as pamphlets, leaflets, broadsheets posters, etc. as well as correspondence. Cabinets come in one-, two-: three- or four-drawer units, usually in metal, although there are some cheap cardboard ones on the market. At a pinch you could always make do with cardboard boxes and used manila envelopes!

Bookshelves, Virtually every information service will have some reference books, varying from a mere handful to many hundreds of volumes. Small numbers can be kept on the enquiry desk itself using bookends (any heavy weight or 'posh' commercial ones), a book slope, or one of those lethal coiled-spring contraptions. Slightly more could be housed on a book trolley and sited conveniently near the desk for quick reference.

Larger numbers will require some form of book shelving, even if it is only cardboard or wooden cartons laid on their side or planks suspended across house bricks. There are an infinite number of commercially made metal and wooden shelving units, either free-standing or wall mounted. Your local library should be able to help you with addresses of library furniture and equipment suppliers. Their shelving tends to be more substantial and you may find that bookshop type shelving is both adequate, attractive and cheaper. Some of the major furniture retailers, like Habitat or MFI, have cheap shelving available in a range of bright colours.

Sloping shelves may be needed for displaying magazines, leaflets or information packs face outwards. Most modem library shelving systems have facilities to incorporate sloping shelves. Murrell's and Point Eight also do sloping shelf units, either free-standing or wall mounted.

Noticeboards. Noticeboards are needed for displaying posters and information sheets for your clientele. Rarely does a community information service have sufficient noticeboard space, so be generous in your estimate where funds allow. Nothing looks worse than seeing a noticeboard with posters all higgledy-piggledy and overlaping. For cheapness, buy a large sheet of pin-board and cut to size to fill empty wall spaces, pillars, doors, etc. Boards do not need too smart a finish since most of the time they will be hidden by posters.

A noticeboard standing or hanging in a window of your centre and visible to the public can be used to feature special events, information campaigns, surgeries, or out-of-hours information. Alternatively, consider using a mobile blackboard or external wall-mounted noticeboard for this purpose. External noticeboards are best covered, using vandalproof glass or perspex. There are many commercially produced free-standing noticeboards.

Leaflet racks and dispensers. Considering the vast number of leaflets available of all, shapes and sizes, the choice of ready-made equipment for displaying them is not wide and what does exist is often expensive. All the more reason for trying to make your own. The following are two cheap suggestions:

Cut stiff manila envelopes of the size required to make pockets, glue them in rows on a large piece of card and pin this onto a wall or noticeboard. An alternative material to use for pockets is adjustable book jacketing, which has an added advantage in allowing all the leaflet to be seen through the plastic front.

Screw cup hooks into a sheet of blockboard or similar material, attach to a wall, and hang leaflets from the hooks by punching a hole in the top of 'them. A copy of the cover of each leaflet could be pasted onto the board to act as an *aide memoire* when stocks have all been taken.

More up-market leaflet dispensers are available from Point Eight Ltd, Shaw Road, Dudley, West Midlands DY2 8TP, including the best one I have seen for holding flimsy A4 leaflets or single sheets. Point Eight also do a range of perspex holders for multiple copies of a single leaflet.

If money is no object, then you might be better off with a custom-designed and made leaflet dispenser.

Display boards. Display boards will be needed if you intend to put on free-standing exhibitions or displays. There are innumerable makes available in a variety of price ranges, many offering special features or accessories. It would pay you to look around first and get advice from someone in the know, such as the publicity officer of a local authority, large firm or other public body. Consider such matters as portability and stability—particularly if you are going to use the boards outside the centre or outdoors—and ease of assembly.

If any display boards can be said to be universal, then it must be those of Marler Haley Exposystems Ltd, who do several different systems that are easy to erect, versatile and attractive. They also have a variety of free-standing noticeboards and a range of accessories such as shelves, lights, leaflet dispensers, etc. which go with both display boards and noticeboards. Prices vary according to range.

Strip indexes. Strip indexes may be used as an alternative to card files or as a way of presenting information for customers to use. They are limited as to the amount of information that can be contained on a strip, although a variety of widths is available. Strips are more awkward to interfile and update but they have the advantage that it is possible to photocopy quite easily the whole file or sections on demand. As personal computers (PCs) become more universally available, it is difficult to see a future for strip indexes. Kalamazoo do a variety of holders and strips but these are a little expensive.

Other furniture and equipment. It is possible to list a great many other items of furniture and equipment that a community information service might need, depending on the nature of the service, the resources available, and the existence or otherwise of back-up secretarial help. Simply note a few items that may be considered:

(a) pigeonholes for storing leaflets; (b) bench or flat surface for assembling packs or publications; (c) typewriter; (d) photocopier (be very careful about leasing a photocopier—preferably get legal advice before signing any contract); (e) machine for recording number of users/enquiries ('clicker'); (f) fax; (g) duplicator—stencil or offset.

Stationery

Pamphlet boxes may be needed for storing booklets, leaflets and other ephemeral materials for use by staff or clientele. They are available in several sizes and varying quality, from cardboard to plastic, closed or open at the top. Lawtons Ltd, 60 Vauxhall Road, Liverpool L69 3AU do a cheap A4-size cardboard pamphlet box, called the Lawco Box, which comes flat and is then folded into shape. A more up-market A4 fold-up file box in brightly coloured plastic-covered card is produced by Esselte Dymo Ltd, Spur Road, Feltham, Middlesex TW14 0TR. The same firm also has a more rigid (and more expensive) polystyrene plastic pamphlet/magazine file box in bright colours, sizes A4 and A5. Library stationery suppliers also have ranges of pamphlet boxes on offer. Addresses from your local library headquarters.

Manila folders and envelopes to file cuttings, leaflets, information sheets in vertical files. Plastic wallets are even better, if you can afford them, as they enable the contents to be immediately visible. They are particularly useful if you want to go in for compiling information packs for your clients. Celsur Plastics Ltd, Drake Avenue, Gresham Road, Staines, Middlesex TW18 2AW have them available in clear and opaque plastic to take A4 documents, and can produce other sizes to your specifications.

Cards: 5in × 3in for subject indexes or brief information, 6in × 4in, and 8in × 5in for recording more detailed information about organisations and services. Cards can be overprinted with a grid for entering information in a standard form. Use scrap cards for cheapness or 'greenness'. Cards are available from most office stationers.

Forms, headed paper, standard letters for collecting information, issuing press releases, correspondence, etc.

Notepads, printed with your logo, opening hours and services, on which to write information for enquirers. These can act as a form of publicity for the service. *Statistics sheets* for gathering information about the use made of the service.

Many organisations, from national campaigning bodies to local tenants' groups, from time to time identify a need to set up an information service to meet the requirements of the following:

— their own staff or membership;
— the general public, as a whole or belonging to a defined geographical area;
— sections of the public with particular needs, such as disabled or elderly people;
— workers and public associated with a particular purpose, e.g. a redevelopment scheme or anti-dampness campaign.

It may sound obvious to state that, before setting up an information service, you should ask yourself, first of all, some very basic questions—like those a journalist asks when writing a story: who?, what?, when?, where?, why?, and how?—but not necessarily in that order. Surprisingly, there are many instances where these questions have not been asked and services have been set up which were either not wanted, the wrong type of service to meet clients' needs, a duplication of already existing services, too ambitious for available staffing or resources, or lacking in commitment from the organisation's management or staff. The moral is that careful thought and preparation at the outset can save a lot of wasted effort and be the sound foundation on which to build a successful service. It is always better to start modestly and grow, than to be too ambitious and have to retract or fail completely. This book tries to follow the same principle in the way its information is presented, moving from simple, cheap solutions to the more sophisticated. But first of all, let us consider those basic questions.

Everybody has information needs but not everybody is equally capable of satisfying those needs. This is increasingly so in what has been termed our 'information society', with its complexity and rapidly accelerating rate of political, social and economic change. Information is now also seen as a commodity, with a market value that may well put it beyond the reach of the 'have-nots'. More and more, it is being made available in electronic forms which may require the possession of special skills on the part of those wishing to access it. Therefore, a good reason for setting up an information service may well be to make it easier for individuals or groups of people who do not have their own adequate information networks to gain access to information that can be of benefit to them.

Some places or groups that warrant particular attention are the following:

— *inner-city areas* where multiple deprivation exists - bad housing, high unemployment, inadequate schools—or where there is a greater proportion of ethnic minorities and transient populations;

— *housing estates* which lack basic social and other amenities—meeting places, recreational space, shops—where transport is inadequate or expensive, housing is bad, repairs deficient and vandalism rife;

— *rural areas* where facilities—shops, post offices, doctors, clergy, local government services, transport—are fast disappearing;

— *groups with special needs—low-income* families, elderly and disabled people, ethnic minorities, young people, patients, community and social workers.

It is not a good idea to set up an information service because other agencies are doing so and you do not want to be left out. There has to be substantial evidence of need for such a service in the local community or amongst your clientele to justify provision. This leads in turn to the next question.

Who needs an information service?

Rarely will the need for an information service be readily apparent or clearly voiced by your clientele. More often than not, that need will have to be identified and assessed. There are several ways of finding out who needs an information service, ranging from the simple to the sophisticated. Here are a few methods you may care to consider:

Talk to the 'gate-keepers' in your community—these are the people to whom, because of the nature of their work, their knowledge, approachability or status, others go for information and advice. A typical list of 'gate-keepers' might include community workers, trade union stewards, youth leaders, headteachers, Women's Institute secretaries, or GPs. A word of caution: you should not rely on the views of these people alone, as they may well be biased or blinkered. It is important to check out the views of community leaders or 'gate-keepers' against those of your potential clientele and by using some of the other methods below.

Contact groups and attend meetings. Find out if there are any groups which represent the people you wish to serve, as they will most likely be aware of the needs of their members or of the community. Particularly useful arc 'umbrella' groups like Councils for Voluntary Service (CVSs), Rural Community Councils (RCCs), councils for the disabled, trades councils, and community associations. Look out also for less formal groups such as luncheon clubs for community workers, youth leaders or advice workers. Attending meetings of groups like these will give you a feel for the kind of problems that arise and for which provision is lacking. Such meetings might also be a useful forum to discuss the need for any proposed information service.

If your 'community' is a closed one, such as the staff of a particular organisation, then it is important for you as information officer or librarian to be thoroughly conversant with the issues of concern to that organisation. One way of achieving this more quickly is to have the right to sit in on committee meetings. This will help in identifying what the organisation's information needs are likely to be and how to meet them. However, you may need to convince committee members of the desirability of this. One of the best ways is to prove your worth by providing them with some information, possibly on subjects under discussion in the committee.

Arrange an informal meeting of representatives of groups in your community and other interested or useful people, at which you can discuss your ideas for an information service and then take things further if there is a positive response. Out of this meeting might well be set up a steering committee or working group which could canvass wider opinion, either informally by calling an open meeting, or by conducting a survey of the community. Such a group might also prepare a feasibility study.

Call an open meeting at which your 'community' can hear about the proposals and make comments. If the meeting is not being called by the kind of steering committee suggested above, in some circumstances it may be helpful for it to be held under the auspices of a neutral body; for example, where your organisation, rightly or wrongly, is perceived by the community as representing one particular viewpoint. Wide publicity for the meeting is essential, using whatever means are available—word of mouth, posters, leaflets, local press, periodicals, newsletters, etc. Try to get the publicity into those areas where large numbers of your 'community' arc likely to see it.

Any publicity should give details of what the meeting is about, when and where it is being held and at what time it starts. Choose a date and venue that is convenient to most of the people you want to reach, taking care to avoid other events or activities that are likely to prove a counter-attraction. This may even apply to what is on television at the time! It is wise to give some thought to the ambience of the venue for, in some cases, an imposing room or 'official' building may inhibit attendance or discussion. If at all possible, avoid holding the meeting in a room that is not accessible to disabled people. Refreshments, if only a cup of coffee, help to stimulate a feeling of informality and encourage discussion. Put yourself in the place of someone who might attend the meeting and ask what would attract you. Make careful preparations before the meeting takes place, including a plan of how you would like the meeting to be structured, so that discussion does not waffle on aimlessly and yet is flexible enough to encourage responses from the audience.

Graphic displays, audiovisual presentations and speakers from similar projects elsewhere can add another dimension and help to get your proposals across.

Some further tips about the meeting:

— you will need someone, preferably a respected figure in your community, to open the meeting, explain what it is all about, and chair the proceedings;

— keep items as brief as possible—people soon get bored with lengthy speeches; encourage questions and contributions from the floor even to the extent of planting a few 'stooges' to break the ice;

— end the meeting before people get restive or discussion degenerates into irrelevancies;

— make it clear what the next step is going to be. If there is support for your ideas, then you may want to form a committee from those present. Alternatively, this step may still be premature, in which case arrange a further meeting of interested parties. Take note of the names and addresses of those expressing an interest so that you can keep them informed of future meetings and developments.

So, by the end of the meeting, you should have some measure of the support for and/or interest in your proposed information service from the community. It is important that the community or users of the proposed service are given an opportunity to participate in both its planning and running, so that it matches their needs and is responsive to changing circumstances. If there is no support, it would be unwise to go ahead, at least in the form that was proposed.

Conduct a survey of potential users to establish their information needs. This can be done instead of or in addition to holding an open meeting. It is essential from the start that you have a clear idea of what you want to learn from the survey and at whom it is aimed, for this will determine the kind of questions you will want to ask and the form in which you present them. It is a good principle always to try to make the wording simple and unambiguous, with alternatives spelled out where appropriate, as in the example from South Molton shown here which was used to establish the need for a multi-agency information and advice service in a small market, own in Devon. When Terence Brake set up a community information service at South Hackney School in London, he rightly surmised that many of the pupils would not understand or use the term 'information' and some might even react with hostility to an emotive word like 'need'. Consequently, he devised a range of simple questionnaires related to the youngsters' interests, such as the one on use of leisure time illustrated here which elicit the information in a way which is less formal and with which the young people can identify.

The drafting of surveys and questionnaires requires a degree of skill not possible to examine here, but if you would like to know more, the following books should help. The method of distributing your survey questionnaire needs careful attention. Ideally, it helps if you can be present when the respondent fills in the form, so that any points or questions not understood can be clarified. Often valuable information is imparted verbally through hints and nuances of conversation that would not be transmitted on paper. However, the ideal is seldom attainable and you may have to be content with mailing out your questionnaires. This obviously saves time but you should not expect a very high response rate. It helps, of course, Where you can afford it, to include a reply-paid envelope for return of the form.

Surveys can be a help in pointing you in the right direction or by adding weight to already formative ideas; however, they should not be used on their own, but only in relation to evidence obtained by other methods. It is well to bear in mind that in the act of setting a framework of questions for your survey, you are already, to some extent, determining the response.

Analyse enquiry statistics to see if there is a demand from any particular group of user which requires special attention, such as a separate information or advice service. For example, recent years have witnessed the introduction of debt counselling services by Citizens' Advice Bureaux as a response to a Vast increase in enquiries in this area. Your organisation may already be operating a more traditional reference or information service. An analysis of its enquiries over a period of time, if these are kept in sufficient detail, may indicate areas of need not being adequately met. An alternative, if your statistics are not detailed enough, is to carry out a short-term monitoring exercise.

As well as your own statistics, you might get some help from those of other information and advice agencies operating in your area of interest. By using some or all of the above methods you should have arrived at an idea of the information needs of your community. However, before making a decision on the kind of service required to meet those needs, it is essential to have as complete a picture of your community as possible. The best way to achieve this is to compile a community profile.

Community profiling

This is a systematic process developed initially by corporate planners and adopted by other agencies, including public librarians, to enable them to plan and provide services which meet the needs of a given community. A typical profile will include:

— *Statistical data* about the population: size, rate of growth, age ranges, sex, marital status, religion, ethnic groups, diseases and mortality, employment, education, housing, etc. Much of this information is obtainable from census documents, supplemented and updated by figures from local authority departments, health authorities, employment centres, police, etc.

— *Socio-economic information:* types of economic activity, community services—statutory, voluntary or private, recreational facilities, meeting places, clubs and societies, etc.

— *Local issues:* redevelopment, unemployment, poor housing, transport problems, racial prejudice, etc.

— *Residents' viewpoints:* letters to the press, community newspapers, local radio and TV, action groups, community noticeboards, graffiti, informal discussions with those who come into contact with a wide cross-section of the community, informal contacts in pubs, shops, public meetings, etc.

The important thing to remember when compiling a community profile is not to rely on one type of information alone as this will give you a biased view. Try to get a fully rounded picture by including both statistical data and subjective assessment, official opinion and residents' reactions, majority and minority viewpoints. Obviously You must tailor your approach to the kind of community you are analysing. Community profiles were initially designed for analysing geographical communities but the same principles will apply, although the techniques and sources of information may vary, if your community is a 'closed' one, such as a school or organisation, or a group with special needs, like elderly or disabled people.

There are also some spin-offs from compiling a community profile. If you do decide to go ahead and set up an information service, the information gathered for the profile could form the basis of your local information file and might also be made available to your clientele in printed form. The valuable contacts made with individuals and groups will form the basis for your information network.

The following conclusions, taken from the above issue of *Library trends,* sum up concisely the right way to approach the question of who needs an information service:

1 Formal and informal methods ... are essential both for developing a clear and useful picture of 'who is out there' and for an understanding of what they need/want.

2 There is no substitute for direct, active information-seeking ... in order to avoid acting on unsubstantiated assumptions about groups of people.

3 Just as different communities will want or need different services, different approaches will have to be used ... There is no single approach which will always work, but respect and flexibility are always essential.

Remember also that some information needs may not become apparent until your community information service is up and running and it ought, therefore, to be flexible enough to adapt to them. Determining needs is not a once-and-for-all exercise but a continuous process.

What community information services already exist?

There is one more step that needs to be taken before you can get down to putting flesh on your ideas and that is to find out if there are any other agencies in your area operating identical or similar services to the one that you are planning. You may, in fact, want to take this step at an earlier stage or you might have found out the information in the course of conducting a community profile. Either way, it is an important stage that should not be omitted, since it is in nobody's interest to duplicate existing services, especially if there are gaps in provision elsewhere.

Information about existing services in a particular neighbourhood can be collected by means of a questionnaire. This will give you only the bare outlines and will need to be expanded by personal visits.

The kind of information you will need to collect about each agency consists of the following:

— location, premises and equipment, opening hours, how to contact the agency;
— staffing, information resources, training;
— the agency's activities;
— referrals, relationship with other agencies;
— the agency's users;
— feedback to policy-makers;
— publicity;
— management and funding.

This list was taken from *Who knows?: guidelines for a review of local advice and information services, and how to publicise them* (National Consumer Council, 1982) which is an excellent guide to conducting such reviews and provides more details under each of the headings. advice services and preparing local development plans.

If it is local agencies that you want to identify and you are not a public library, then try your local library for a start. Other sources might include the Citizens'

Advice Bureau, Council for Voluntary Service, Rural Community Council, Social Services Department, civic information bureau and individuals, e.g. community workers, social workers.

Having gone through the above process, you should now have a clearer picture of which community information services already exist in your community or area of interest and where there are any gaps in provision. You should also have some idea of the strengths and weaknesses of existing services and thus be in a position to make a decision about your own proposed service. At this point there are several choices open to you:

Maintain and strengthen the existing provision. It may be that your community is adequately covered by information services, in which case your efforts might best be channelled towards helping to strengthen and maintain those services. The costs of providing an information service rise continually and finding for many organisations is frequently precarious. Material support or behind-the -scenes lobbying to help existing services will usually be more than welcome.

Extend an existing service. The solution to meeting the information needs of your community does not necessarily have to be your direct responsibility. It may not be appropriate, anyway, if your staff do not have the training, flexibility, time or independence to provide the kind of service that is required. There may well be an existing information and advice service which is prevented from providing an adequate service or extending its work through badly located premises or lack of funds for staffing, training, information resources, etc. Your organisation could make an appreciable difference by:

— offering free use of suitable accommodation to relocate the service in a place more accessible for the public;

— offering similar accommodation for the location of extension services;

— offering the use of mobile service points, where feasible, so that remote areas of the community can be reached;

— providing help with staffing or resources, e.g. you may have staff who can offer a particular expertise on a surgery basis or you might be prepared to supply loan collections of more expensive reference materials;

— providing access points for the public in unserved areas on behalf of the information service, e.g. by having available postal enquiry forms or providing a direct-line telephone link to the service's central office.

Cooperate. Although your analysis may show that there are gaps or shortcomings in existing provision, that should not be a signal to leap in immediately and set up a new service. At a time of financial stringency, it makes sense to explore first of all the possibilities for cooperation and thus to get a more rational and coordinated use of resources. This could take the form of one or more of the following suggestions:

Sharing information. Public libraries, for example, could explore ways of putting their extensive information resources, both materials and staff, at the service of other information and advice agencies by agreeing to keep and update files of local information or by producing a directory of local information and advice services.

Joint collection, processing and dissemination of information. Often several agencies in a community will be collecting local information. This is wasted effort, as the information needs to be collected only once, and causes annoyance to those supplying the information. A joint approach is called for, either one organisation collecting the information on behalf of the others, or a consortium of organisations sharing the task.

Shared premises. There are distinct advantages in several agencies sharing premises, in addition to that of economy. It provides better access for the public who can see a number of agencies in one place without a time-consuming and often expensive run-around. Referral is made easier, which is particularly useful in multi-problem cases. There is the possibility of not only shared accommodation but also shared information resources, shared publicity, shared case-notes, etc. Sharing can make the service available for longer hours than one agency on its own could possibly attain.

Support groups. Cooperation of the kind listed in this section can be fostered by the formation of an 'umbrella' group which brings together all the community information agencies in a particular community or area of interest. Such a group could take on activities such as information sharing, joint collection of information, cooperative approach to funding, shared publicity, training and generally creating a greater awareness and understanding of each other's work. Sometimes a number of agencies in an area, who are heavily involved in handling problems of a particular kind and do not have the resources or time to cope adequately with them, can benefit from the creation of a specialist support group to provide training, research, practical assistance (e.g. tribunal work), information materials, current awareness services, or expertise in certain areas, such as law, debt counselling, housing, planning, tax, etc. Many public libraries have been involved in setting up and-running 'umbrella' groups.

Face-to-face contact with clientele

This is the passive function, whereby a community

information service is located in a particular building or room and the clientele call in person to seek information for themselves or from the staff by enquiry at an information desk. It has the advantages that the most up-to-date information is available, provided the service has carried out its information-gathering efficiently; the client can be questioned to reveal exactly what information is required; and a member of staff familiar with using the files or databases is on hand to search out information, to make contact with services, or to suggest further possible courses of action.

There is some evidence to suggest that many people prefer information to be transmitted verbally, especially if they have low literacy skills. Some disadvantages to having one defined location are that, unless it is prominently sited (in the High Street or shopping centre), it may be difficult to bring the service to the attention of potential users without a continual publicity campaign; moreover, it can be expensive to operate in terms of the resources needed to staff the enquiry desk continually and to stay open outside normal office hours.

Dealing with people face-to-face requires a certain amount of skill but, above all, is needed a pleasant and approachable personality, a characteristic that is not so easily learnt. The following guidelines may be helpful in dealing with clients:

— First of all, try to make the enquirer feel at ease, so that s/he is not afraid to ask questions or discuss a problem. It may seem a trivial enquiry to you but could be causing the client much anxiety.

— Do not exhibit feelings of shock, horror, amusement, disbelief or repugnance at anything the enquirer says. It is not part of your job to pass judgment on a client whose behaviour or ideas are contrary to the norms of society.

— Listen to the whole query and don't start jumping to conclusions before the enquirer has finished. Listen 'actively' by asking appropriate questions to clarify what is specifically being asked, since most people tend to phrase their questions in general terms. What the client seems to want may not necessarily be what s/he needs.

— When you think you know what is being requested, state it in simple terms so that the enquirer can confirm that you are on the right track. I once spent ages looking through modem dance manuals to answer a request for information on 'how to jive' only to find, after proudly presenting a suitable book, that the enquirer had a speech impediment and really wanted to know 'how to djive a car'!

— Try to identify with the enquirer's problem, at the same time remaining impartial and emotionally uninvolved. Such a counsel of perfection is probably unattainable but is only a warning that sometimes people ask the impossible or want confirmation or support for a course of action when they are in the wrong. Even where a service sets out to be impartial, it cannot support clients irrespective of whether they are right or wrong. It may be necessary at times to give information or advice that is contrary to what the client expects to hear.

— Before any information is given it should, wherever possible, be double-checked to ensure that it is correct and, if reasonably brief, written down to give to the client.

— Where there are alternative courses of action, explain these to the client in simple terms and leave her/him to make the choice unless you are specifically offering an advice service.

— Never leave the client with a negative response even when you cannot answer the query. Suggest where else the client may go to find an answer, even making a telephone call, if necessary, to fix an appointment or make an introduction. If the enquiry needs further investigation and is not urgent, take down the details and offer to phone or write with the answer as soon as possible. Suggest that the enquirer calls back after a certain interval if they have not had a reply.

By telephone

The facility to transmit information by telephone can be an advantage, especially where clientele have difficulty in reaching your service because of its location, hours of opening or their own physical disabilities. Some people actually prefer the greater anonymity of the telephone. The physical location of a community information service whose work is mainly or entirely conducted on the telephone is less important. Staff can be occupied with other work in between calls and do not have to be tied to an enquiry desk; thus it may be possible to offer longer hours. With the additional use of an answerphone, a service could offer a 24-hour, sevendays-a-week service. A conference-phone facility enables three-way link-ups to be made and clients can be put in direct contact with a service that can help them. If in order to answer enquiries you need to move away from the telephone or for periods of time it has to be left unstaffed, then you may need to consider the convenience of a cordless phone. However, telephones are still by no means universally available in Britain and public call-boxes are frequently inconvenient because of location, continual use or lack of privacy.

Some people are deterred from using telephones because they experience difficulties in expressing themselves via this medium or the cost of making calls is a financial burden. Some services have overcome the latter difficulty by offering a Freephone or 0800 number, or by a policy of ringing back the caller as soon as contact is made. Telephones are best suited for answering enquiries that are brief, clearly stated and uncomplicated. Time does not allow for lengthy interviewing of the client over the phone, nor is it possible to pick up those non-verbal signals which often help in assessing the true need of the client. Likewise, the client cannot see you—so make your voice welcoming. Here are some tips on answering the telephone, based on an English Tourist Board booklet supplied to Tourist Information Centres, called How can *I help you?*:

— Make sure you always have a supply of pens and paper near the telephone and that the most used sources of information are readily to hand.

— Answer the telephone promptly. You may think that letting it ring and ring is a smart way of getting over the message that you are busy, but it only annoys the caller, who imagines that you are either drinking tea or having an interesting discussion about last night's television programme or football match.

— Never use 'Hello!'—it is too casual and, at this stage, the caller may be uncertain whether they have got through to the right service or not. State clearly the name of your service, your name, and offer to help, e.g. 'Exville Information Service. This is Joan Smith. Can I help you? If you don't want to give your name straight away, it can be left to the closing remarks, such as 'If you need to ring back, my name is Joan Smith. Thank you for calling.' If the caller gives their name, always use it.

— Do not smoke, eat, or drink when speaking on the phone, and definitely not all at the same time, as it impedes your speech.

— Jot down the details of the query as it is given and confirm with the caller the essence of their enquiry before answering.

— If you have to ask the caller to wait or need to leave the telephone to look up information, explain what is happening, how long you might be and, when returning, thank the caller for waiting.

— If it is obvious from the start or after an initial search that the query may take some time to answer, offer to ring the caller back—*not* forgetting to take down their telephone number and name (if you haven't got it already). If the enquirer is ringing from a public call-box, either ask them to phone back later (try to specify a time or length of time) or take down name and address and post the reply.

— When answering an enquiry by telephone, ask the caller to read back any crucial information such as amounts of money, telephone numbers, etc. as a check that they have been taken down correctly

— At the end of the enquiry, thank the person for calling. Be positive even if the reply is negative. It's better to say 'Sorry, we haven't been able to help you on this occasion but thank you for calling and please get in touch again if you have any other queries' than 'Sorry, can't help you'—click.

A very useful adjunct to the telephone is a fax machine which will enable you to transmit and receive documents to and from other information services.

By post

Requests for information by post do not as a rule figure

prominently in the work of a community information service, but they are just as important. There is a temptation to assume that postal enquiries are less urgent than the client who is breathing down your neck or hanging on the end of a telephone and so can be dealt with whenever there is a spare moment—in other words, never! However, every enquiry is important to the person making it and should be dealt with expeditiously. A fairly common type of postal enquiry from individuals, organisations and commercial concerns is for lists of clubs and societies on a particular topic or in a particular area. It is obviously an advantage if you have a filing system or a computer database which enables you to print out a section on request.

An alternative for frequently requested information is to have it pre-printed as a list, broadsheet or leaflet. Where a postal request is likely to take a little time in being answered, send off a pre-printed acknowledgement slip on receipt of the enquiry, saying something like: 'Thank you for your enquiry, which is receiving our attention. We will send you a reply as soon as possible.'

By display

People have an innate tendency to browse, picking up information in a casual fashion. An information service can take advantage of this by providing well-sited, attractive and interesting displays for putting over information to clients and passers-by. There are four main aspects of display: noticeboards; thematic displays; window displays; and outside display.

Noticeboards. A great deal of information is available in poster or broadsheet format. Some of it is free, some will come unsolicited and there are a few posters for which you have to pay. There are basically four types of poster:

— the event poster gives details of something that is to take place at a particular time;

— the *service* poster gives details of a service that is available—its opening hours, location, who is eligible, how to contact, etc.—and is not, as a rule, restricted to a finite date;

— the *information* poster presents hard information in an encapsulated form—benefit rates, changes in legislation, health education, eligibility for grants, etc.;

— the *persuasive* poster seeks to sell a product, change opinions, or enlist sympathies.

The displaying of posters is an activity that can frequently arouse great passion, particularly those posters concerned with moral, political or religious issues on which strong opposing views are held. This applies not only to campaigning posters but also to ones presenting straightforward information, such as an event or hours of opening of a service, e.g. family planning clinic. You need also to be sensitive to the location of a poster. A poster showing how to fit a condom may be appropriate for display in a youth information centre but not on a board just outside the children's library. Ideally, a community information service or its parent organisation should draw up guidelines on what is or is not allowed to be displayed. Try to avoid the overly simplistic approach of displaying either everything or nothing at all. An open door' policy may, in theory, sound fine but in practice it can throw up just as many problems, such as your right to refuse to display a poster which may not be in the public interest but does not necessarily contravene the law. It has been usual to rule out commercial advertising posters, although some services now accept these but make a charge in order to raise money for the service.

There is more to displaying posters or other notices than simply sticking in a few pins. The following are a few points you might find useful:

— You can never (or rarely) have enough noticeboard space, so in planning your service— think BIG!

– If you have several boards, categorize them: coming events, sources of help, places to visit, official notices, etc.

— Don't overcrowd your noticeboards—posters should never be overlapping and obscuring each other. If you have only a limited space, change the posters regularly to give each one a chance.

— Arrange posters to look attractive—contrast posters of different shapes or colours to add interest. Move long-term posters around from time to time to give the impression of change.

— Check noticeboards regularly to ensure that out-of-date posters are not left on display and long-term posters have not become faded or tatty.

Thematic displays. Displays devoted to a particular topic or theme, if well produced, can be a useful way of drawing attention to information that is available. The theme may (a) concern a problem area identified from an analysis of enquiries; (b) relate to a current change in legislation or benefit rates; (c) be aimed at improving public awareness of an issue of current concern; (d) draw attention to benefits, grants, services or rights of which your clientele may not be aware; (e) canvass support for a cause; or (0 educate your clientele on personal matters, e.g. health, finance, etc.

Use noticeboards or—better still—free-standing boards to mount displays. There is some skill required in preparing materials and mounting an effective and attractive -display. Identify someone in your organisation who has a flair for this kind of work and is willing to help.

There are a number of organisations and government departments which have displays that can be borrowed free of charge or with carriage paid one way.

Window display. If your information centre is blessed with large windows looking onto a thoroughfare, then they can be used to good effect in giving out information not only to users of your service but also to casual passers-by. Displays such as those described in the section above, placed in the window, enable the information to reach beyond your own clientele and may even attract use of the service. An external window can also be used for displaying essential information when your service is closed, such as addresses and telephone numbers of emergency services, hotel or bed-and-breakfast accommodation.

A number of commercial organisations have produced microcomputer-driven information points which usually stand in a window and feature local information and advertising. The computer either scrolls pages automatically or is controlled by means of touch terminals mounted on the outside of the window. Windows or glass entrance doors may be also be used to display small ads and job vacancies.

Small ads may seem trivial but they do fill an important information need in most communities and also have an added bonus of attracting people to look in your window and, perhaps, thereby become more aware of the service and of what it can offer. Small ads can also be a useful source of income for your service but, in setting up such a service, be sensitive to other small ads services in the immediate vicinity. A job vacancies board is a much appreciated service, particularly at times of high unemployment and where your service is located some distance from the nearest Jobcentre. Either contact local firms, businesses, shops, etc. and ask if they would be prepared to display their job vacancies in your window—you might even make a charge and earn a bit of income for the service - or contact your local Jobcentre who may be prepared to let you have job vacancy cards on a regular basis. If you can afford to do so, offer to contact the firm or Jobcentre on behalf of any client who is interested in a particular job advertised, to see if it is still vacant.

Outside display. As well as displaying information in your own centre, consider the possibilities of display in other buildings. It may be possible to circulate such displays around a number of centres and thus reach a much wider audience. Some commercial businesses, like banks and building societies, who rarely have anything interesting to show in their windows, encourage organisations to use these for displays.

With displays located on other people's premises, you will have to accept their right to reject all or part of your display if it is objectionable to them or not produced to a high enough standard. Find out first if the organisation or business has a policy on what can or cannot be displayed and whether they have their own display equipment which you can use. For outside displays, other than simply posters pinned to a wall, you will need spare display boards that can be released for a length of time and the means of transporting them.

The display should be checked regularly to maintain stocks of any give-away leaflets, etc., to ensure the currency of the information, and to keep it in good repair. Another possible outlet for information is community noticeboards, which are usually located in prominent positions such as market squares, shopping malls, etc. They are most likely to be owned by the local council but it is not unknown for councils to assign the running of them to a local information centre. The sort of information best suited for this type of board is directional (map of village, town or neighbourhood and street index), showing places of interest and sources of help or coming events.

Selective dissemination of information (SDI)

This is a rather forbidding term to describe a process for transmitting information which many information services adopt quite naturally without ever having heard of the phrase. It simply means taking note of the subject interests of particular individuals or groups who use your service and supplying them with new information on their areas of interest as it becomes available. 'Taking note' can be a fairly organized and formal system involving the sending out of a questionnaire initially to discover users' interests and maintaining a card or computer file (usually arranged by subject) of those interests.

However, more often than not, it is an informal system stored in the information worker's head (I know Joe Bloggs is interested in this, I'll send him a copy'). Good information workers can even anticipate the interests of their clientele. SDI is most often used by services whose clientele are a closed group—a voluntary organisation, for example—rather than ones who serve the general public. Where generalist services operate SDI, it will usually be for other information and advice workers, community workers, professionals or groups.

An SDI service can include regular scanning of new publications, journals, newspapers, press releases, annual reports, product literature and other ephemeral material or it may be rather unsystematic and random. Either way, it is a useful service, particularly for those individuals, organisations and groups who need a supply of new information in their area of interest but do not have the time, resources or expertise to search it out. It is an excellent way to win friends for your information service who in turn may be able to help you on other occasions.

Deposit files and collections

One solution to the problem of having one fixed location from which to give out information is to duplicate your information file or database and make it available to other centres. This would make it more accessible to a wider clientele but has the disadvantages that (i) you need to have a mechanism for keeping these files or databases up to date, especially if you have to rely on someone else to do the updating, and (ii) staff, where they exist, need to be trained in using the file or database so that they can help clients. Files using loose-leaf binders or strip indexes are easier to duplicate than card files.

Computer databases can easily be copied onto floppy disk(s) but depend on the recipient having compatible equipment. Those information services whose databases are stored on a mainframe computer may be able to offer other centres online access. Some community information services have made available collections of books and other material for deposit in centres which have particular needs, such as youth clubs. This is quite a costly service to provide in terms of both resources and staff time in preparing the collections and keeping them up to date. With this type of service, it is desirable to have a monitoring mechanism so that the value of the collections can be appraised.

A good example of an information service that is duplicated and made widely available is that operated by

NACAB. The material consists of specially prepared loose-leaf information sheets; leaflets and booklets.; reference books; a comprehensive index; and other supplementary material, such as sources of leaflets and information about useful reference books.

The system is updated by means of monthly packs containing amendments to the information sheets and leaflets; new information sheets and leaflets; a booklist of new publications; *Update—a* magazine which provides a comprehensive summary of changes in the law, etc.; and new editions of reference books. As the system is so comprehensive, it provides the factual resource for a wide range of advice and counselling services. However, it does require a substantial amount of staff time to update the files each month and occupies several feet of shelving or a whole four-drawer filing cabinet.

For many organisations the costs may also be prohibitive: £644 (voluntary organisations), £900 statutory and commercial bodies) to set up the system, while the annual updating subscription from April 1993 is 040 (voluntary) and £566 (statutory and commercial). For those organisations who do not have this kind of money or do not need such detailed information, NACAB also produces a Basic Pack, contained in two loose-leaf binders, costing £29.50 (voluntary), £ 78.50 (statutory and commercial) to set up, with the annual updating subscription costing £37.00 (voluntary) and £61.50 (statutory and commercial). Further details can be obtained from NACAB, 115-123 Pentonville Road, London NI 9LZ. If your problem is lack of space or staff time to update the hard-copy version or you need an information system that is portable, NACAB also caters for these needs with a microfiche version of the hard-copy pack. Microfiche are 6in × 4in transparent cards which contain up to 60 pages of information.

Publications

These are one of the best means of making your information more accessible to a wider range of people than you could ever hope to reach through a static service point. Well-produced and attractive publications enhance the image of an information service and help to attract custom. The commitment of information to print inevitably attracts corrections, additions, etc. which enable your service to maintain an even more accurate and up-to-date database. Producing publications of reasonable quality can be costly in terms of both time and money, depending on the system used for storing your information base and access to in-house printing facilities.

If your database is stored on computer then there are a number of options, as follows:

If you have a word-processing or desktop publishing package on the same computer or access to these within your organisation, it may be possible to transfer the whole or sections of the database file into these packages and manipulate them to produce the required format and layout for publication; at which point there are again several choices:

— print out the publication on demand or in small quantities (assuming your computer has a printer)—not practical for lengthy documents;

— print off one copy on your computer printer and photocopy best for short documents with a limited run where quality is not critical;

— produce printed master copy for printing in-house or by a commercial printer using offset litho—master copy needs to be produced on good quality laser or bubblejet printer; (Tip: You can improve the appearance of text produced on a dot matrix printer by reducing it slightly on a photocopier or, better still, asking the printer to do it photographically—don't forget to allow for this by making your document format slightly larger.)

— copy the document to a floppy disk and take it to a printer who has equipment and software compatible with yours.

If you don't have access to word processing or desktop publishing, you may still be able to copy your database or sections of it to a floppy disk which can be read by a commercial printer with compatible equipment. The production costs will be higher as the printer will need to format, design or lay out the publication according to your specifications. When you are planning the computerisation of your information system, it is worth ensuring that all your software packages are compatible not only on your computer but also with systems that are to be found in most printing firms nowadays. It may be worth investing A little more to get an integrated package that offers a suite of facilities—database, word processing, spreadsheet, graphics and communications service—that allows you to swap documents or bits of documents from one facility to another with ease. If you have a manual database then a lot more work is necessary to transcribe the data into a form suitable for printing.

Once you are at that stage, and if you do not have in-house printing facilities, it will pay you to shop around for printers. Get at least three estimates - you may be surprised at the variations in both price and the size of the publication (if this has not already been determined). Ask to see examples of the printer's work so that you can get an idea of quality. If you have a limited budget, look out for community printers or resource centres which offer services at virtually cost price of materials, though you may have to do much of the work yourself (with guidance).

Alternatively, explore the possibilities of: (a) joint publication with other organisations; (b) obtaining a grant from an appropriate body who may have an interest in your publication; (c) sponsorship; and (d) advertising, or a combination of these. Once information is printed, it is static and, therefore, liable to date in a short space of time. When producing a publication always consider your ability to sustain not only one issue but also any future new editions which may be necessary, to distribute copies, either as a one-off or regularly, or to handle sales. All these can be very time-consuming. It is an acceptable strategy, of course, to publish one issue in the hopes that its value will be recognized and future issues will attract funding.

The frequency with which you need to update the publication should determine the format you choose—whether it should be loose-leaf or not, a leaflet or a booklet. Publications may be aimed at basically two kinds of user: those whose work or status consists wholly or in part in informing others and those whom we might term your general clientele. They may be the public, a section of the public, or members of a particular organisation or group. The major differences between the two in respect of publications will lie in the degree of detail and the way the information is presented.

How do you know what to publish?

— The kind of enquiries your community information receives will be one indicator. Frequent requests for the same type of information, e.g. addresses of playgroups, could be answered more quickly if a printed list or leaflet is available to give away.

— Identification of a gap in the coverage of a topic as a result of analysing enquiries or seeking information.

— Recent development or change which has not yet spawned any interpretative literature.

— Local issues.

— Discussions with other information and advice workers.

— Identification of specific groups who have defined information needs, e.g. elderly or disabled people, parents with children under five, school leavers, or the unemployed, which might be met with a suitable publication.

Types of publication

These are the simplest forms of publication to compile, often arising out of repeated requests for the same kind of information. A list can be just a single side of paper or several sheets stapled together. The arrangement is usually straight alphabetical or alphabetical under subject or place headings, depending on the topic. Lists are given out in response to an enquiry, so do not require a great deal of creative design in their production.

The use of an attractive pre-printed headed paper with the logo of your service, if you have one, its address, telephone and fax numbers, can make a humble list a little more attractive and helps to publicize the service. Small numbers of lists can be run off on a photocopier or, where you have a computerized database, printed out on demand; for longer runs use a stencil duplicator or an offset litho printer. If you do not have print facilities yourself, most towns of any size nowadays usually have at least one instant-print shop where good-quality copies can be obtained at a fairly reasonable price and quickly.

Leaflets

A leaflet in one respect is a kind of extrovert list; it goes out of its way to attract attention—and thus encourage people to pick it up -through design and format. This is the *information* type of leaflet, the contents, of, which may be much the same as a list. The two other main, types are the *educational* leaflet, the objective of which is to increase understanding or awareness of a particular subject, and the *campaigning* leaflet, which sets out either to convert someone from one point of view to another, to gain sympathy and support for a cause, or to change a certain state of affairs for the better.

Thousands of leaflets are produced each year by all kinds of organisations. The quality of these leaflets varies from the extremely glossy and eye-catching to the cheap and nasty. If you are going to enter this arena, then it is important to give as much attention as possible to the design of your leaflets as to their contents, since they will have to compete for attention with commercially designed products. However, you do not have to be an artist or designer to be able to produce an attractive leaflet. Look -around at examples of commercially produced leaflets for inspiration.

Advertising can also be a source of abundant 'free' or non-attributable art to illustrate and add impact to your own leaflets. Other sources of material might include old engravings (particularly of the Victorian era), drawings of the great masters (Leonardo da Vinci, Durer, Michelangelo, etc.) and instant art books. If you have access to a computer, the possibility is opened up to you of investing in a graphics package which enables you to draw and design your own artwork or to buy in copyright-free art files that can be manipulated for your own purposes. Lettering in a wide variety of styles which can be rubbed onto artwork is available in large and small sheets from most stationers, or your organisation may well have invested in a lettering machine. Use cartoons, diagrams, graphs and photographs to liven up the text. Keep wording simple and short. Standard sizes of leaflets are A5 (149mm × 210mm) and 1/3A4, but experiment with unusual sizes based on standard sheets for added impact. Have enough copies printed to give a wide circulation and distribute them through as many outlets as possible, particularly those which attract large numbers of people. If the leaflet is aimed at a particular group in the community, identify specific ways of reaching them. Investigate other means of distribution that might give you an even wider coverage, such as insertion in a free community newspaper, with the council rates demand, or through organisations which regularly send out to a large mailing list.

Posters

The aim of a poster is to present a small amount of information with the maximum amount of impact so that 'he who runs may read'. Use posters to advertise events or your service, to draw attention to a few sources of information and advice, or to point out eligibility for a service or benefit. Much of the advice given above about the design of leaflets applies equally to designing posters. The design of a poster should emphasize and complement the information that you want to convey. Remember that some of the most successful posters contain no words at all. Let the image do the talking. Don't make the poster too—big as this may create problems for those whom you might wish to display it, since most organisations do not have unlimited display space. A3 (297mm × 420mm) is the most popular and useful size; A4 (210mm × 297mm) is a little small to make a great deal of impact but may be more acceptable if you want organisations to display the poster for a long time. Ideally, you should produce posters in a variety of sizes to suit varying locations. A one-off poster can be prepared -by hand if you have someone artistically inclined, but for any quantity you will need to have access to printing facilities or a good photocopier capable of enlarging and reducing. Use coloured copier paper for effect if you are printing only in black.

Colour photocopiers are becoming more widely available but copies are considerably more expensive and may only work out cheaper than printing for very short runs. Another method of reproduction for posters is silk screen, which is a kind of stencil process. Some community arts centres make silk-screen facilities available to groups and will show you how to go about it.

Directories

A directory is one of the most useful publications that a community information service can produce. It may cover the whole of a community, be confined to the interests of a particular client group, or contain information about a certain type of organisation, e.g. social welfare agencies, local government services, etc.

A directory plays an important role in community development by informing people about the services that exist and thus encouraging them to take a more active part in community life. It helps newcomers fit into the community and is a tool for those people to whom others turn for help and advice. A directory will usually be based on an information service's database but reproduced in a format that is easy to understand and use. There are a number of decisions to make before you embark on producing a directory, regarding such as the following:

Who is it aimed at? The general public (i.e. all households), sections of the public with special needs, community groups, community leaders, etc.

How many copies will be required? This will depend on whether you decide to distribute to everyone, in which case you need to obtain an estimate of your target group. If it is not feasible to give it such a wide distribution, then you must decide on how many copies it is realistically possible to produce within your budget.

You will need to work out as accurately as possible what size the directory will be so that estimates can be obtained from printers. Allow for advertising space if you are using this method to finance the directory. Newspapers work on a formula of two thirds advertising to one-third editorial (information) but they have greater overheads to, contend with. Half-and-half or even less may be an acceptable proportion, depending on your advertising rates and whether the advertising is intended to cover the whole cost.

How is it to be funded? From your own budget? By special allocation from a parent body? Joint funding with other agencies? Grants from outside bodies? Sponsorship? Advertising? Sales? Or a combination of several of these? Local newspapers often take a strong interest in producing directories of their communities. These are generally paid for by advertising and are distributed free of charge either as a pull-out supplement or as an integral part of a particular issue of the newspaper. It may be worth pursuing this alternative at the outset as it could save your information service much time and expense, and ensure that the information is made widely available.

What format? This will depend to a certain extent on the number of copies to be produced and the target group. A directory aimed at the whole of a community and containing a lot of information will need to be produced as a book, rather like a telephone directory. An alternative is to publish it as a supplement to a newspaper, but this carries the danger that it will be discarded with the newspaper and not kept for reference.

If you intend to produce just a small number for use by other information centres and agencies who have contact with the public, then a loose-leaf format may be more appropriate, since it allows you to send out updated sheets as information changes. Consider any special needs of your target group, e.g.. elderly people will require larger type, people with disabilities will require a format that can be handled easily.

How is it to be distributed? Delivered free to all households? Supplement in local newspaper? Insert in a community newspaper? On request or sold at certain specified centres? Through individuals who have contact with the public or target group, e.g. social workers, health visitors, teachers, etc.?

Content and arrangement It is not possible here to go into detail about the scope and arrangement of directories because these will vary depending on the nature of the directory, but the following guidelines may be of help:

Scope. This should be clearly defined before you start. Decide the geographical area to be covered and the topics included. The majority of space will be taken up with entries for organisations, clubs, societies, agencies, services, etc. but some directories may include a certain amount of 'hard' information, even if this is simply a profile of the area. There is a thin line between what constitutes a directory and what a handbook.

Detail of entries. This will depend on the directory's target group. If you are producing it for use by other information agencies or community workers, then you may need to provide the full range of information collected for your database, as those using the directory will need as much information as possible in order to assess the usefulness of an organisation to their clients. For general use, it is best not to give too much information as this may result in confusion and render the directory too cumbersome for efficient use. The minimum amount of information for each entry should give the name of the organisation, persons to contact, address and/or telephone number, and a brief description of the aims of the organisation where this is not self-evident from the name. The examples listed here show a full and a short directory entry.

Arrangement. Directories can be arranged in a number of ways fairly common method is alphabetically by name of organisation under broad subject groups which in turn may be further subdivided. Where the directory covers a number of distinct and separate towns or neighbourhoods, you may want the primary arrangement to be geographical. Other possibilities include one alphabetical arrangement by name of organisation, with a subject index if required or an A-Z by subject. A contents page at the beginning may be necessary to locate sections quickly. Also include at the beginning any information that may be required, urgently, such as emergency services. Directories are used mainly to locate specific items of information quickly, so if the arrangement is not clear and well signposted, you may need to provide an alphabetical index. Certainly, in a directory aimed at other information services, there will be a need to index by the subject interests of agencies, groups, etc. as well as by their names. If there is more than one entry per page, then each entry should be given a running number to which the index should refer, rather than a page number.

Current awareness bulletins

Pleas for up-to-date information are often made by workers in many spheres of activity who do not have the time themselves to search the literature. Community workers, social workers, information and advice workers, doctors and health visitors are just a few of the groups which might benefit from a regular flow of information.

Current awareness bulletins are one of the best ways of supplying that information in an easily digestible awareness bulletin is a duplicated listing of items of information which would be of use to a certain group or groups of workers. Where a publication or periodical is available locally, it is helpful to state this at the end of each item using for brevity, if necessary, some sort of code to indicate location, with a key provided at the beginning or end of the bulletin. Each item should be given a distinctive number so that requests for further information, photocopies or loan of material can be identified clearly and simply.

The usual method is to use a combination of the year and a running number, e.g. 83/1, 83/2, etc. The most common way of arranging the entries in a current awareness bulletin is to group them under subject headings with a contents page at the beginning. Under each subject group arrange entries alphabetically. Before deciding to compile your own current awareness bulletin, find out what is already produced both locally and nationally, to avoid carrying out work that is already being done elsewhere. It may be possible, with permission, to adapt an existing bulletin to your own local use. Seek help from other agencies with compiling and finance.

The bulletin shown here was produced jointly by an Advice Workers' Group and the public library, with finance from the local CVS. If necessary, to cover costs or postage, the bulletin can be made available on payment of a subscription. You might be able to save on postage by using another organisation's distribution network, e.g. CVS, library, local government.

Handbooks often contain directory-type information but mainly the text comprises descriptive information, e.g. about services, rights of individuals or groups, advice on personal matters, courses of action, etc. Handbooks are usually aimed at groups of people who have particular needs—elderly people, people with disabilities, parents of children under five, young people—or they may cover a defined geographical area. You may have to get help with writing the text from people who have knowledge of the subject.

The arrangement of a handbook will depend to a certain extent on its subject but a simple method is to use broad headings arranged alphabetically. A contents page and index are essential for locating specific items of information quickly. Use illustrations to break up the text and add interest. Handbooks can be expensive to produce and you will probably need to get help with finance.

Packs are an increasingly popular form of making information available, especially to people who perhaps do not have a habit of reading books. They are also useful for community information services that have limited staff resources and where the service offered is mainly of the self-help type. Packs vary from a simple plastic bag to specially embossed or printed folders. Their chief attraction is that they enable a number of flimsy items on a related theme such as leaflets, information sheets, small booklets, flowcharts, sample forms and letters, booklists and address lists, etc., to be brought together in such a way that the whole is greater than the sum of the parts. Sometimes it is necessary to link items with a specially prepared text.

Packs are easily duplicated for distribution to outlying centres and, if well produced, can entice people to browse through them who otherwise would not use a more conventional book form. Some organisations even produce them to give away. Some, disadvantages to packs are that they need to be displayed face outwards for maximum impact; they need to be regularly checked and updated (less easy the more they are dispersed); and without careful and attractive presentation they can so easily appear to be just a rag-bag of assorted ephemera.

The following guidelines may be helpful in preparing packs:

— *Choose the topic*—this might well be (i) a subject of frequent enquiry, e.g. buying and selling a house, adoption, writing a CV; (ii) a subject on which there is very little information in book form or that which exists is not readily understandable to the layperson, e.g. pensions, VAT registration; or (iii) a subject that meets the needs of a particular group e.g. one-parent families, those with debt problems.

— *Identify* suitable material and obtain in required quantities.

— *Write or compile* any linking material, lists of addresses and further sources of information. Get help from people who have special knowledge of the subject, if necessary.

– *Number* items and list them on a contents sheet.

— *Design* a title sheet which can be inserted into or stuck on the pack.

Manila wallets for packs can be obtained from most stationer, usually in A4 or foolscap sizes. You may also be able to find a stationer who stocks ready-made transparent plastic folders but, if not, Celsur Plastics Ltd stock these and will make them to your specifications, if necessary. If your funding will stretch to it, then you might like to go in for custom-designed plastic or manila folders.

The media

Newspapers, local radio and, latterly, cable television can be important vehicles for getting information to the public, in addition to their usual fare of sensational stories. The media will often readily accept offers of free material from outside organisations, provided it is presented to them in the right way and would be of interest to their readers, listeners or viewers.

The great advantage in using the media is that your information will reach a much wider audience than it ever would by any other means of dissemination, even if said means is not a very permanent one. Of course, the decision as to how that information is presented to the public will be out of your control. However, we have found that in the case of regular articles, columns or scripts, provided you have clear guidelines on what is required by the particular media in terms of length, style and content and keep to them, the material will not be altered very much.

The kinds of topic in which the media might well be interested are (i) forthcoming events, either generally or of a particular kind (e.g. sports, arts, etc.); (ii) information on new services or groups; (iii) important changes in legislation affecting people's lives; (iv) reviews of new publications; (v) general rights education; (vi) general services knowledge; (vii) information for young people (jobs, education, rights, recreation, etc.). Think carefully about taking part in 'live' phone-in programmes on radio, if this is offered. You will not be able to bring your information service into the studio and you can lay yourself open to all kinds of trouble by giving instant advice or information over the air without being able to check its accuracy first.

8

Rising Fifth Generation

Japan's Fifth Generation project will use faster, denser circuitry to create a new class of superintelligent computers. The 24 projects in the Fifth Generation concentrate on artificial intelligence, a goal of American computer scientists for more than a quarter century. Although the Japanese are highly regarded as superb engineers, Japanese computer scientists have often been faulted for failing to develop innovative computer software. But in a break with tradition, Kazuhiro Fuchi, the Fifth Generation project director, has deliberately assembled a young team: "The question was who would adapt most easily to this research," says Fuchi. "Young people have fewer fixed ideas." The project, headquartered in a downtown Tokyo skyscraper, will focus on computer architectures, software, and the symbolic logic necessary to build thinking computers. The Microelectronics and Computer Technology Corp. (MCC) Last year William Norris, the founder and chairman of Control Data Corp., convened a meeting of top computer and semiconductor industry executives at the Grenelefe Golf and Tennis resort in Orlando, Florida, to discuss setting up a hugh research cooperative.

The companies agreed to form a nonprofit joint venture so that they could pool their resources and share the cost of doing long-range research. Twelve major us corporations joined the new organisation, including

Honeywell, Motorola, RCA, and Control Data. MCC is a bold departure from the way research is usually done in American universities and corporations, and it will probe the limits of the nation's antitrust laws. The venture partly follows the Japanese model: the companies will donate scientists and researchers to MCC, loaning them for up to four years. The corporate co-owners will also put up the money to fund MCC' research, in return for the rights to use the results. Whether the scheme will work is an open question. The 12 companies in MCC are competitors in fast-moving, high-technology markets, and ordinarily they jealously guard any technological edge they gain. In fact, many top us firms—Cray Research, Texas Instruments, Intel, and others—chose to stay out of MCC.

MCC's directors chose retired Admiral Bobby Ray Inman, former director of the National Security Agency and former deputy director of the CIA. Inman is widely respected for his managerial abilities and is an adept politician besides. Over the past five months, Inman orchestrated a competition among 57 cities for the MCC headquarters; the winner was Austin, Texas, after private donors, the state, and universities put together a generous package of incentives.

The consortium will have a budget of about $75 million a year and a staff of 250. Its first projects include programs in semiconductor packaging and interconnect technology, advanced software engineering and computer-aided design and manufacturing (CAD/CAM) for the electronics and computer industries. Most ambitious is a 10-year program aimed at breakthroughs in computer architecture, software, and artificial intelligence.

MCC will own the licenses and patents to the technologies; the manufacturing and marketing will be left to the companies that sponsor the projects. MCC win give them a competitive edge on the market-they will have exclusive rights for three years before the research is published and other firms are allowed to buy licenses.

Over the past three years Japan has captured a vital segment of the world semiconductor industry, the market for so-called RAM (random access memory) chips, a technology invented in America. Japan now supplies 70 percent of all 64K RAMS sold, and it appears that, as the next generation of memory chips, the 256K RAMS, is being readied for market, the Japanese semiconductor companies are threatening to take a big share of sales.

Over the past 20 years, DARPA has poured half a billion dollars into computer research, in the process virtually creating the science of artificial intelligence. The first supercomputer, built in 1964, was a DARPA project. Computer time sharing, a fundamental advance, came out of work sponsored by DARPA. So did packet-switched networks, the workhorses of today's telecommunications data networks. And computer graphics—now used on desktop computers and video-arcade cockpits—is a DARPA-sponsored invention.

DARPA plans to do everything the Japanese have set out to accomplish-and more. Earlier this year DARPA proposed a "Strategic Computing and Survivability" project, which it hopes will lead to a variety of new machines. "Other kinds of systems are good for logic processing. We want architectures that can do very rapid signal processing [and] structures that can handle very, very large amounts of data in communications." Smart robot weapons—drone aircraft, unmanned submarines, and land vehicles—that combine artificial intelligence and high-powered computing can be sent off to do jobs that now involve human risk. "This is a very sexy area to the military, because you can imagine all kinds of neat, interesting things you could send off on their own little missions around the world or even in local comba. The Pentagon will also use the technologies to create artificial intelligence machines that can be used as battlefield advisers and superintelligent computers to coordinate complex weapons systems. An intelligent missile guidance system would have to bring together different technologies-real-time signal processing, numerical calculations, and symbolic processing, all at unimaginably high speeds-in order to make decisions and give advice to human commanders.

The same technology that can be used to simulate an antitank missile smashing into a heavily armored tank can also be put to work on less martial arts. Instead of shooting a commercial the conventional way—a costly photo session-Digital can create the "pictures" it needs in detail so precise that it's impossible to distinguish between the supercomputer's graphic image and the real photo. As the commercial market grows, the Japanese believe that their strategy of building supercomputers for the general-purpose market will pay off. The Cray X-MP contains a dense pack of 240,000 silicon chips arranged to shorten the distances the electrical signals must travel, thereby decreasing the time it takes to perform an operation; the new Cray X-MPs will run at 400 million operations per second. And Japan's superspeed goal is 10 billion operations per second. Because of the cost of supercomputers—Cray's X-MP will sell for $ 11 million—the market will remain limited. Japan's Fifth Generation project, however, plans to build "super personal computers." These huge increases in raw computer power are just the first step.

The most profound changes brought by the new technologies will be the development of reasoning computers that will use superspeed symbol manipulation to simulate human thought. The Fifth Generation the field is not new: scientists in the us have been studying artificial intelligence for 25 years, struggling to understand the nature of knowledge and how to represent it in forms adaptable to computer usage.

Digital Equipment Corp. the nation's second largest computer firm, uses an AI program called X-CON to make custom designs of its, computer systems. Using a set of more than 2500 rules programmed into the system, X-CON examines a customer's specifications, determines whether all the necessary components are included, then draws a set of diagrams showing the proper spatial relationships among the components. Scientists studying artificial intelligence have been aided by advances in computer hardware, too. In 1980 a group left MIT's Artificial Intelligence Laboratory to found a company, Symbolics Inc., of Cambridge, Mass., to build computers specially designed to run LISP, a language used to develop artificial intelligence programs; and Xerox has begun to sell similar computers. Symbolics has been selling its machines, the Symbolics 3600, to a broad range of university and industrial research labs. The company has another customer as well: the managers running Japan's Fifth Generation project have bought 10 Symbolics machines-and they have 15 more on order. In exploring the brave new world of artificial intelligence, computer scientists are concentrating on several important problems. "Knowledge engineers" are building so-called expert systems that can mimic human expertise in a narrowly defined area.

The program is, in effect, a computer replica of Courtés expertise; the computer will ask the drilling-rig foremen questions, just as Courté would. Once it gathers the information it needs, the computer will make recommendations by drawing images on the screen and giving suggestions on how to retrieve the bit. Because daily drilling costs are high, Elf Acquitaine may well recover the program's development costs the first time it is used successfully. General Electric is building a software program that will provide expert advice on repairing locomotives.

The Pentagon would like to build artificial intelligence programs that could serve as a pilot's assistant in the cockpit. Stockbrokers and insurance agents may also soon get help: "Some people are beginning to see a gold mine in financial services," says Patrick Henry Winston, chairman of MIT's Artificial Intelligence Laboratory. And savvy software designers for the personal computer industry are beginning to look at artificial intelligence as the next big wave that will sweep the market. Despite the successes, there are problems ahead as researchers attempt to move beyond the building of narrowly defined "experts."

Computers have always been maddeningly literal machines, subject to the absolute tyranny of the binary codes they use to do their calculations. (The switches are either on or off, simulating ones or zeros, nothing else.) That literal-mindedness can transform a problem that would seem trivial to humans into a nightmare. Consider the simple statement "Mary had a little lamb." For a computer to translate the text into another language—a function scientists are now trying to develop—it would have to sort through what is, by one count, 28 possible interpretations.

The statement "Ronald Reagan is president" carries a number of immediate meanings to a flesh-and-blood American, but a computer would have to rummage through its silicon memory chips in search of dozens of facts-what the word "president" means and biographical facts and details that tell who Ronald Reagan is. And the biggest challenge of all-teaching computers to learn to acquire knowledge on their own-is nowhere near being solved.

Mankind has long been enchanted—and frightened-by the prospect of creating machines that think. All the mechanisms for human intelligence are present. Already machines can think just like people—in a limited sense. Man isn't unique in that respect." Moreover, many machines may soon possess sight, touch, hearing (in the form of voice recognition), and speech, thus imitating humans' sensory capacities along with their intellectual ones. But whole areas of the human thought process-volition, emotion, the creative uses of error—still lie well outside a computer's experience.

Japanese planners view the computer industry as vital to their nation's economic future and have audaciously made it a national goal to become number one in this industry by the latter half of the 1990s. They aim not only to dominate the traditional forms of the computer industry, but to establish a "knowledge industry" in which knowledge itself will be a saleable commodity like food and oil.

The Japanese plan is bold and dramatically forward-looking. It is unlikely to be completely successful in the ten-year period. But to view it therefore as "a lot of smoke," as some American industry leaders have done, is a serious mistake. Even partially realised concepts that are superbly engineered can have great economic value, pre-empt the market, and give the Japanese the dominant position they seek.

Technology targets

The Japanese Fifth Generation project aims to design and produce computer hardware and software for knowledge engineering in a wide range of applications--including expert systems, natural language understanding by machines, and robotics. To accomplish these goals, the Japanese must improve present computing capabilities dramatically, but they must also make major innovations in existing technology that will enable Fifth Generation computers to support very large knowledge bases, allow very fast associative retrievals, perform logical inference operations as fast as current computers perform arithmetic operations, utilise parallelism in program structure and hardware to achieve high speed, and develop a machine-user interface that allows significant use of natural speech and images.

All experts systems built by knowledge engineers to date consist of three main parts. First is the subsystem that "manages" the knowledge base needed for problem solving and understanding. Second is the problem-solving and inference subsystem, which discovers what knowledge is useful and relevant to the problem at hand, and with it constructs—step by step—a line of reasoning leading to the problem solution, the plausible interpretation, or the best hypothesis. Third are the methods of interaction between human and machine, in modes and languages that are "natural" and comfortable for the user. Ordinary human natural language is often preferred, but the stylised notations of some fields like chemistry are also desirable for specific groups of users. Knowledge-based management, problem solving and inference, and human interaction—these have all been approached in our present expert systems via software innovations, innovations that have pressed traditional von Neumann hardware architectures to their limits.

The Fifth Generation plan organises its work around these three subsystems, but with a critical added dimension: for each component subsystem there is a hardware level and a software level. And between the levels the Japanese designers must define a "language" with which the software and hardware interact. The knowledge in the knowledge base must first be represented in symbolic form, and in memory structures, that can be used efficiently by the problem-solving and inference subsystem. This representation can take many forms.

A typical kind of associative network is the taxonomy, known as "The... is—a (*hierarchy*)." For example, "The sparrow is—a kind of bird." In this case, both sparrow and bird are objects within the knowledge base. If the knowledge base is informed that "The bird is—a kind of animal that can fly," the knowledge base management system must automatically propagate the deduction that sparrows can fly.

A rule consists of a collection of statements called the "if" part, and a conclusion or action to be taken called the "then" part. For example, "IF the fog ceiling is below 700 feet and the official weather forecast calls for no clearing within the hour, THEN landing is dangerous, will violate air traffic regulations, and diversion to a neighboring airfield is recommended." To find out if a rule is relevant to the reasoning task at hand, the problem-solving program must scan over the store of "ifs" in the knowledge base. That search can be immense in the size of knowledge base the Japanese plan to make possible. Here again, the knowledge-base management subsystem will be designed to organise the memory in ways that will reduce the amount of processing to be done.

Parallel processing capabilities in both the software and hardware levels of the system will also speed associative retrievals. In the Fifth Generation plan, knowledge will be stored electronically in a large file known as a relational data base. The job of automatically updating the knowledge in the file, and of organising appropriate searches for relevant knowledge, will be performed by the knowledge-base management software. The Fifth Generation prototype knowledge-base subsystem will handle a modest knowledge base—thousands of rules and thousands of objects—about the size needed for current expert system applications. Each object will be allotted 1000 characters of file storage space. Within the ten-year trajectory of their plan, the Japanese goal is to develop knowledge-base capacity in their systems that will be able to handle tens of thousands of interference rules and one hundred million objects! What could so much knowledge encompass?

Since the Fifth Generation is so far-reaching, it demands dramatic improvements in other technologies that support the main-line knowledge information processing systems (KIPS) goals. Essential to the future of the enterprise, for example, are extremely high-speed processors, capable of processing by orders of magnitude faster than anything now available. Artificial intelligence made its debut on first-generation machines and has been implemented subsequently on second- and third-generation machines, but not yet on fourth-generation supercomputers.

The Japanese aim for chips with 10 million transistors. Chips in current production carry a few hundred thousand transistors at most. Such processors are being developed in the course of another MITI effort, the SuperSpeed Computing Project, and will be adapted into the Fifth Generation machines. In addition, the Fifth Generation depends on access to knowledge bases in many locations, so its technology will ultimately be fused with the most advanced communications technologies.

The whole area of intelligent interfaces—the ability the machines will have to listen, see, understand, and reply to human users—will require extensive R&D in natural language processing in speech understanding, and in graphics and image understanding. All these have been concerns of artificial intelligence research from virtually its beginning some 25 years ago, and basic research in each of these fields has made reasonable progress. Because nonexperts will be the largest group of users, natural language processing is one of the most important research goals of the Fifth Generation.

Research here will cover speech wave analysis, phonetic and syntactic analysis, semantic analysis, and pragmatic analysis, which derives understanding by extracting themes or foci in a given sentence, detecting focus shifts, and so on. For speech output, sentence generation will also be studied. Text analysis is also considered a part of natural language processing by the Japanese, although they are quite aware that the techniques used for large-scale text analysis are different from the techniques needed to smooth the way for an individual user to talk to his machine.

The Japanese see knowledge systems as a potential solution to the steadily increasing amount of text and documents that must be handled by computer. Our research on intelligent man-machine interface will help to solve this problem," reported a group of Japanese scientists at a Fifth Generation project meeting. Present artificial intelligence research suggests this can be done—in a prototype system, intelligent automatic analysis has been successfully applied to a wire news service in the us, for instance-but the sheer scale of the automatic analysis planned by the Japanese dwarfs any existing systems.

All this research in natural language processing will proceed in three stages, beginning with an experimental system, followed by a pilot model implementation stage that is connected with the inference and knowledge base machines, and concluding with prototype implementations. At that point the machines will be expected to understand continuous human speech with a vocabulary of 50,000 words from a few hundred or more speakers with 95 percent accuracy. The speech understanding system is also expected to be capable of running a voice-activated typewriter and of conducting a dialogue with users by means of synthesised speech in Japanese or English.

The machine's capacity to respond intelligently to users, known as its question-answering system, will first be designed to handle queries in the computing field, but it is expected to be a prototype for such systems in many professional fields: in addition to the query system's 5000 or more words of vocabulary, it will have 10,000 or more inference rules.

Images

Picture and image processing are considered almost as important as language processing, especially as they contribute to computer-aided design and manufacture (CAD/CAM) and to the effective analysis of aerial and satellite images, medical images, and the like. Here again the research will take place in three phases, beginning with an experimental phase to tackle such topics as the hardware architecture of "feature extractors"—for example, to distinguish the boundaries of objects-display generators, and the image data base.

The second phase will produce a pilot model, and in the third and final phase a prototype will be built, integrated into the Fifth Generation machine, and applications will be studied. One obvious use is in constructing robots that can see, understand, and act under novel circumstances. The bulk of robotics R&D, however, will be done in a Robotics National Project. Eventually, the image understanding system is expected to store about 100,000 images.

There are both positive and negative sides the Japanese project. First, its flaws. The science upon which the audacious Fifth Generation plans are laid lies at the outermost edge and beyond what computer science presently knows. The plan is risky; it contains several "scheduled breakthroughs." There are major scientific and engineering challenges in every aspect, from artificial intelligence through parallel architectures and distributed functions to VLSI design and fabrication. The project demands early successes to maintain its momentum and funding, and that could be a problem.

Conversely, meeting or exceeding the goals of the first three-year period might well propel the Japanese ahead of their timetable, bringing increased support from the participating companies. Central to the success of the project are the Japanese managers, both governmental and industrial. Generally conservative and risk-averse, they are now to be charged with managing a very ambitious, high-risk project based on technology they hardly understand. Most of the breakthroughs the Fifth Generation project must achieve are basically innovations in software concepts.

The key ideas in the approach to knowledge information processing systems came out of the software world—ideas about the creation, maintenance, and modification of large and complex symbolic data structures in computer memories and the discovery of symbolic lines of reasoning. A quick fix to the problem is to work on the intermediate territory of the so-called firmware—intricate and detailed "programming" of the hardware-switching functions that sit at the bottom of the computing process. This is not a desirable final solution, however, since interpreting and executing the "firmware program" consumes time and slows down the machine.

Japanese computer specialists and managers are not, and never have been, comfortable with software-it's intangible to them, and its production is notoriously difficult to manage "on schedule and on budget." The Japanese lack the experience base in knowledge engineering and expert systems from which to draw as they begin to work out the details of what to build. In addition, the Japanese lack a large corps of university

Finally, from the AI viewpoint, two elements of the plan are questionable. First, the priority given to the highspeed logic processor. Are all those millions Of Lips needed? Second, is PROLOG the best choice for the machine language of the logic processor? In the American engineering experience, few applications have been limited by the number of inference steps per second that could be performed. Rather, limitations in performance arise from limitations in the quantity and quality of knowledge available to the machine (too little and not well refined); the facility with which it can be managed and updated; and the speed with which it can be searched and accessed.

A second plus for PROLOG is that it solves problems by proving theorems in first-order predicate calculus using computationally fast methods. The user never has to be concerned with the details of the problem-solving process. But PROLOG detractors see this as a serious flaw. The major successes of AI have come from mastering the methods by which knowledge can be used to control the search for solutions in complex problems.

The last thing a knowledge engineer wants to do is abdicate control to an "automatic" theorem-proving process that conducts massive searches without step-by step control exerted by the knowledge base. Such uncontrolled searches can be extremely time-consuming.

The parallelism that can be brought to bear is a mere palliative, because the searches become exponentially more time-consuming as the problem complexity increases. One can't keep up with exponential growth simply by lining up a hundred or a thousand more parallel processors.

Creating the knowledge industry, with hardware, software, and knowledge system applications, is a great bet. Indeed, it is one of the few great bets sitting out there now in the information processing industry, ready for a major push toward exploitation. Of course, the traditional modes of numerical calculation and data processing will continue to develop and prosper. But these will see steady incremental growth, not explosive growth.

The exponential growth will be seen in symbolic computation and knowledge-based reasoning by computer. MITI's key economic insight is correct. For an island trading nation, exports create wealth and in the knowledge industry the value of exports is enhanced by indigenous resources-the intelligence, education, and skill of people. Further, knowledge information processing systems will significantly enhance the productivity of many other industries, thereby indirectly contributing to the value added.

The creating of ICOT, the pooling of talent in a cooperative endeavor, plus the well-coordinated transfer of technology between ICOT and the parallel labs of the firms, seem inspired. The ten-year planning horizon is excellent. Ten years is a long time in the information processing industry. Ten years ago pocket calculators cost hundreds of dollars, video games were primitive laboratory toys, and the

Japanese had yet to produce their first viable microelectronic chip. As we live through it, we tend to underestimate the speed of technological change. MITI's concern for nurturing the innovative talents of Japanese computer scientists appears well placed. The us and the advanced European nations have become wary of providing the leading technologies upon which Japanese technical achievements have hitherto relied.

Trade wars are under way, and blockades are inevitable. Though solutions to the technological problems posed by the Fifth Generation plan may be hard to achieve, paths to possible solutions abound. The Japanese are rich with excellent engineering talent and have an adequate supply of cutting-edge computer scientists. The mix of talents enables (but does not guarantee) a good chance of success.

What's real?

Managers of the Fifth Generation project have said that it would not disturb them if only 10 percent of the project goals were achieved; others have remarked that the ten-year planning horizon should not be taken too seriously; that the project goals are so important that an extension over another half or full decade would not be unreasonable. Partially realised concepts that are superbly engineered can have great utility and be of great economic benefit. At the very least, a partial success can pre-empt the area and make it not worthwhile for others to enter playing catch up.

The first 20 percent of the technical achievement may skim off 80 percent of the potential economic gain. If true, firms in the American industry might never find it in their economic interest to enter the arena. Being late might put them out of the contest. Consider this: though videotaping was invented in the us, the lengthy and expensive R&D process for the consumer-oriented video cassette recorder led to an all-or-none market share result, with American industry getting the "none." No matter how partial its success may be, the Fifth Generation project will provide a decade-long learning experience for a new generation of Japanese computer scientists.

They will be called upon to confront and perhaps solve the most challenging problems facing the future of information processing, rather than re-engineering traditional systems. They will be learning advanced software concepts in a way that has never been done before in Japan and has never been widely done in the us or Europe. The Fifth Generation project, in its short life, has emplaced the technology transfer mechanisms necessary for Japanese industry to move effectively to bring its developments to market. Right now, the us has a substantial lead in virtually every area of Fifth Generation work.

Of course, the answer depends on what one substitutes for "XXX." Readers who filled in, say, "national socialism" could have supposed that these words were spoken, as a warning to German intellectuals who had not yet appreciated the glory of the Nazi revolution, by Josef Goebbels on the occasion of the book burning in Berlin on May 10, 1933. Readers could substitute "the ideas of the great leader and teacher" for "XXX" and leave open what particular revolution is being talked about. Leaders who come to mind, and whose names would render the quoted paragraph plausible, are, to name just a few: Karl Marx, General Pinochet, Stalin.

The Germans, by the way, had a word for what intellectuals are here being warned to do: *Gleickschaltung*, which is translated as "bringing into line" or "coordination." But, implausible as it may seem at first glance, "XXX" in the quoted passage stands for "this new instrument," meaning the computer. The authors of

The Fifth Generation maintain that intellectuality, the creative use of the mind engaged in study and in reflection, will soon become inevitably and necessarily dependent on the computer. They are astounded that American intellectuals aren't rushing to enlist in their revolution.

A professor of computer science at Stanford University and a cofounder of two commercial companies that market artificial intelligence software systems, and Pamela McCorduck, a science writer, give the reader an idea of what's happening in the world of computers. They make the following claims. First, certain American computer scientists have discovered that, if computers are expected to intervene in some activity in the real world, then it would help, to say the least, if they had some knowledge of the domain of the activity in question. For example, computer systems designed to help make medical diagnoses had better know about diseases and their signs and symptoms.

Second, other American computer scientists have described designs of computers, "computer architectures," that depart radically from the industry's traditional design principles originally laid down by the pioneer computer scientist. The new architectures allow computational chains to be decomposed into steps which can be executed as soon as the data for executing them are ready. They then don't have to wait their turn, so to speak. Indeed, many steps can be executed simultaneously. Computation time is in a sense "folded" in such machines, which are consequently very much faster than their orthodox predecessors.

Third, still other computer scientists, mainly French and British, have created a computer language which they believe to be well suited for representing knowledge in computers in a form that lends itself to powerful logical manipulation. The Japanese hope that the conjunction of this computer language with the new architecture will allow ultrarapid computation of "inferences" from masses of stored knowledge. Fourth, these developments have taken place at a time of continuing dramatic progress in making computers physically smaller, functionally faster, and with increasing storage capacities.

Finally, the Japanese, who already dominate the world market in consumer electronics, have seized on the resulting opportunity and decided to create entirely new and enormously powerful computer systems, the "Fifth Generation," based on the developments described above. These systems, as the book jacket puts it, will be "artificially intelligent machines that can reason, draw conclusions, make judgments, and even understand the written and spoken word." This appears to be a very ambitious claim. But not to seasoned observers of the computer scene, who have long since learned to penetrate the foggy language of the computer enthusiasts.

In other words, the most recent ambitions of the Japanese were already close to being realised according to leaders of the American artificial intelligence community a quarter of a century ago! All that remained to be done—and it would be done within the "visible future"-was to extend the range of the problems such machines would solve to the whole range of the problems to which the human mind has been applied. That ambition remains as absurd today as it was twenty-five years ago. In the meanwhile, however, much progress has been made in getting computers to "understand" the written word and even some words spoken in very highly controlled contexts. Is the Japanese project then really not very ambitious?

A geriatric robot that frees old people from the murderous instincts of their children and is programmed to lie to them systematically, telling them that it understands their petty stories and enjoys "listening" to them. Mechanical doctors we can be utterly candid with and which won't disapprove of us as human doctors often do. Technical devices in our own homes that gather information about us and determine to what group we ought to belong and which ones we should hate.

Technical systems that permit us to exchange knowledge "engagingly" with our fellow creatures while avoiding the horror of having to look at them or be looked at let alone touched. This is the world Feigenbaum and McCorduck are recommending. In fact, they haven't told us the whole story. Professor Tohru Moto-oka of Tokyo University and titular head of the Japanese Fifth Generation project promises even more:

> . . . first, [Fifth Generation computers] will take the place of man in the area of physical labor, and, through the intellectualisation of these advanced computers, totally new applied fields will be developed, social productivity will be increased, and distortions in values will be eliminated [emphasis added].

We are well on our way to the kind of world sketched here. Already, we are told, and it is undoubtedly true, many people prefer to "interact" with computers. Schoolchildren prefer them to teachers, and many patients to doctors. No one seems to ask what it may be about today's doctors and teachers, or with the situations in which they work, that causes them to come off second-best in competition with computers.

The computer has long been a solution looking for problems—the ultimate technological fix which insulates us from having to look at problems. Our schools, for example, tend to produce students with mediocre abilities to read, write, and reason; the main thing we are doing about that is to sit kids down at computer consoles in the classrooms. Perhaps they'll manage to become "computer—literate"—whatever that means—even if, in their mother tongue, they remain functionally illiterate. We now have factories so highly computerised that they can operate virtually unmanned.

Devices that shield us from having to come in contact with fellow human beings are rapidly taking over much of our daily lives. Voices synthesised by computers tell us what to do next when we place calls on the telephone. The same voices thank us when we have done what they ask. But what does "the same voices" mean in this context? Individuality, identity, everything that has to do with the uniqueness of persons—or of anything else!-simply disappears. No wonder the architects of, and apologists for, worlds in which work becomes better and more engaging to the extent that it can be carried out without face-to-face interaction, and in which people prefer machines that listen to them to people, come to the conclusion that intellectuals are irrelevant figures. There is no place in their scheme of things for creative minds, for independent study and reflection, for independent anything.

Aside from whatever advantages are to be gained by living our lives in an electronic isolation ward, and aside also from the loss to "them" of a market ,(we" now dominate, what good reasons are there for mounting our own Fifth generation project on a scale, as Feigenbaum and McCorduck recommend, of the program that landed our man on the moon? -if you can think of a good defense application,"

One chapter of the book is devoted to "Ai and the National Defense." However, the chapter is only six pages long, and is mainly a song of praise-perhaps gratitude is a more apt word-for the Pentagon's "enlightened scientific leadership." Laid on thick, the praise tends to betray its own absurdity:

> Since the Pentagon is often perceived as the national villain, especially by intellectuals, it's a pleasure to report that in one enlightened corner of it, human beings were betting taxpayers' money on projects that would have major benefits for the whole human race.

The corner mentioned is the Defense Department's Advance Research Projects Agency, DARPA, also often called just ARPA. Well, there is reason for workers in AI to be grateful to this agency. It has spent in the order of $ 500 million on computer research, and that certainly benefited the AT community—the artificial intelligentsia—enormously. But "major benefits for the whole human race")

The military, however, has good reason to continue, just as generously as ever, to provide funds for work on the fifth generation, as Feigenbaum and McCorduck make clear: The so-called smart weapons of 1992, for all their sophisticated modern electronics, are really just extremely complex wind-tip toys compared to the weapon systems that will be possible in a decade if intelligent information processing systems are applied to the defense problems of the 1990s.

The authors make five points. First, they believe we should look "with awe at the peculiar nature of modern electronic warfare," particularly at the fact that the Israelis recently shot down 79 Syrian airplanes with no losses to themselves. "This amasing result was achieved," they write, "largely by intelligent human electronic battle management. In the future, it can and will be done by computer.

Second, we cannot afford to allow the "technology of the intelligent computer systems of the future . . . to slip away to the Japanese or to anyone else. . . . Japan, as a nation, has a longstanding casual attitude toward secrecy when it comes to technological matters." Third, with the ever-increasing cost of military hardware, "the economic impact of an intelligent armaments system that can strike targets with extreme precision should be apparent . . .fewer weapons used selectively for maximum strike capability."

Fourth, "it is essential that the newest technological developments be made available to the Defense Department." Finally, "the Defense Department needs the ability to shape technology to conform to its needs in military systems. Here, perhaps more than in any other argument of the book, we are close to what it's "all about." A much shorter, and better, account of the Japanese Fifth Generation project appeared recently as a cover story of *Newsweek* magazine. People generally should know the end use of their labor.

Students coming to study at the artificial intelligence laboratories of MIT, my university, or Stanford, Edward Feigenbaum's, or the other such laboratories in the us should decide what they want to do with their talents without being befuddled by euphemisms. They should be clear that, upon graduation, most of the companies they will work for, and especially those that will recruit them more energetically, are the most deeply engaged in feverish activity to find still faster, more reliable ways to kill ever more people—Feigenbaum and McCorduck speak of the objective of creating smart weapons systems with "zero probability of error" (their emphasis). Whatever euphemisms are used to describe students' AI laboratory projects, the probability is overwhelming that the end of their research will serve this or similar military objectives. To underline the importance of the computer as the "main artifact of the age of information," Feigenbaum and McCorduck instruct us just wherein the importance of the computer lies: [The computer's] purpose is certainly to process information—to transform, amplify, distribute, and otherwise modify it. But more important, the computer produces information. The essence of the computer revolution is that the burden of producing the future knowledge of the world will be transferred from human heads to machine artifacts [emphasis in the original].

How are we to understand the assertion that the computer "produces information"? In the same way, presumably, as the statement that a coalfired electric power station produces energy. But that would be a simple and naive falsehood. Coalfired power stations transform energy, they do not produce it. Computers similarly transform information, generally using information-*losing* operations. For example, when a computer executes an instruction to add 2 and 5, it computes 7.

Social impact of machines

Since then, it has had some notable successes, enabling computers to perform—albeit in a very limited way—some of the tasks normally done by our minds. Some AI workers see AI as a way of helping us understand human psychology; they try to write programs that tackle their tasks in the sort of way in which we do. Others see it as an approach to a theory of intelligence in general, human (and animal) intelligence being a special case. Still others simply want to write programs to do something (to understand language, to describe visible objects, or to solve problems of various kinds), irrespective of how we do it.

And most of these hope that what their programs do will be not only interesting, but useful. The technological aspects of AI have suddenly become more visible. Public interest in AI, and media coverage of it, have increased enormously over the last two years. More and more people view it as an incipient technology of great potential power and social significance. The public interest dates from the announcement in 1981 of Japan's ten-year national plan for developing "Fifth Generation" computers. These are defined as incorporating AI techniques (as well as large-scale parallel processing).

Since then, large sums of money for AI-research have been made available also by governments and industry in the Western industrialised nations.

Developments

Several core research areas are likely to make solid progress within the next decade. Each of these is already being worked on in various countries, and progress does not depend upon the success of Japan's ambitious "Fifth Generation" project. One is low-level vision, based on techniques using parallel hardware and cooperative processing.

Current "connectionist" research in this area differs in its approach from work on two-dimensional pattern recognition by "property lists," and from-the-top-down "scene analysis" of three-dimensional scenes. Based on detailed studies of image formation, it is able to extract from the ambient light information about three-dimensional features (such as shape, depth, texture, and surface orientation) which in previous approaches could have been computed only, if at all, by way of high-level knowledge of the expected scene. Some of this work is being done in the context of human psychology and neurophysiology, some in a more technological context.

Dedicated (massively parallel) machines are being designed for this research, and major advances depend upon such hardware. A second area in which we can expect significant progress is robotics. This includes problems of movement control, trajectory planning, and visuomotor coordination (and will take advantage of advances in low-level vision). As in the case of vision, some projects will rely on "artificial" means to ensure success (such as light stripes for automatic welding machines, capable of recognising different sorts of weld joint and guiding the welder accordingly), while others will relate more closely to psychophysiological theories of motor control and visuomotor coordination in living organisms. Knowledge-based "expert" systems will multiply enormously in the next decade, not least because there is considerable commercial interest in them. Different domains of human expertise may require different approaches to knowledge engineering. In domains less fully covered by an explicit scientific theory, it may be easier to extract knowledge from human experts who are competent but who have not yet achieved the "intuitive" mastery of the domain that topflight experts enjoy.

The latter give the right answer more often, but cannot easily introspect their reasoning processes, which happen very fast and are not consciously accessible. The former take time to come to a decision, after consciously weighing distinct considerations against each other and verbally identifying areas of unclarity. Domains (such as medical radiology) that depend on the comparison and interpretation of complex visual images are especially difficult to automate, since low-level visual processes are not open to voluntary inspection or control.

Indeed, experts often give highly misleading advice about how they may be carrying out the relevant comparisons. (Eye movement studies show, for instance, that expert radiologists do not scan x-ray photographs in the way they say that they do.) In tandem with the increasing experience of AI-trained knowledge engineers, further psychological studies of the organisation of knowledge in different domains should be useful. Research on expert systems will also focus on the computational architecture required to deal with large, complex knowledge bases.

Current systems are relatively simple and inflexible, and are restricted to very narrow domains. They can be incrementally improved, but only up to a point. Eventually, the interactions between the increasing number of independently added rules become too difficult to control, and the system's reliability and intelligibility are jeopardised. Current systems have no access to higher-level representations of the knowledge domain and their own problem-solving activity (see below). Special problems arise if a system has to work in real-time, where unexpected events can require quick switching from the current activity to some other.

The next ten years will see some general work on powerful (IKBs) architectures (as well as the production of more examples of specific commercially useful systems), including parallel-processing devices. Progress can be expected also in natural language processing, both of individual sentences and of texts. Key issues include syntactic parsing, the integration of syntax with semantics, and the understanding of connected text.

Machine translation could in principle benefit from advances both in single-sentence parsing and in text analysis. Current work on parsing is motivated both by theoretical (linguistic) interests and by the hope of improving the man-machine interface so as to make it possible for nonspecialist users to communicate with programs in (some reasonable subset of) natural language. Where a program is used for some specific purpose, semantic factors can be more readily used to help in the parsing and disambiguation of queries and instructions input by the user.

Verbal interchanges about lunar geology, or about airline reservations, are already reasonably "natural" because of the exploitation of semantic constraints, and further domain-specific semantics will be developed over the next decade. More generally applicable (theoretical) research will continue into the best point at which to use semantics in parsing: from the beginning of the sentence, or spreading out from the middle, or only after an initial parse of the entire sentence? Text-analysis programs can already give a precis of most short news stories about specific topics (such as earthquakes, hijackings, and road accidents). But they rely on rigid, preprogrammed schemata, which provide the semantic skeleton of the types of stories concerned.

Some recent research is aimed at enabling a text-analysis program to learn new schemata for itself, to integrate one schema with another so as to understand a story combining both, and to use a given schema to reason analogically in an unfamiliar context. A high degree of success cannot be expected within the next ten years, but our understanding of the relevant problems should be advanced. A variety of educational applications is already receiving attention.

Some are focused on particular curricular subjects, and require both a model of the theory of that subject and a model of the student's knowledge of it (which varies in level and in organisation, from person to person and from time to time). Others are less specific, and aim to use AI-based techniques to improve the pupil's attitude to intelligence in general. There is some evidence that both normal and handicapped students can attain greater self-confidence and intellectual achievement by experience with these specially designed programming environments. Controlled research into the classroom effects of AI-based systems has recently been initiated, and this can be expected to bear fruit within the next decade. An extremely important area, which is increasingly being studied because of recent hardware developments, concerns the computational properties of large parallel systems. At present, we understand very little of the potential and limitations of such systems. Some of the connectionist work mentioned above suggests that cooperative processing may have some highly surprising properties.

For example, the number of individual processors required to make the "human" range of visual shape discriminations appears to be markedly less than one would naturally assume. Again, making a connectionist system stochastic rather than deterministic improves its chance of finding an optimal solution. The computational properties of parallel machines will not be well understood for a long time, but experience with these new systems in the near future will doubtless lead to some advance.

Sciences and technologies

The impacts of AI on other technologies will include many different examples of applications to individual problems. For example, an olfactory chip is being designed using AI techniques of pattern recognition. Given advances in very large-scale integration (VLSI), instruments and products of many different kinds will come to include chips whose design makes use of AI methods. Any commercial-industrial task that could benefit from even a limited degree of intelligence could in principle be performed better with the help of AI, so the technological applications of AI will be extremely diverse. AI will influence other sciences in their general philosophical approach as well as their specific theoretical content. Indeed, psychology and (to a lesser degree) biology have already been affected by computational ideas. And, contrary to what most people assume, Ai has had a humanising effect in psychology. AI's influence will be especially strong in the psychology of vision and language, and, as noted above, it is likely that robotics will engage with the psychophysiology of movement. Psychological research will feed back into AI; for example, insofar as psychologists arrive at a better understanding of the organisation of knowledge, their work may he useful in designing computerised expert systems.

Social impacts will be of various types. First, there will be effects on individuals and institutions brought about by specific applications of AI, such as expert systems for medical diagnosis, legal and financial advice, or educational help. These programs will not merely provide a service (whose adequacy should be very carefully monitored), but will very likely change the social relations of the profession or institution concerned.

For example, if general practitioners, or nurses, can use an AI program to aid in various aspects of patient care, the social image of the specialist physician may be profoundly affected. (And legal responsibilities for medical decisions may be assigned in a way very different from today.) Likewise, legal programs may undermine the status of lawyers, and alter the nature of their work.

In both cases, while the mystique, of the human experts may be lessened, their opportunity for exercising their specifically human powers may be increased. The general public might come to be less dependent on human experts than they are today. Reducing the power of professionals such as doctors, lawyers, and teachers would certainly have advantages. But replacing human professional advice by computer programs is dangerous to the extent that AI systems in public use are inadequate—and/or ill-understood. Systems that have taken several man-years to develop (and whose original programmers may be retired, or dead) are often very difficult to evaluate or alter, because even computer scientists do not fully understand how they work.

A second type of social impact concerns general social trends brought about by applications of AI and information technology (IT). These include changes in the proportion of the workforce in service and leisure industries, changes in the division of labour and sexual roles, and changes in general lifestyles and patterns of interaction.

But other potential consequences of AI point in the opposite direction. The widespread use of home terminals, for instance, threatens to have an isolating influence even more powerful than that of television. If people are encouraged to work, and to shop, from their sitting-rooms, there may be unfortunate psychological effects in terms of personal stress and loneliness. Community computer centres could offset these effects to some extent, providing a social meeting place outside the confines of the home and nuclear family.

Some writers even predict that commercially available (and highly profitable) AI systems will be heavily used not only in task-oriented ways, but as surrogates for human contact. On this view, the strong tendency to anthropomorphism that most of us share will result in patterns of interaction being skewed away from human beings, and towards quasi-human computer systems (with naturalistic, "voices," and sometimes even "bodies").

Long-range AI research

There will be "more of the same," in that the areas

mentioned above will provide perplexing problems for many years to come. Especially hard problems include learning, high-level vision, naive physics, and abstract work in computational logic.

For instance, expert systems are at present unable to "plain their reasoning except by "backwards-chaining": giving a resumé of the chain of inferences (rules) that led up to their conclusion. They cannot relate their conclusion to the domain in general, or rely on an overview of the problem to assess the relative theoretical reliability of different hypotheses.

Nor can they monitor and adjust the structure of their own problem-solving, for they have no high-level representation of it. They are unable, too, to integrate different knowledge domains, and to use concepts and patterns of inference taken from one domain to reason (analogically) in another. Nor can current systems explain their conclusions differently to different users, taking account of the specific user's knowledge.

The user can ask for a "deeper" explanation (a more detailed inference resumé), but the program has no user-model in terms of which to adjust its explanations to the human's particular range and level of knowledge. For this reason also, the pattern of interaction between user and system is at present very limited. The user cannot offer his own conclusions for comment and criticism, for example, as students can do with human teachers. A special case of human knowledge is "naive physics," one's everyday knowledge of the properties and behaviour of different sorts of physical substances, and the nature of the causal relations between them. This knowledge enters into vision and motor control, and also into natural language.

For example, a language-using program would have to understand the differences in meaning between verbs such as pour, flow, spill, drop, and the like if it were to give instructions or understand texts about activities dealing with liquids. Similarly, a robot capable of seeing that a container was just about to spill its contents onto the object below, and of adjusting its movements accordingly, would need some representation of the behaviour of fluids. Very little work has been done on these issues so far, and they are likely to provide a challenge for many years.

"Computer-aided design" is typically thought of as involving the graphical display of precise three-dimensional specifications of various products (from machine tools through cars to buildings), taking into account a wide range of values of many parameters. But a recent form of computer-aided design involves suggestion rather than specification, in the sense that the design program originates novel ideas—ideas that are not merely quantitatively different from previous specifications.

For example, heuristic programs are already being used to suggest novel experiments (described at the intramolecular level) in genetic engineering, or to help design new sorts of three-dimensional silicon chips. The potential of systems like these should be further explored. The computer modelling of creative thinking will require long-term research, especially with respect to domains whose crucial concepts cannot be so readily defined as the concepts of molecular biology, chip circuitry, or set theory. Machine learning is a pressing problem for the future. If a program cannot learn for itself, its development is limited by the time and ability of the programmer to provide it with new information and ideas.

9

E-commerce

Electronic Commerce is a rapidly growing research and development area of very high practical relevance. A major challenge in successfully designing EC applications is to identify existing building-block technologies and integrate them into a common application framework. The last decade has witnessed major efforts towards generalizing the functionality of transaction-based applications, and this has been one of the roots of today's workflow technology. Thus, an important objective and, to some extent, achievement of workflow technology is to reconcile rich specification languages for the control flow (and data flow) of complex, long-lived, often widely distributed, organizationally decentralized applications with the industrial-strength dependability features of transaction processing systems. To this- end, workflow technology does itself make intensive use of database systems and transaction services. Thus, we believe that workflow technology today provides the most mature and promising basis for becoming the backbone of EC applications.

A second overriding requirement of EC is the need for interoperability among largely autonomous, often heterogeneous subsystems. This can span a spectrum from widely established standard protocols between information servers all the way to "intelligent agents" that have capabilities for negotiation, sophisticated exception handling, etc. Again, we believe that the database and transaction technology has a fairly good success story in dealing with heterogeneity and interoperability issues. Thus, workflow technology inherits a number of these salient properties, and this is why it can integrate almost arbitrary application programs into a unifying execution framework. However, there are still major deficiencies in the interoperability between different workflow management systems. These need to be overcome to provide full-fledged support for enterprise-spanning applications including EC applications.

Initial ideas along these lines do exist, but more research is needed. It should be noted, in any case, that the highly structured, rigorous yet dynamically adjustable nature of workflows make them an excellent candidate for addressing the interoperability problems, as opposed to say a general-purpose, arbitrarily complex, distributed programming language such as Java.

We discuss the state of the art in workflow research and technology with regard to its applicability to and benefits for EC. We identify necessary extensions to workflow management systems to support EC, and sketch the research issues towards these extensions. The chapter is organized as follows: the next section discusses properties and requirements of workflows in the EC context. Then, we discuss contributions of workflow technology to address these requirements. For the sake of concreteness, we will occasionally refer to our own prototype system, Mentor, as an example for what state-of-the-art workflow management systems can do for EC.

Workflow technology aims to provide as much computer support as possible to the modelling, execution, supervision, and possibly reengineering of business processes. Such computer-supported processes are then referred to as workflows. It seems natural to consider EC as the glue between previously independently modelled business processes. Hence, it is beneficial to model major parts of EC applications also as workflows. Following this approach, we can identify several specific requirements that EC applications pose on workflow technology.

The probably most important requirement is *dependability,* which subsumes a reliable, fault tolerant, secure, and provably correct execution on a highly available platform. While these requirements are ubiquitous in mission-critical computer applications, there are a few key technologies that have achieved substantial progress towards these goals over the last three decades. In particular, database and transaction systems are the backbone of today's mission-critical commercial applications such as banking and insurance businesses, travel planning and booking, or financial trading.

Workflows that capture (major parts of) EC applications have specific properties. In the following, we denote such workflows as EC workflows for simplicity. In this section we discuss these specific properties of EC workflows and derive from them specific requirements on workflow management systems. The discussion is broken down into build-time issues that arise in the modelling and analysis of an EC workflow, and run-time issues that are relevant during the execution of EC workflows.

Build-time Issues

We can identify a number of specific properties of EC workflow specifications:

— The core part of EC workflows, which is typically

centered around the payment scheme (i.e., the sales phase), is rather static. So there is no need for supporting dynamic modifications of running workflows. On the contrary, this core part can be viewed as a specific protocol that has been agreed upon by all EC partners at one point, and thus must not be changed further on. In fact, it is highly desirable that certain properties of the payment protocol can be verified in a formal manner. This is only feasible for static workflows.

— Both the pre- and post-sales phases of EC workflows should, however, allow for flexibility at run-time. So a workflow model for these phases is more likely to be a skeleton that is dynamically enriched by introducing additional activities along with their control and data flow, and also possibly skipping parts of the prespecified workflow skeleton. The need for such improvisation is particularly evident in the pre-sales phase that includes filtering ads, bargaining, etc.

— In all phases, EC workflows involve multiple parties. In the pre-sales phase, there are rather loose interactions between customers and merchant. In the sales and post-sales phase, customer and merchant and banks or credit card companies are more tightly coupled. The coupling is based on standard interfaces, enabling the establishment of the sales and post-sales phases without complex negotiations.

The core part of EC workflows can be fully automated. So none of the underlying activities should require human intervention, other than simple typing of initial input parameters. In contrast to certain high-value workflows in banking (e.g., approval of company loans), for example, EC payment schemes rarely involve intellectual decision processes. Such automation is indeed an important factor in promoting EC as a mass opportunity.

From these properties we can directly derive the following requirements that EC workflows pose on the underlying workflow management systems:

— *Verifiability (Provable Correctness):* For the core part of an EC workflow, guaranteeing the correctness of the specification is of utmost importance. This involves proving both safety and liveness properties, examples being "the customer's credit card number is not shown to anybody other than the merchant's bank" and "money is eventually credited on the merchant's bank account", respectively. So, unless such critical properties are formally verified, an error-prone specification bears the risk of exposing confidential information or even losing money. Superficially, it may seem that the required correctness guarantees can also be given intellectually by "carefully looking at the specification", but it often turns out that such distributed payment protocols can raise a fairly large number of different exceptions all of which need to be handled correctly as well. Once the effect of multiple of these exception handling methods can interfere with each other or with the "mainstream" of the workflow, it is often extremely hard to capture all the resulting effects intellectually. Thus, automatic verification methods or at least support tools are called for. These should be able to deal with the complete control flow specification, including all exception handling, and also the data flow specification.

— *Composability of Building Blocks: As* we discussed above, the payment scheme itself, albeit constituting the core part, is only one phase of an entire EC workflow. Both the pre- and post-sales phases require much more flexibility, and may involve subworkflows that are provided and have been designed by different parties. Thus EC workflows are inherently heterogeneous in that independently designed workflows have to be composed into more comprehensive higher-level processes. The specification method must support this kind of composability in an easy-to-manage manner.

— *Interoperability:* Interaction between different parties involved in an EC workflow is required in all phases. However, the type of interaction differs, which requires different interfaces for interoperability. The loose coupling of customer and merchants in the pre-sales phase can be supported by a web-like interface, posing little requirements on specifications. As the customer has to face incomplete and outdated information anyway, the focus is on a fast access to information with low overhead, not on dependability. In the sales phase, the picture changes completely. As correctness and dependability are of utmost importance here, it must be possible to specify the corresponding interoperability protocols.

Run-time Issues

As for the run-time issues of EC workflows, we can again highlight certain properties. These are not exclusively specific for EC workflows, but they are of absolutely crucial importance in the EC area and play less of a role in most other application areas of workflow technology.

— EC workflows in-the-large usually involve several autonomous parties and would therefore often run in a truly distributed manner on several, possibly heterogeneous workflow management systems.

— The actual EC workflow will be accompanied or surrounded by state-of-the-art security protocols for encryption, authentication, digital signatures, etc. Without confidentiality or even anonymity and, especially, the guaranteed value of "cybercash" currencies, EC applications cannot be successfully established.

— EC workflows will ideally become mass operations: millions of customers initiating billions of workflows every month or even week, with heavy load peaks in certain popular time periods.

— Frequent failures and unavailability of EC workflow servers would immediately weaken the market position of the merchant (or the EC provider that acts on behalf of one or more merchants) and eventually result in significant financial losses.

From these properties we can infer the following execution-related requirements that EC workflows pose on the underlying workflow management systems:

— *Scalability:* The mass-business characteristics of EC workflows requires a high-throughput execution engine. Thus, load distribution across multiple workflow servers is necessary to ensure this kind of scalability.

— *Dependability:* This subsumes a number of technical requirements: fault tolerance, reliability, availability, and also security. The execution environment for EC workflows must be fault tolerant in that transient failures of system components (e.g., workflow servers) do not lead to incorrect behaviour of the workflow execution. Further, failures that hamper the progress of workflow executions should be very infrequent; that is, the overall execution should be highly reliable. This may already call for redundant components within the system, so that many failures can be completely masked. In addition, the few failures that cannot be completely masked should be repaired sufficiently fast, for example, by restarting system components based on logged data. The net effect should then be very high availability of the EC services: customers are satisfactorily served without noticeable delays with extremely high probability. Finally, security measures such as encryption must be well coordinated with the other system components to ensure the desired overall dependability.

— *Trackability*: Comprehensive traces of EC workflow instances must be available for documentation purposes and possibly also for data mining towards better marketing. This calls for an elaborate workflow history management component with powerful temporal querying. On the technical side, extremely reliable and long-lived archiving must be provided, too.

Workflow specifications serve as a basis for the largely automated execution of business processes. They are often derived from business process specifications by refining the business process specification into a more detailed and executable form. Automated and computer-assisted execution means that a workflow management system (*WfMS*) controls the processing of work steps, denoted as activities, within a workflow. Some activities may have a manual or intellectual part, to be performed by a human. But the workflow management system is in charge of determining the (partial) invocation order of these activities. In contrast to business process specifications, this requires a formal specification of control flow and data flow.

Build-Time Issues

The use of workflow management systems in different application areas has led to different approaches for specifying workflows. There exists a wide range of languages including script-based, net-based, rule-based, and logic-based languages. They differ widely in their expressiveness, formal foundations, and ease of use. Beyond the "pure" approaches that fit into the given categories, hybrid methods have also been proposed. Because of its designated role as an industry standard, the Workflow Process Definition Language (WPDL) of the Workflow Management Coalition is especially notable among these hybrid methods.

Provable Correctness

For specifying the sales phase of EC workflows, a high-level specification language with mathematically rigorous semantics is required, Its semantics must be sufficiently expressive for the complex protocols executed during the sales phase, Control flow as well as data flow must be captured in order to model all aspects which are relevant for the correctness of the EC workflow. On the other hand, the specification language should be simple enough to support automatic verification of workflow properties by means of verification tools.

The formalism of state charts and activity charts meets these demands. In the Mentor project, we have explored its use for workflows, and it seems that state and activity charts are gradually finding wider use and acceptance. They have been adopted for the behavioural dimension of the UML industry standard.

State and activity charts comprise two dual views of a specification. *Activities* reflect the functional decomposition of a system and denote the "active" components of a specification; they correspond directly to the activities of a workflow.

An *activity chart* specifies the data flow between activities, in the form of a directed graph with data items as arc annotations. *State charts* capture the behaviour of a system by specifying the control flow between activities. A state chart is essentially a finite state machine with a distinguished initial state and transitions driven by Event-Condition-Action rules (ECA rules). In the Mentor project, we have investigated the feasibility of verifying certain properties for workflows specified as state and activity charts. A prerequisite for the verification is the modelling of these properties in a formal language. For this purpose, variants of temporal logic are well established.

Temporal logic extends predicate logic by temporal operators. With these operators, invariants (both safety and liveness properties) can be modelled, such as: 'If p was true in the past, q will be true at some point in the future'. A temporal logic with an expressive power suitable for properties of workflows (according to our experience) is CTL *(Computation Tree Logic).*

Once the critical workflow properties are formally stated, they can be verified against the formal specification of the workflow. Two different approaches are possible here. The first approach is using theorem provers, which automatically verify that a given specification has the desired properties. However, in many cases this approach is computationally infeasible. As a less powerful, but much more efficient approach, model checking can be used. In essence, *model checking* verifies whether a given finite state automaton (the workflow specification) is a model of a given temporal logic formula. The most efficient variant of model checking is known as symbolic model checking. Symbolic model checking is based on a compact, symbolic representation of a finite state automaton in terms of an *ordered binary decision diagram (OBDD).* Because state charts are closely related to finite state automatons, model checking can be applied to state charts. Tools for symbolic model checking already exist (at least as research prototypes) and are used mainly in hardware design and for reactive embedded systems. In the Mentor project we have used a tool for symbolic model checking described in. Although the resource requirements were high, we found symbolic model checking to be suitable even for the interactive verification of workflow specifications of non-trivial size.

As EC workflows involve multiple parties with already existing business processes, the specification language has to provide means for combining existing workflows into higher-level specifications that provide more comprehensive EC support.

Starting with a skeleton workflow, e.g., only specifying the existence of the sequence of pre-sales, sales, and post-sales phase, workflow composition can be used to dynamically refine the workflow, even during execution. The mechanism of nested states, i.e., substituting states by entire state charts provides this composability for state and activity charts. The semantics is that upon entering the higher-level state, the initial state of the embedded lower-level state chart is automatically entered, and upon leaving the higher-level state all embedded lower-level states are left. In addition to the composability of workflow specifications, EC workflows need a flexible exception handling. Exception handling code should not be sprinkled throughout the specification.

Otherwise, the specification can easily become unmanageable. In state and activity charts, orthogonal components provide a convenient means for incorporating exception handling in an easy and clear (i.e., truly orthogonal) manner. Orthogonal components denote the parallel execution of two state charts that are embedded in the same higher-level state.

Both components enter their initial states simultaneously, and the transitions in the two components proceed in parallel, subject to the preconditions for a transition to fire. Using this concept, an execution handling for a "watchdog" component would simply stay in its initial state until a certain condition becomes true or a certain event is raised.

Run-time Issues

The run-time requirements for EC workflows stated previously are quite similar to those for current business workflows in large enterprises. Workflow management systems supporting such workflows or even workflows that span several enterprises also have to face scalability, dependability and trackability problems.

At the merchant's and at the bank's or credit card company's site, a large number of EC subworkflows have to be executed concurrently. This is usually not the case at the customer's sites, as a customer will typically be involved only in the purchase of a small number of items at a time. However, this does not mean that the issue of scalability is limited to the merchant and the bank or credit card company. In fact, the need for scalability may arise in three different forms:

1. *Upward scalability is* needed mostly from a throughput perspective, that is, to cope with larger numbers of workflow instances simultaneously while still guaranteeing acceptable response times. This is the kind of scalability required for the merchant and the bank or credit card company. Upward scalability is usually achieved by using distributed, multi-server workflow management systems.

2. *Downward scalability is* desirable towards the lower end of performance demands in environments with scarce resources, the goal being a light-weight workflow management system with a small footprint. As a customer is typically involved only in a limited number of EC workflows at a time, and rarely uses advanced functionality like analysing the history of a workflow, light-weight and tailorable workflow management systems are the systems of choice at the customer's site.

3. *Sideward (or horizontal) scalability* aims at a high degree of interoperability with other workflow management systems. This is of crucial importance for EC workflows.

In all phases, EC workflows involve multiple parties, which will typically use different workflow management systems. The Workflow Management Coalition (WfMC) has proposed a standard interoperability interface for workflow management systems. However, this interface is currently in a proposal stage. It remains open how suitable it is for EC workflows.

Dependability

The sales phase of EC workflows requires a highly dependable execution platform. This subsumes the following issues:

1. *Fault tolerance:* In a fault tolerant execution, system failures do not harm the correctness of workflow execution. When a failure occurs, the system is rolled back to the most recent consistent state. Workflow execution can then be resumed from this state. In data systems, fault tolerance is achieved by atomic transactions. Workflows are typically more complex, consist of more activities and are of longer duration than database transactions. Workflows are

usually executed as sequences of short transactions. In case of distributed workflows, distributed transactions are required. Middleware services like T? monitors or OTS transaction services are used for controlling the execution of distributed transactions, also in case multiple different database systems are involved. Reliable message queues provide the "glue" between transactions implementing the steps of a workflow. Their usage guarantees that after a transaction has successfully finished, the next transaction is eventually started.

2. *Reliability:* In reliable systems, failures must be infrequent. Obviously, this requires well designed and rigorously tested software, running on reliable hardware platforms. Workflow management systems rely on database management systems as one of their core components, which have proven to be among the most reliable software products. In addition, redundancy can be used to increase reliablity. For example, a failed server process can be dynamically replaced by a "standby" process that has access to the underlying persistent data (i.e., a database and/or a log file) which may again be replicated if necessary. This way, even less reliable components can be used in a system with high reliability demands.

3. *Availability:* Highly available systems ensure that users find the system operational with very high probability. This can be achieved by ensuring that complete system failures are sufficiently infrequent and by providing very fast recovery and restart after such failures. In addition to very low system downtimes, a workflow should almost never be delayed in a user-noticeable manner-Redundant workflow servers are again an appropriate means to increase availability. For less demanding worknows,

for example in the pre-sales phase of EC workflows, simpler modes with lower or no redundancy should be supported to improve the cost/performance ratio of the overall system. Such a configurable approach has been studied in the Exotica project as an extension to IBM's Flowmark.

4. *Security*: EC workflows probably have the highest demands on security among all classes of workflow applications. Up to now, this issue has only received limited attention in the workflow community. Hiding confidential workflow data from unauthorized third parties can be achieved by using encryption protocols. In addition, specific secure payment and negotiation protocols have to be implemented, for example, as a special high-security class of workflows.

In all environments where non-trivial amounts of money are handled, trackability is a major requirement. The need for archiving the history of workflows is already considered a major requirement in many workflow management systems, because the history can also be used to improve the underlying business process model, e.g. by determining workflow steps that frequently miss their deadlines, involve more resources as expected, etc. Improving the overall workflow is typically based on aggregated, statistical data, whereas tracking EC workflows requires detailed data on a per instance basis. Workflow management systems can provide the necessary archiving service for this purpose as well.

Research demands on workflow technology

The previous sections have shown that using workflow technology in EC applications is promising and already solves many of the encountered problems. However, substantial further research is needed to solve problems that are not yet addressed by workflow technology and arise in the new application environment of EC.

Dynamics

The need for dynamic adaptation of workflows has already been recognized independently of EC. For example, in medical applications, the treatment of patients can usually not be determined in advance. Instead, the corresponding workflow has to be constantly adapted to new diagnostic results. The current generation of workflow management systems still provides only primitive support for such dynamics. Systems supporting modifications of control flow and data flow at runtime are often weak in other respects such as administration, correctness of execution, reliability, scalability, and security.

EC workflows involve multiple, autonomous parties. Thus, interoperability is crucial. A specific kind of interoperability has already been addressed by most workflow management systems, as they have to provide access to arbitrarily heterogeneous applications. This is achieved through the wrapper/mediator paradigm, that is, encapsulating the actual application, surrounding it with a standard-compliant interface, and invoking applications through a broker service (the mediator in this case). Usually appropriate middleware such as CORBA or DCOM is employed. Only little work has been done, however, on the interoperability between different workflow management systems. In this regard, EC workflows have higher demands than most other workflow applications, since EC involves multiple, autonomous parties by definition.

The most promising approach to address the interoperability between different workflow management systems seems to be again a wrapper/mediator architecture, where each system is encapsulated and enriched by a common language for process definition, state introspection, and manipulation. Once such a common language were established, different systems could communicate in a straightforward manner, possibly again through some "broker" or "mediator, services. More research is needed along these lines.

Security issues have to be addressed jointly with the security research community. The challenge is to integrate security protocols into workflow management systems in a seamless yet easily maintainable manner. This is not a straightforward task, as multiple components of workflow management systems such as communication managers and history managers are involved. Modifying these components accordingly may conflict with existing solutions for scalability and availability. In addition, different levels of security have to be supported in order to execute, for example, information gathering workflows in the pre-sales phase as inexpensively as possible. If different security levels are used in different phases of an EC workflow, we have to make sure that the security of the critical workflow parts is not compromised by parts executed at low security levels or by transition problems between security levels.

Electronic commerce (EC) can be regarded as a specific kind of business process involving several enterprises. As workflow management systems have been developed to implement such business processes, EC can largely benefit from current workflow technology. In particular, the core of electronic commerce, sales and money-handling transactions, can be modelled as special kinds of workflows. We have identified the main requirements that EC poses on workflow management systems. Pre-sales and post-sales phases of EC workflows require highly flexible, light-weight workflow management, whereas the core sales phase including money transfer has to be executed in a highly fault tolerant, reliable, and secure manner on a highly available system.

10

Internet Marketing

The Marketing activities, concepts and strategies are bound to change due to changing situations and environment. Since 1985 a competitive, customer driven economy has been emerging in India. The abolition of Licensing and liberalisation of market entry regulations since July 1991 has further added impetus to this process. It has been given the final shape by the formation of WTO at markesh. Most of the people and the industrialists have felt that whether a company wants to go for global competition or not, in the present liberalised situation the global competition will arrive at their door step. By endorsing the final act of the Uruguay Round the developed world has in effect endorsed free trade in a multilateral setting a phenomenon that will work to the advantage of developing countries that need new markets. Countries like India will get an opportunity through W.T.O. to negotiate better deal for itself. This can be possible only when the quality and standard of the products is improved. The policy of liberalisation has created a situation in which companies like Uniliver, Glaxo, Pepsi, Whirlpool, Phillips have increased their stake of equity. New products new brands and new formulations are being announced virtually every week, mergers and acquisitions like Brook-Bond-Lipton designed to build competitive fortress have become more common. "Down Seizing" restructuring and engineering are the words that have potent force for emboldened executives. Thus the whole market environments has under gone a severe change. India has become one of the largest emerging markets attracting substantial flows of equity investment and also consumer goods. It focuses that there are challenges of improved products of advanced nations on the one hand and on the other hand if the executives have vision foresite and creativity there can be enough opportunity for domestic products both in India and in other emerging markets.

The first challenge by opening up the Indian market is of survival of Indian companies and Indian brands. Brand here understand should be considered as a brand created for the Indian market and owned by a company of Indian origin. Brand building is directly related to the scale of business. Indian companies like Lakme or Nirma do not have financial boost or technology like Hindustan Lever or Colgate Palmolive. It has been the experience in the past that whichever country has permitted multinational companies to enter their market their Local brands have been wiped away. Indian brands cannot have a different situation. Though Swaminathan, S. Anklesaria Aiyar editor of the Economic times feels 'A very large number of low and consumers have never heard of foreign brands and are not hungering for them". The magic of the foreign brands cannot be denied. A section of new middle class definitely runs after them. If the foreign brands in the long run become Indian or perceived as Indian like Lux, Surf, then the matter is different but a Coake will always remain foreign. What attracts the consumer towards the foreign brands produced by multinational companies (MNC) is firstly the quality and secondly the status symbol and a new way of life.

The survival of the Indian brands will depend not only on brand, but on product, the company backing it, and the people who run that company. Each of these factor determines the state and future of the brand. For example Amul has been promoted so consistently that no MNC will easily shake its grip on Rs. 160/- crores butter market. However, majority of Indian companies do not invest consistently and also adequate amount, they want quick harvest. Those Indian brands will survive which have a very clear positioning. Brands which depend not only on the advertising buck but on the entire gamut of brand building activities and what the consumer perceives as the value delivery. The technology difference wont be as important as the speed of action, the right package at the right price, the right upgradation at the right time. The products in which aesthetic function is more valuable than the physical attributes will face sever problem of survival. One may recall that recently American consumers forum has protested on the import of Indian Shiffon Skirts and the USA government has issued notification to stop their imports.

Another important issue related to survival of Indian brands is that there is lack of commitment to product quality in the Indian producers. What is important is that the product should meet the consumer need. You may recall that when American Cars were best those who could afford bought them. To day when Japanese cars are the best every one wants to buy them. This is the function of quality not of origin or of brand alone. Indian brands have been isolated of 40-50 years therefore the product quality does not stack up to international standards. In fact, branding is a process for adding distinctiveness to products or service which offer the consumer quality, value and satisfaction. Apart from Superior Quality what foreignness also signals is status and a new way of life. The producers will have to take care of this need. If they do not look after their consumers need some body else will take care for their need. By 2000 A.D. If the Indian producers do not realise these facts, they will face serious threat of loosing the market. In the liberalised economy a market once won can not remain for ever for a particular company or product unless the company is continuously engaged in innovation of Technology and products as per need of the consumers.

Another important challenge is from the technology side because people look for a product that has a good image and is backed by good technology. It is believed that the multi-nationals have better technology to back their products. Indian producers have always imported technology and have never made any attempt to Indianise them improve upon them and have a better technology of their own. Technology imports have been costlier and will definitely increase the cost of production. To meet the challenges posed by the multi-nationals it is essential that the Indian producers should also use better technology. Bajaj is on example inspite of the fact that Bajaj entered in business of two wheelers with the imported technology, they have Indianised it and they have also continuously made effort to improve the technology and improve the product. The Bajaj Scooter is one of the quality product backed by a better technology. No multinationals can make Bajaj to loose its market. If a company has invested in technology and in quality of its product it will survive like Bajaj & VIP Luggage because they have ensured that the product lives up to promise that they have made. Hence, the Indian producers have to up grade, update, renovate and improve their technology to have quality product which can match the forcing products and meet the consumers need both in domestic and foreign markets. This will definitely depend upon a company's access to the technology, if it can buy the technology it is better if not will be compelled to enter into joint ventures or alliance with foreign companies to have access to technology. Only having the technology is not enough. There is need to invest in technology improvement and continuous upgradation of technology. Technology and its development has become one of the essentials of economic development. We are aware that only one company of Japan invests an amount in R&D of technology which has been equal to the total amount of investment in R&D in India.

The opening of Indian market for world producers and the market of other countries for Indian producers will have any meaning only when the Indian producers have any product backed by a good technology and superior in quality to match the competitors product. Hence Indian producers need continuous innovation and investment in innovation to survive.

Everyone, who is a student of marketing might have found that in Indian market premium brands are flooding the market to block the entry of the products of MNCs several premium brands in the last two or three years have been priced up to 10 times higher than the popular brands. This is based on the idea that as incomes of middle class increase there will be demand for products which may have distinction and life style. Thus, the premium brands of Indian producers will pose a challenge to the other products. The premium brand producers are happy as they quote the survey report of National council of Applied Economic Research that "there are 6,5 million middle class house holds earning over Rs. 18,000 per annum out of which 3.7 million earn over Rs. 78,000 per annum. One million house holds earn more than Rs. 1 lakh a year "In 1993 the purchasing power of average Indian had been equivalent to $ 1,150 (Rs. 35,650) per year. Thus, they have been guessing about the market of premium brands good among these "Maruti Millions" or the status seekers. A host of products like Lacoste's shirt priced for Rs. 750/-, Park Avenue shoes for Rs. 1600 and so on will meet the demand of the new status seeker middle class consumers. It is true that only a minscule of Indian populations will buy. These products will have a core group of buyers and large number of floating buyers. Thus the premium brand products are posing challenge to other products. Let us call it Intra-country competition. The challenges will be compounded because the consumers may buy the usual brand and also the premium brands for occasional use leading to low frequency of repeat purchase of premium brands, secondly the fast moving consumer goods consumers will float not only between brands in a product category but also between the categories themselves. Hence even the producers of premium brands will have to face problems in selling their products. Lastly the introduction of intellectual copy right will be introduced by 2000 hence the imitation of product will be beaten down and out. The premium products producers will have to adjust to the socio-economic conditions of the country and produce products for higher price which will give value to consumers for the money paid.

Thus the changing economic scenario opening up the Indian market for the global producers has definitely forced the domestic produces to adopt a new production strategy and a new marketing technique. The change definitely throws some challenges but it provides some opportunities also.

The Liberalisation of Indian economy and going for global and entering into an agreement to be a member of World Trade Organisations, India will now have an Institution—WTO, to negotiate better deal for itself through discussion and creating concencions among the contacting parties. As Mudra's Krishnamurthy puts "the globalisation of the Indian market need to be seen as an opportunity to become MNC, not as a problem "Building competitive advantage through exposure to international markets should be a conscious strategy. Companies from countries like Japan and south Korea have learnt from the West and then successfully marketed world class brands globally. The Chief Executive of a Japanese car manufacturing company which was established with the help of Technological assistance of General Motars after fifteen years visited General Motors on return he called, his executives meeting and told them that they can go for World Market now. His executives expressed doubts. They were sent to visit General Motors and on return they confessed that they have improved over General Motors and can easily compete in the World Market. Now Japanese cars are in American market and in European Marketing competing successfully and in some cases sharing major portion of automobile market. Japan had imported Technology for Watch manufacturing from Switzerland. It is Japan which added day and dates music and varieties of alarm sounds and finally automatic and quartz and captured major shave of world watch market. Indian producers will have to learn from Japanese experience to avail the opportunity of going in foreign market. Clarity of thinking and a single mined focused strategy on improved Technology and Superior Products are key to realise the potentials and avail them. In fact the policy of globalisation has been adopted with an idea to make Indian producers competitive globally. Hence the opportunity for Indian companies to become efficient MNCs has been provided by this situation.

Mr. Balkrishna Zutshi Indian representative at WTO expressed that the changes in economic policy and signing of agreement with WTO provides access to global market. There is tremendous opportunity for India to integrate itself with the Global market. It is now upto Indian industries and to some extent the government, to adopt the right policy to exploit the countries potential in the world market and to improve its export in different areas.

One of the new are for achieving some share in world market is the service sector. In the recent agreement some concessions have been provided for the export of services. They form a good basis for further development. This particular area which can interest India, the movement of natural persons as service provider has tremendous opportunity. Further we can increase our exports in textiles, but we have to modernise our textile industry in next ten years. The export of textile will pick up.

India has great potential in agricultural sector. The government can subsidies upto 10% of the value of production on fertilizer water, pesticides, seeds and electricity. It can help in improvement of quality and quantity of product. India can export rice and other agricultural products to Japan and Korea upto 4% of their demand.

The probability of export of agricultural produce has increased, exports of spices has great potential. India exported 1,50,000 tonnes of spices totaling worth Rs. 500 crores last year 1993-94[10]. Following table will show the upswing in Indian Exports in general and Agro-products in Particular:

Table -I

India's Export an upswing (Rs. in Crore)

YEAR	VALUE
1990-91	53,350
1991-92	69,546

1992-93	53,648
1993-94	72,886
1994-95	74,766
1995-96	75,826

Table - II

Export of Agro Products (in $ Million)

Particulars	1991-92	1992-93	1993-94	1995-96
Spices	150	127	160	176
Cereals	356	342	370	410
Oil Cakes	399	574	555	575
Vegetable & Processed Food	375	349	455	525
Sugar	165	112	176	216

Cashewnuts, tobacco, cereals processed food, Sugar & Tea can have greater potential for increased exports. The quality, size of packing and value addition is the need. If a group of exporters who are quality conscious who can keep pace with international changes and bring in technology make efforts may open opportunity for growth of exports.

There is another area where Indian producers can think of entering into global market, the ready made garments. The Gokal Das Exports have been exporting shirts, to Europe, Australia, middle east Singapore, U.S.A., Canada and are regular supplier to Levi Straus and Warnglar. Even while international brand names like Pierre Cardin, Benetton, Van-Heusen Lacosta ad Arrow are making inrodes in domestic market Indian companies are betting into high technologies to tap emerging global opportunities. Indian companies have no choice but to invest heavily in developing exclusive brands and entering into non cotton fabrics. However, India can be a potential exporter in this area. There is enough scope of exports of shoes and other Leather garments. Liberty shoes and Namaste Exports have shown the way. Korean Leather garments have become costly and European markets have started opening up mainly due to the closure of tanneries there. The scope of export of leather products has increased. According to study conducted by the federations of Indian Export organisation "Indian exports are extremely competitive in special are like leather, garments, handloom, jewellery and engineering goods where it is much easier to adopt to changing trends of a foreigning buyer who suddenly asks for a different auto components, or a different fashion of handloom cloth or leather garments it is much easy for a small producer to change his production process. The only need is to understand the consumer need, improve the quality of the product and add value through packaging and design. The competitive edge can be added by adopting and innovating required technology and a marketing strategy for the changing situation.

Issues

One can now clearly feel that the issues in marketing in 2000 AD are, to understand the consumer needs and anticipate their expectations whether they are in domestic market or in other countries market. In fact in an ACME Seminar of Top executives the conscientious has been that all the successful brands have designed and developed products on the basis of the anticipation of consumers needs and expectations. The second important issue which was emphasised at the seminar by these executives was the need of being "unique", innovative", "Positioning and therefore becoming competitive, whether they were "offering" themselves or the way they were presented and communicated to any prospective buyer. Thirdly the executives of the companies of successful brands have confessed that the secret of the success of their company has been the product itself rather than any other marketing technique or imputes such as salesforce, advertising, promotion, quality of over all managements etc.

It one examines, a few domestic products of wholly Indian companies one may be able to bring home the important issues of marketing for 2000 AD, such as Nirma (Popular priced washing power) Titan watches, Onida (TV), Videocon Washing machine and Maruti Cars, Maggi Noodles, and "Close Up" Tooth paste each one of them presents some significant break through in terms of product development and market process.

Nirma, the most often quoted brand in almost any marketing forum in the past ten years entered with almost no backing or background in consumer marketing, in a period of five years, emerged as the greatest competitive threat ever faced by Unilever's flagship company in India, Hindustan Lever. Ignored by all those in the detergent market for nearly five years as being not in our segment, not our kind of product, this brand launched at almost third of the unit price of Unilever's Surf grew explosively almost ten fold in a ten years period overtook everyone else i the process. Titan a company launched by Tata India's largest private sector entrepreneurial group repositioned the watch and especially the Indian made watch in the eyes of the consumer, and made it into a stylish personal accessory to both men and women. In just four years, it grew to 2.6 million watches and No. 1 in the quartz segment and No. 2 overall, behind the much older and slower, HMT, it also rewrote the 'rule book' of conventional wisdom in watch marketing, that the best watches are imported (legally or illegally).

Some of them created new segments in the market and new usages and users. You may recall Ketchup, for example had long been thought of and used as an essentially western product, which could not easily be blended with Indian cuisine. Maggi by Nestle not only introduced alternatives to the tomato sauce, which has generally too blend for the discerning India plate, but showed it in association with a number of essentially Indian snacks such as samosa and vada. An even greater innovation was the 2 minute noodle. Long known both in Europe and the Far East as a meal by itself, the noodle could not be expected to replace rice or the home made forms of wheat such as pooris and chappatis. However, interestingly presented and positioned as an afternoon, after school snack, it caught the imagination of children and mother to become an almost unique product that virtually owned the territory it developed.

A few of them took competitive standards several noiches higher, for example; The Maruti small car (800 cc) gave the Indian motorist a stylish, maneuverable and modern alternative with a compact design. Of course, the fact that the technology was several decades ahead of the Fiat and Morries oxford versions (Premier Padmini and Hindustan Ambassador), ensured that it virtually had no competition. The Maruti 1000 which followed in the late 80's had an almost unique position as "Japanese quality premium personal car. The latest offering is the Maruti Zen, the first Indian car to incorporate the jelly bean shape and rounded edges, to reduce wind resistance and increase fuel economy, along with five speed transmission all with the full impact of Suzuki of Japan now the majority owner of this company. Three out of every four cars sold in India, now come from Maruti. In the home appliances field little known Videocon emerged in a period of 4 years as the major share leader with 27% of the colour TVs market and 50% of the washing machines market. They flooded the market with Japanese style product introduction rate, concentrating on wooing the dealers with substantially higher margins and array of incentives and beating the competition on price. In this last aspect, they had much in common with Nirma in the detergent market and Hero in bicycles and mopeds. For India's largest and most successful consumer product company, Hindustan Lever,, "Close Up", brought success at last to the personal products division in the enternal battle against Colgate in the toothpaste market. Relaunched as a gel with variants it attained a 15% market share. Only two of the above brands "Maggi" and "Close Up" are owned and marketed by multi national affiliates in India. All the others are not only from wholly owned Indian companies but in many cases from entrepreneurial first generation business group. Neither the Dhoots of Videocon nor Mr. Patel of Nirma started with any accumulated experience in a related industry. Nor did they have the warchests from promotional onslaught which a coke, a pepsi or a Proctor & Gamble would subsequently bring to the Indian Scene. The above examples of products and their marketing way clearly gives any one to understand that being multinational per se cut no ICE with Indian consumers that sheer power of resources is not a pre requisite for success and competitive edge; That what is important for being competitive in the future is to be innovative in product as per need and expectations of the consumer and therefore, there is urgency of improving the product and service quality standard; finally that innovation will have to be applied to every segment of business, retailing, general management quality structure and even financing over and above this speed through which it is implemented.

The success of the five brands mentioned above proves that there is the need to understand consumer behaviour in the Indian context and to change the approach of strategic marketing. That to succeed in any competition market whether domestic or global the application of the same approach applied prior to 91 will not be effective. What ever may be the individual ingredients of success strategic style or approach must concentrate on rewriting the 'rule book'. In earlier decades the dictum was that marketing orientation meant not only doing things differently (the USP School) but better and more memorably (as emphasised by David Ogilvy and Ries and Trout in the brand personality and its positioning eras). To day beyond just being different or better thinking about the market and conceiving the future differently from once predecess, seems to be at the core of successful strategic marketing. The core & key factor in the above five brands has been innovation to meet the future opportunities and understanding the needs of the consumers also has a high position. Innovation should not be taken as more and more intensive and extensive research in the status quo of consumer; No amount of quantitative analysis of consumer motivation or market segment on quantification can be said to be real alternative of innovation.

Innovation; therefore, seems to come more from internal thinking daring and sevendipity than analysing the industry in two by two matrix in mind numbering detail.

Very recently the executives have started talking about the fifth 'P' The pace with which you adopt a & improve a product launch and relaunch a product use a technology how speedily your plans implement any strategy is more important . Now they feel the fifth P only can form the base of new marketing strategy.

I wish to point out at this stage that student and teachers of marketing should develop a technic of marketing forecast to foresee or have understanding and perception of what marketing in India in 2000 AD and after would demand of them. We find that the need to understand consumer behaviour in the India's context leads the rest of things behind Assessing the relative effectiveness of different forms of marketing inputs on a cost benefit equation. Conventionally marketers have always tended to think of most marketing inputs other than the soft area of Advertising as fairly measurable in terms of sales response. Every company has its own rules of thumb developed over the year from their own or their international affiliates based on experiences on how much is desirable to spend on promotion distributions, product launched, or percentage of sales required to sustain market shares of stable on going brands, and so on. In the changed situation the question obviously is whether the old rule will be valid in changing context and how far such rules will apply in the changed situation. Here then is a rich area for constructive and continuous collaboration in research between the thinking manager and the user-friendly academics.

Strategic Marketing is a dynamic concept and it is still under evolution. In India situations have been changing, liberalisation policy, opening up of Indian market for multi-nationals, and the Government vacating the board rooms, the customer being ushered in effect being given a place of pride, has brought changes in Economic environment. It has posed three major challenges. Increasingly competitive market with new entrants providing Superior product and service, a subsequent change in most industries from a seller market to buyers market with quality and price conscious consumers; and necessity to succeed in globalisation economy by exploiting potential sales market.

Marketing even in a global situation is a process of perceiving, understanding, stimulating and satisfying the needs of specially selected target market by channelling an organisation resources to meet those needs. Marketing is thus matching dynamic inter relationship between a company's products and services, the consumers want and needs and the activities of competitors.

Peter F Druker has also mentioned that old system of marketing cannot be useful today. He said "But the right marketing knowledge won't be of much help in this turbulent, competitive fast changing decades. It requires the right marketing actions. Japanese define market by the use of their product. The customer rather than the makers determine the market and Japan became a forceful competitor in the global market of automobiles, T.V. etc.

Hence even in India most of the Chief Executives have now been focusing on developing consumer oriented marketing strategies and brands. One is reminded of Peter F Drukers view "Marketing is business seen from the view of the final result, that is, customer point of view". The advocates of this view have been now talking of customerisation. There is another approach also for competitive strategy. As in a competitive market there is fight between the rivals in every retail shop for each customer bot from domestic and international producers some executives feel watching the rivals move only can help in developing a competitive strategy. Wayne-Calloway has pointed out "Nothing focuses your mind better than the sight of a rival who wants to wipe you off the face of the earth". Can Druker and Calloway both be correct? Can the classical marketing which involves studying the consumer alone be a tool for successful marketing in the liberalised market?

There is a battle for the market, every marketer is trying to retain orgain market. Hence in their own way they are adopting various strategies. It is now time for Indian producers to think new about their strategy, the way they conduct their business. The Indian marketing has come to an age. In 90s the marketers often seen as intent on getting each other as they are on getting consumers. Some ten years ago there was hardly any competition.

Each market was dominated by one producer. In some fast moving consumer goods there was some kind of an armed truce rival marketers kept themselves out of one another way. By the late 80s the stream of new brand launch and flood of MNC products has gathered force. And the flood gate opened after 1991 upset the whole statusquo. Each year an established brand had to deal with many new factors that could affect its fortune.

Though in a number of seminars executives have emphasised that firstly the basis of success is the product and its quality rather than any other marketing input, secondly the executives have emphasised the improved Technology as the basis of the successful strategy of marketing and quote the success of a few Indian Products e.g. Bajaj and Maruti. The continuous improvement and updating of technology by Bajaj has proved, "Nothing can beat Bajaj" and the continuous change in technology has made maruti as one of the most desired car and now it occupies a place of pride. Out of every four Cars sold today in Indian market three are the Maruti Cars—The product and technology has placed products in a unique situation and made them competitive whether they were the offering themselves or the way they were communicated to any prospective buyer. Thirdly executives have been quoting the strategy of distribution adopted by Videocon washing machine as the key of success of the product in occupying 50% share of the Washing Machine market. The most successful products; Nirma, Titan, Maruti, Maggi, Videocon washing machine and 'Close Up' have been quoted to prove that product, Technology, Price, the process of offering the products and understanding the need of consumer have been the cause of their success. Fourthly the executives have expressed that the product innovation and the technology innovation have been to satisfy the consumer. One cannot deny these facts.

Now it is no longer limited to watch the consumers only it is also essential to watch your rivals. Today marketing has become a battle of perception and not just a product which explains why competitive marketing is gaining ground in the over all strategic process. The product innovation or technology adoption may be one aspect but not as important as 'Watching your rival' and 'the speed of Action' the right package at the right price, the right upgradation at the right time. Hence in a competitive marketing 'Watching the Rivals' and the 'pace' with which you react are two strategies seem to be important and have been deliberated here in this paper.

Watching the Rivals: Now it is not enough to watch the consumer only it is essential to watch your rivals. Product differentiation is lowering its sharpness hence watching the action of rivals about distribution and such other things have become crucial, and the 'Pace' of marketing is quick really quick, like combatants in power tennis, marketers have to anticipate where the opponent will place the ball. Trying to get it after the ball has been struck is too late.

Intense competition has forced the companies to be more specific in watching their rivals. Now companies try to have resource audit, interfirm comparison, checking rivals financial cos-price analysis, profit margins, man power cost, in fact everything under the microscope. The route to consumer is always through competition. Since rivals are targeting the same consumers, marketers must anticipate possible retailiation in the execution of their own strategy.

By watching the rivals offerings you will ensure that you have not missed out something that may affect sales. For example; If Bajaj Auto would have reacted earlier to ailing LML attempts to fragment the Scooter market by LML, might have been unable to 'turn it round' and share some market of Scooter from Bajaj. There is another more vivid example of not watching the rival and facing a disastrous consequence by 'Farex' of Glaxo when Nestles baby food Cerelac cam. Cerelac being milk based was preferred by doctors and mothers, Cerelac offered a range of variants. Cerelac was preferred because milk shortage can be managed. Doctors recommended ceralac because if Farex upsets the baby's stomach it was difficult to identify which cereal has caused, and ceralac offered a range of variants. There are other examples of not watch in the rivals such as; 20 year ago milton appeared, by continuous Innovation, Segmentation and sub segmentation of market Milton has acquired the position of No. 1, in Rs. 250 crore, thermo ware market. In 1986 Cello joined, is now no. 2, Eagle lost the market of thermoware, except flask to Milton and Cello.

We have example of BPL which anticipated the arrival of Global brand and quickly expanded its consumers electronic range to cover a wide spread size and price segments and block as many entry points of MNCs as possible. Another example is of the Proctor and Gambles which in August '95 quickly flooded the Bombay market with its 'Paper Brand' of daipers to pre empt the launch of Kiberly Clark Huggies marketed in India by Kimberly Clark Lever Ltd. by watching its rival and by acting quickly, really quickly Proctor and

Gambles threw its rival marketer off its strides. If you are not watching rivals you are doing only half the marketing.

Unfortunately in India it is still informal, not data-based. 'Indian Companies are still like babies—tend to fiddle with their navels, instead of studying the external environment; rivals move rather than theirs. In fact any strategy cannot be made in isolation of environment, existing market situation. Broadly speaking a marketer has to monitor three 'Cs' Consumer, Competition, Cost. In responding the competition the company's cost can be affected and in turn influences company's try to damage the competition example is of 'Times of India' Changing its advertising rates every time. In fact extensive attention by a rival-specially if it is a larger one can Unnerve the marketers example of Standard Batteries Ltd. coming with 'Signature' and two years guarantee unnerved the Exide. The Exide people were in so much hurry that they did not even change the warranty card and directed the wholesale and retail outlets to issue two year warranty. When standard introduced Calci charge, a maintenance free battery, Exide tracked its performance for four months and it brought its new product, 'Exide Freedom' for Rs. 200 below calcicharge. Exide is compelled to scrutinise standard's activity. When Jhonson and Jhonson was planning to relaunch SAVALON an antiseptic liquid brand bought from ICI. Dettol felt its monopoly threatened. It's marketer RCI created a media blitz and launched Dettol medicated plaster which coincided with savalon's launch. The strategic objective was to heightened brand salience for dettol while forcing Jhonson & Jhonson to splurr for defending its leader Band Aid.

However rival watching is a complex phenomena. Number of parameters on which they have to be watched have grown. Rivals have to be watched and their move is to be anticipated well in advance. Rivals have to be watched cautiously and properly other wise many a times marketers end up in watching the wrong kind of competition. In any case quality product and improved technology alone can not help the marketer in a competitive market. Watching the rivals is very essential. Further watching the rivals may be important; but the product attribute the technology difference and rival watch wont be as important as the 'Speed of Action' - the right package at right price, the right upgradation at the right time, and the right action to put the right blockade for the rivals at a right moment i.e. the pace strategy.

Pace Strategy: The fundamental four 'Ps' have been found insufficient for developing any marketing plan & marketing strategies in the changing competitive market. The smart and intelligent executives have discovered that 'PACE' is another strategum by which they can have an advantageous position in the competitive, crowded market created by the policy of liberalisation.

In their opinion 'Pace' or Speed is the many edged weapon to be used on all fronts; whether product innovation, Technology up gradation, Promotion or pushing the product in the market. "Every marketing man can match the four Ps of marketing. But the ultimate differentiator is the speed to market".

This was never realised by corporate sector in India before liberalisation and globalisation of Indian market they were contended with sporadic launches of products. A company like Hindustan Lever had never relaunched its product untill four years after its introduction knowing that it would milk its money making potential. With the open economy and open market, traditional tools have lost their significance. All marketers are trying to adopt 'Pace strategy' to protect their market share

Speed strategy is being recognised as the important element in a competitive market of next millennium specially because it is becoming easier for corporate sector to catch upon other fronts . Peter F-Druker has also mentioned that the winner in competitive world economy is going to be the firm that most effectively shortens the product life of its own product that is the which organises most systematic abandonment of its product. It must be done quickly without loosing any opportunity. Indian producers in the present situation of global competition should identify PACE as one of the important element in marketing strategy.

What Pace Means?

Pace means; Increasing the speed of Launch of new Products and re-launch of old ones. It indicates that be innovative in product quality, but be fast.

Secondly it means reduction of gap between one Launch and another Launch and making several brand launches in a short period of time.

Thirdly it means quick response to changes in consumer needs and preference by creating brand variations, time consuming test marketing and product fine tuning may be anti PACE but consumer need had to be judged. The use of qualitative research can offer quick insight into buyers perception for quick response and help in reducing marketing time.

Fourthly it means adopting a fast system design to keep fast track and PACE with the emerging global trends and control the quality of manufacture. It will help to squeez the time in product development for effective speed marketing. A new product must be ready almost as soon as it is launched globally. Lastly it means increase in the pace of promotion to maintain high frequency. The high frequency of promotion keeps the consumers interest high in the product.

The PACE means the rapidity of quality management, product development, technology adoption and creating fast brand wave and increased frequency of promotion. Hindustan Level -Denim after Shave lotion, Lux White, Surf Easy wash. Domestic floor clean, Confident tooth brush, Walls-Ice cream, relaunches of the entire range of Kishan, Life Boy Liquid, are the few examples. Even Britania launched six brands of biscuits between January 94 to July 94. e.g. 50-50, Little heart, Bakers choice, Joshesps thin etc. PACE means the right product of right quality, the right Package at right price, the right promotion at right time. Executives in India have identified PACE as a priority strategy to meet the global challenges.

In Indian market the PACE Setters are Hindustan Lever which has floated a variety of new product and re-launched its old products and has gone into hyper-drive in a very little time. Lever has been followed by Proctor & Gambles, I.T.C., Rickett and Colman, Britannia Industries, Coco-cola India, and Videocon International. (Except Videocon all the above companies are multinational having global market).

These firms are not only pushing the pace, they are also increasing their risk, Under researched brands launched are merely to flop. Obsession for speed however should not affect adversely the contents or substance and quality of product. However the occasional failures are the price that the new generation of speedsters is willing to pay. It is also known that in flooding the brands not all products will succeed, and the winners will carry the burden of failures.

What PACE Can Do?

PACE knocks down your competitor out even before he can get going. Let us recall the Hindustan Lever's rushing of its liquid 'Life Boy' anti bacterial soap in market and at the same time the Launch of Gel verson of Liril and Lux International. Let us also examine why did Proctor and Gamble race to Launch its whisper ways sanitary napkins in August '94 choosing to dispense with its elaborates test marketing?

Both were Proactive because launches from competitors were imminent. Hence they used PACE to blunt their competitors edge for instance the life Boy Liquid shop earned edge over the RCI 'Dettol' hand wash liquid which came Later. Similarly Proctor and Gamble's rapid fire Launches we are preempting the paper products that the Lever- Kimberly Clark joint Venture Planned to Launch soon. There are examples of MESLOS and REBOCK Shoe companies MESLOS used space to block Rebock Sports Shoe market.

As soon opportunities arise the producer must go out into the market place to exploit them. For the faster you react to the consumer the better it is for the bottom line. A series of quick launches hurts your rival in many ways (a) It raises his cost of entry since he must catch product you have launched, (b) forces the rival to dedicate additional resources, which is bound to affect his profitability.

PACE Helps to Create a New Segment and Dominate in that Segments:

In consumer products where there is fierce competition quality and tactical move at market place oriented have been dominating. So far. The B.C.G. Strategy of segmentation and product market matrix helped producers to find segment or adopt segmentation. Now the producers are adopting 'Appeal Segmentation' for example Maggi the two minutes noodle created an appeal segment. The school going children prefer it as after school meal. It has become very popular Indian dish.

The Hindustan Lever has been designing a series of product attributes taking each one to a brand extension for creating an appeal segment. Occupying a new segment first is the best way to ward off the competition. Similarly the first innovation of 2 minutes 'Maggi' created a segment of its own and ruled over.

PACE Wins Over Promiscus Consumer

The example of Britania Co. illustrates it very clearly. In 93 it did not launch any brand. In 1994 Britania launched one brand every three months eg. Little Hearts, 50-50, Bakers choice Bake Sandwitch bread, and josheps thin are example of it.

As increasingly fikle consumers show low brand Loyalty particularly for Premium or Low involvement product. PACE is providing a panacea for the harried marketers. Instead of fighting the customers propensity to experiment with new products that offer novel appeal, Savvy companies are Launching string of products at regular intervals different from one another to ensure that consumers stay with them. The example of 'Classic' Cigarette of ITC is before us. It is Launching flavour based premium brands at rapid pace, four brands of classic brands have already been launched. In fact using brand extensions at a quick pace is an effort to push down a customer every time when he gets restless and fidles with the idea of switching to other brand. Speedy launching the variants of a strong brand, instead of new brands satisfies the customers panchant for Loyality as well his urge for new experiment. Thus it helps a producers in creating an appeal segment and also in retaining the segment even in the situation of global competition.

PACE Revives Dropping Brand

It is but natural that even the best brands may go on the

downward life cycle stage in the market. In an open competitive market with global competition brand life cycle is being more compressed today. It may be further compressed in the next millennium. A brand must have multiple lives today. Attempts for speedy action of rejuvenating your brand is essential. Velocity alone will ensure that the revitalisation of the brands will hammer away at the consumers consciousness without allowing his interest to slacken in the brand due to long intervals between relaunches. This can be observed by the relaunches of Cadbury's four chocolates, cadbury, dairy milk, 5 stars, Eclare and Gems. Cadbury has used speed of its relaunch to bounce into the consumer awareness. Just in seven months in 1994 Cadbury redefined 'Dairy milk' as an adult food to unconventionally, 5 Star as a Snack. The pay-off from this was rewarded by renewed interest of the consumers.

PACE Can Compensate for Being Last One

An organisation which comes into operation at a later stage can definitely become a formidable competitor by setting dizzying pace of product launches. For late entrants pace is the only antidote, If competitors have deployed preemptive strategies of their own. It is trademill. Once you have stepped on to it you cannot get off. Tour the front line of Cola Wars for a first hand taste of Pace. Anticipating the Launch of Coke, Pepsi Foods has unleashed a blizzard of Promotional activity preceding its entry in every market possible. When Limca 300 ml was launched in August '94 thums up 300 ml was also launched alongside the Limca in the market next week. President of Cocacola remarked that Cocacola India has changed its strategy to PACE. He remarked "our actions and reactions time has been reduced nil ." Earlier the marketer worked to the slogan of 'ready aim, and fire.' Today it has changed to ready, fire, aim. Thus pace not only helps an organisation to earn a segment but also to be one of major share holder of the market even the organisation is a late starter.

PACE Lends Products a Life Long Technological Edge

Present is the age of technology. A number of products are based on technology and are flooding the market eg. Timex watches,, MNV's televisions, pump dispensers for liquid soap. It is essential to catch the hi-tech wave before rivals adopt it. Titan watches did it. Titan made watches as personal accessories and it became leader of the Quartz segment of watch market, pushed HMT to second position. It also rewrote the Rule Book of Conventional Wisdom in watch market that the best watches are imported one, legally or illegally . Videocon International has adopted the pace strategy in this area. It has rushed into market the first product in every segment created by technology, from picture-in-picture to frost free refrigerators. Videocon international believes in being first with a new concept, using a tactical and strategic marketing in compressed time frame. Videocon by adopting speed in technological adaptation has become technology Leader. Thus speed marketing has carved out an advantage to Videocon and has provided a Life Long technology to its product.

Conclusion

The success of Nirma (Popular priced washing powder). Titan Watches, ONIDA (T.V.) Videocon Washing machine, Maruti Cars, Maggi Noodles and Close-up tooth paste, each one of them presents some significant break through interms of product development. Their success also proves that there is need to understand consumer behaviour in the context of global competition and change the approach to strategic marketing. That to succeed in any competitive market whether domestic or global the application of the traditional approach will not be effective. The strategic approach must concentrate on looking at the market differently than what was being done before liberalisation. The companies must be innovative from the point of future opportunities and understanding of the needs of consumers also. It is something more than USP School. Innovation should not be only quantitative. It should be quick, daring, dynamic than analysing the industry in two by two matrix. It should be qualitative and must be based on watching the performance of rivals .

Now it is clear that the product innovation, the quality management and technological updating can matter only when you watch your rivals action and they are adopted with speed. Pace only can increase market share, increase turnover, enhance dealers motivation, improve product viability, improve corporate image, lead to new technique, a new position in the market.

Futures, February 1983. A review of the literature on possible urban/regional problems.

Watson, Tony. *Management, Organisation and Employment Strategy*. Routledge & Kegan Paul, 1986.

Wedderburn, D. and Crompton, R. *Workers' Attitudes and Technology*. Cambridge University Press, 1972.

Weizenbaum, Joseph. *Computer Power and Human Reason*. W. H. Freeman, 1976.

Whisler, Thomas, *The Impact of Computer on Organisation*. Praeger, 1970.

Woodward, Joan. *Industrial Organisation: Theory and practice* (2nd edn). Oxford University Press, 1972.

Work, Colin, 'The future development of campus-wide information systems: towards the virtual campus', *Journal of Information Networking*, 1(1), 1993.

Zuboff, Shoshana. *In the Age of the Smart Machine*. Heinemann, 1988.

Index